DATE DUE			
AUG 0 4 1999			

Religion and the Modern Mind

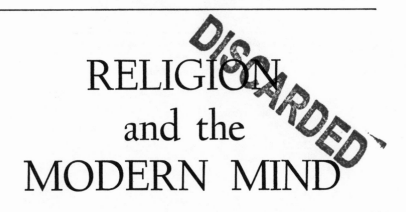

RELIGION
and the
MODERN MIND

W. T. Stace

GREENWOOD PRESS, PUBLISHERS
WESTPORT, CONNECTICUT

Library of Congress Cataloging in Publication Data

Stace, Walter Terence, 1886-
  Religion and the modern mind.

    Reprint of the 1st. ed. published by Lippincott,
  Philadelphia.
    Includes index.
    1. Religion--Philosophy. 2. Skepticism--
  Controversial literature. I. Title.
  BL51.S6256 1980   201   80-24093
  ISBN 0-313-22662-8 (lib. bdg.)

This is a reprint of the first edition.

Reprinted with the permission of Lippincott and Crowell
Publishers.

Reprinted in 1980 by Greenwood Press
A division of Congressional Information Service, Inc.
88 Post Road West, Westport, Connecticut 06881

Printed in the United States of America

10 9 8 7 6 5 4 3 2 1

PREFACE

THE MIDDLE CHAPTERS OF THIS BOOK DISCUSS HOW SOME OF THE most important characteristics of the modern mind, with its special religious, moral, and philosophical problems and perplexities, can be traced back to the seventeenth century scientific revolution. But though the book is thus in some sense historically oriented it does not profess to be history, even intellectual history, as the professional historian uses that term. To understand these problems it is necessary to know how they arose, but the emphasis of the book is always on logical connections between ideas, or the lack of logical connections, and on the problems themselves rather than on their history. And the purpose of the earlier chapters is to lead up to and into the final two chapters in which an attempt is made to throw light, so far as the writer can, on the solutions of the problems which have thus come to bedevil the modern world.

I owe some facts recounted in the earlier chapters to Professor J. H. Randall's book, *The Making of the Modern Mind*. My great indebtedness to A. N. Whitehead's *Science and the Modern World* will be obvious to anyone who has read that book. My thanks are also due to Professor A. G. Shenstone, of the Princeton Physics Department, who kindly read through the chapter on the rise of modern science and helped me to make corrections in it, and to Mr. George Stevens, of J. B. Lippincott Company, who gave me helpful criticisms of my first draft of the whole book and especially made valuable major suggestions regarding the arrangement and expression of the ideas of the final chapters.

W. T. Stace

Princeton
January, 1952

CONTENTS

Part I

The Medieval World-Picture

❋ 1 ❋

THE MEDIEVAL WORLD-PICTURE

THE THOUGHTS AND ACTIONS OF MEN TEND TO BE GOVERNED, or at least influenced, by some set of general ideas about the nature of the world and man's place in it. A set of general ideas of this sort may be called a world-picture or a *Weltanschauung*. Sometimes, by scholars, scientists, or philosophers, a world-picture is more or less explicitly articulated. But in the majority of men it works unseen, a dim background in their minds, unnoticed by themselves because taken for granted. Usually a particular epoch in a particular culture will have some such set of ideas which is peculiar to it and which pervades the whole culture at that time. Sets of general ideas change in the course of history under the impact of the incoming fresh experiences of the race of men.

Such changes are usually slow. But in the seventeenth century of the Christian era there occurred a series of events which caused what seems in retrospect like a sudden revolutionary change in the world-picture of European man. This was the century which saw the birth of modern science. It was the century in which the main work of Kepler, Galileo, and Newton was done. Of course science had its roots in the past. Revolutions, whether political or intellectual, are never so sudden as they are apt to appear at a quick glance. But in this book we shall be concerned with the

11

consequences of the seventeenth century scientific revolution, not with its causes, which we can therefore leave unexamined. Hence any over-simplification which is involved in speaking of the rise of science as "sudden" can be ignored. And although the process of history is an unbroken stream of events, exhibiting continuity and slow change, yet there are periods during which the rapidity of change is greatly accelerated. Thus without too great a distortion we can speak of the modern mind as something clearly distinguishable from the medieval mind. And we need not make too much of the fact that what we here call the medieval mind itself underwent great changes during the centuries. What the thirteenth century thought was not exactly what the tenth century thought. But still we can say that the world-picture of medieval man was dominated by religion, while the world-picture of modern man is dominated by science—which is not to say, of course, that in medieval times there was nothing which could be called science, nor that in our own age there is no religion. With this broad contrast, ignoring for the present the innumerable detailed qualifications which might well be made in it, we may profitably begin our discussion.

We may remind the reader first of some well-known facts. Throughout the middle ages the geocentric theory of astronomy held undisputed sway. The earth stands motionless at the center of the universe. Sun, moon, planets, and stars revolve around it in circles. In the ancient Greek world the idea that the earth is a moving planet had been more than once suggested. In the sixth century B.C. Pythagorean philosophers speculated that the earth, along with other heavenly bodies, moves round a "central fire" which is always hidden from us because it is on the other side of the earth; the central fire was thus not the sun. At a later date the Greek astronomer Aristarchus definitely proposed a heliocentric view. But in the middle ages these ideas were ignored and forgotten, chiefly under the influence of Aristotle who espoused the geocentric theory. No one, at any rate no one of importance, from the rise of Christianity to the time of Copernicus, doubted that the sun and the stars move round the motionless earth.

The world was created by God in the manner set forth in the early chapters of Genesis. The date of its creation was uncertain. A popularly accepted date was 4004 B.C., derived by adding together the ages of the generations of Adam as given in the Bible. But other dates were sometimes proposed. Dante believed the creation took place in 5200 B.C. The universe was in any case only a few thousand years old.

At some not far distant date in the future, on the day of judgment, the material universe would be brought to an end. This might happen in 4004 A.D., so as to make the history of the world symmetrical, with the life of Christ in its exact temporal center. Dante again differed. He thought that the world would come to an end in 1800 A.D. In any case the whole history of the universe, from its first day to its last, would be only a matter of a few thousand years.

This whole world history, from the creation to the day of judgment, would constitute, according to St. Augustine, a sort of religious drama in which three great crises could be discerned. The first was the Fall of man. Man, having eaten of the forbidden fruit, became sinful and accursed. In the justice of God atonement for man's sinfulness was required, for without such atonement all men would have to be condemned to limbo or eternal torment. Hence the second great crisis came with the incarnation of the Son of God in Jesus and his death upon the cross, which constituted the required atonement. The third and final crisis, the denouement of the world-drama, would be the day of judgment. On that day the wicked would, in Santayana's words, "behold with dismay the Lord visibly coming down through the clouds of heaven, the angels blowing their alarming trumpets, all generations of the dead rising from their graves, and judgment without appeal passed on every man. Whereupon the blessed would enter eternal bliss with God their master and the wicked everlasting torments with the devil whom they served."[1]

The world-drama was enacted and controlled by purposes in

[1] *The Philosophy of Santayana, Selections,* ed. Irwin Edman (New York: Charles Scribner's Sons, 1936), p. 177.

the mind of God. Everything which happened somehow fitted into the divine plan. Why was the world ever created at all? This seemed very puzzling since God had existed by himself through an eternity without needing a world. This, of course, was beyond human comprehension, but presumably creation was in some way for the purpose of the glorification of God. Or perhaps man and the world in which man was placed, were needed as objects of God's love. Or perhaps God's superabundant being simply overflowed itself in such a manner that the overflow became the universe.

Not only must the existence and history of the universe as a whole have a purpose. Every object which exists in the universe, every event which occurs in it, must have its purpose. And every such detailed purpose must fit into the grand scheme and the general plan of the whole. To some extent one could see the purposes of things. The sun obviously existed to give man light during the daytime, the moon to provide him with illumination at night. Herbs and animals existed to be man's food, water to assuage his thirst. Rainbows, as we are explicitly told in the Bible, were put in the sky when it rains in order to remind man of God's promise never again to destroy the human race by flood as he did in the days of Noah. Why bugs, mosquitoes, serpents, dirt, warts, and tornados exist one cannot say, though they may have something to do with punishment for man's original sin. The puny mind of man cannot, of course, expect to unravel all the mysteries of God's plan. While in a few cases, such as the existence of the sun and the moon and food-providing animals, the purposes are obvious; and in other cases, such as rainbows, their purposes have been revealed; for the most part we have to take the purposes of things on faith. But one can be sure of the general principle that everything has a purpose.

❈ 2 ❈

GOD AND THE WORLD-PURPOSE

THE MEDIEVAL WORLD-PICTURE WAS A MIXTURE OF SCIENTIFIC and philosophical ideas. The geocentric theory, for example, is scientific in character, since it belongs to astronomy. But if one leaves on one side the scientific conceptions, one finds that there are three main philosophical ideas left—God, world-purpose, and the moral order of the world. In the next two chapters I shall examine these conceptions. Our purpose is not history, and nothing further of their history will be mentioned until we come, in later chapters, to discuss what happened to them as a result of the seventeenth century scientific revolution. For the present I shall concentrate on their meaning and logical implications. If we are in any way to attempt a solution of the problems which beset our own age, the first essential is to pin down, so far as possible, the exact meanings of the conceptions which are our cultural inheritance and which, coming down to us from the past, have set our problems.

The first idea is that of God. The important thing for us to understand is what this word, inherited by us from a long past, has commonly meant in men's minds. In other words we want to know what kind of a being God has been believed to be. And the main point to be stressed is that he has been thought of as personal, that is to say, as a conscious mind or spirit.

This implies that God's mind must be something like a human mind. It makes plans and has purposes. It must be conscious. It must have thoughts and ideas, perhaps also emotions, such as love and anger, though perhaps it has no physical sensations since God as pure spirit has no physical body. Of course theologians may not say quite these things. But the point is that it is impossible to think of a mind at all except in some such terms. The sophisticated may say that psychological words like "idea," "purpose," "thought," "emotion," are only used of God in some allegorical or symbolical sense, and that in reality God's mind must be entirely different from any mind known to us. But in that case it becomes a question whether the use of such psychological words as applied to God has any meaning. It becomes a question whether to call God a mind or a spirit, or to attribute to him a purpose for man or for the world, conveys any true thought to our minds at all. One may quite legitimately use a word or a phrase in a metaphorical or symbolic way. But one must in that case be able to say what the non-metaphorical meaning is. For instance, you can speak of a "sea of troubles." If you are asked how troubles can constitute a sea, you can explain that the word "sea" is a metaphor which here stands for the manyness, the multitudinous character, or perhaps the overwhelming nature, of the troubles. You have then given the literal meaning. The rule is that a metaphor is meaningful if you can give the literal meaning of it. But if you cannot, then it is a "mere" metaphor, and is meaningless.

If one were to say of an object, "this is a tree," and were to add that by the word "tree" one did not mean anything like any of the things which are ordinarily called trees; and if at the same time one could not say in what other sense the word was being used, it would then be obvious that the word "tree" as thus used had no meaning at all. And it cannot be otherwise with psychological words as applied to God. Either they mean, when applied to God, the same things as they mean when applied to men; or, if they are metaphors, we must be able to say what the metaphors literally stand for; or they mean nothing at all.

The purpose of these remarks is not to be skeptical, or to ridicule the idea of God as a spirit. But we have to face up to the difficulties which are implicit in our thinking. It may be said that the real nature of God is beyond human conception, that we cannot give the literal meanings of the words we use in such a manner as to satisfy a logician, but that nevertheless these words "spirit," "purpose," and so on, *hint* at some meaning to which we cannot give explicit expression in language. Perhaps something of this sort may be true. But what I am at present trying to do is to ascertain what—apart from the thought of profound theologians or mystics—the ordinary thoughts and words of plain men have meant and implied; what they must have believed when they believed that God is a mind or a spirit. They must have believed what their words logically imply, that God is a consciousness having a psychology basically similar to human psychology, so that mental processes such as those which we denote by such words as "idea," "thought," "purpose," "love," "anger," can be properly attributed to him. Of course God's mind is thought of as much larger, greater, more powerful, wiser than any human mind—it has been orthodox to speak of God's wisdom, love, knowledge, and power as infinite—but still it must be of the same kind as a human mind.

Sophisticated thinkers, whether theologians or philosophers, are aware of the tremendous difficulties wrapt up in this ordinary anthropomorphic conception of God. Hence they have attempted to substitute other more abstruse conceptions, and these may possibly possess very great philosophical merits. But it is impossible that, however sophisticated or erudite, they can ever wholly escape from anthropomorphism. If you think of God as in any sense a person, a mind, or a spirit—however much you realize the inadequacy of such words, however much you try to avoid their ordinary crude meanings as applied to human beings—you cannot help being anthropomorphic, you cannot help conceiving of God in terms of your conception of human minds, because you have no other materials out of which to form your conception of him. In short, ·the idea of God is incurably and *necessarily* anthropomorphic.

To say this is not to criticize. Anthropomorphism may be true. Or it may not. The question lies quite open before us, entirely unprejudiced by anything that has been said. What is at present apparent is simply this: that men who believe in God believe in a mind which must have consciousness, thoughts, ideas, purposes, and other mental states; that this is what the idea of God means; that it must have meant this for the medieval mind; that this is what it means now; that in popular religion, then or now, it is obvious that this is what it meant; and that even the most elaborate and learned constructions of theologians or philosophers cannot refine the idea of God in such a manner as to avoid some element of anthropomorphism.

This psychological being, God, created the world at some time in the past. According to medieval belief it was only a few thousand years ago. According to modern thinking it must have been billions of years ago. The period of time which has elapsed since the act of creation is of no importance in our present context. The point to which attention should be directed is that in this account the word "creation" must have its ordinary English meaning or none at all. To create means to make. Men make houses, machines, furniture. God made the world in just this sense. For the same arguments which showed that the word "mind," if used of God, must have its ordinary meaning or none, show equally that the word "create," if used of God, must in the same way, and for the same reasons, have its ordinary meaning or none. God then made the world in the same sense as men make houses, the only difference being that he made the world out of nothing whereas men make their artifacts out of pre-existing materials. This difference, however, presents no difficulty to the mind. Though we do not happen to have the power of making something out of nothing, the idea is nevertheless quite easy to understand. Making a thing with no pre-existing material could only mean deciding that it should come into existence, whereupon it does come into existence. The biblical text according to which

"God said, 'Let there be light': and there was light" precisely expresses the thought. That we ourselves cannot do a thing in no way prevents us from understanding what is meant by saying that it is or was done. Exactly what a magician appears to do when he takes an object out of an empty box is what God actually did. This is the original basic idea of the creation of the world, however much learned men may have tried to refine upon it or alter it.

The second idea, the meaning of which we have to discuss, is that of purpose as applied to the world, and the consequent attempt to explain natural phenomena teleologically. "Teleological" means "purposive," and the teleological explanation of a phenomenon means the explanation of it in terms of a purpose. Thus if a man commits a theft, his action is an event in nature just as much as would be a flash of lightning, and we may ask for an explanation of the one event as of the other. We may ask "why" the event, either the lightning flash or the theft, occurred. If the theft is explained by the consideration that the man was hungry and that he stole the money for the purpose of buying food, this would be called a teleological explanation. Teleological explanation is usually contrasted with "mechanical" explanation. To give a teleological explanation of an event is to give the purpose of it; to give the mechanical explanation is to give the cause of it. Mechanical explanation may also be defined as explanation by laws of nature. For to explain by a law and by a cause are the same thing. That the water froze in accordance with the law that water freezes at such and such a temperature, and that the cause of its freezing was such and such a temperature, are equivalent statements.

To return to the distinction between teleological and mechanical explanation, consider the following case. Suppose that a man is observed climbing a hill. We ask *why* he is climbing, that is, we ask for an explanation of the event. There are two different kinds of answers which may be given, both of which appear to be quite sensible. One would be: "He is climbing the hill because he wants to see the view from the top." This would be a teleological explanation. A physiologist, however, might answer the same question by giving a chain of causes and effects ending in the movement of the man's legs. The food he had eaten caused energy to be stored in certain parts of his nervous system. Some external stimulus caused the release of this energy, resulting in nerve currents which caused the contractions and relaxations of his muscles, which finally caused the propulsion of his body up the hill. This would be called a mechanical explanation of his movement. It should be noted, merely as a matter of terminology, that the word "mechanical" is used wherever the explanation is by causes, whether the object caused to act is what is ordinarily called a machine or not. This is evident from the example of the man climbing the hill.

By way of emphasizing the opposite natures of the two kinds of explanation some philosophers have thought of causes as pushing the event from behind, and of purposes or goals as drawing the event after them from the front. The cause of an event happens before it in time. In a chain of causes and effects one follows another in a time series. First I swallow the poison, then it coagulates my blood, then this stops my heart, and then I die. When the man climbs the hill the stimulus comes first, and after it the contraction of the muscles. But it has been supposed that, if we give a teleological explanation, the purpose or goal comes after the event in time, and not before it as a cause would. The seeing of the view from the top of the hill, which is the goal of the man's climbing, comes into existence after he has done the climbing. It is in this sense that the cause has been said to push the event from the past, while the purpose draws it from the future.

This contention, which is not justified, is nevertheless one which it is important for us to understand. For it has contributed to the widespread belief that teleological and mechanical explanation, being opposite in nature, are mutually exclusive, so that if a mechanical explanation is true, a teleological explanation must be false, and vice versa, a view against which we shall have to protest. The contention is unjustified because it is the result of a simple confusion between the idea of a purpose and the idea of a goal. When the man is climbing the hill, the goal, it is true, is in the future. The goal is the actual seeing of the view which does not occur until the man reaches the top. But the purpose which drives him to climb the hill is something which characterizes the man while he is climbing the hill or, indeed, before he begins to climb. It is roughly identical with the desire to see the view, which he had before he began to climb, and which persists in him while he is climbing.

The belief that the two kinds of explanation are mutually exclusive opposites, which cannot both be true at the same time, is part of (not the whole of) the reason why many scientific men have a prejudice against teleological explanations and consider them "unscientific." An event, it may be said, is fully and completely explained by its causes. Suppose that all the causal conditions of a phenomenon are known. Let us call them A, B, C, and D. If this is a complete list of the causal conditions, it is a complete explanation. It is also a mechanical explanation since it mentions nothing but causes. There is therefore no room and no necessity for any other kind of explanation. Any attempt to introduce purposes or goals, as well as causes, into the explanation will result in an incongruous jumble of incommensurable conceptions and irrelevant considerations.

It is true that the introduction of the idea of future goals into an explanation has this effect, since goals lie in the future of the event and therefore cannot be among its causes. But the introduction of purposes in the sense of present desires for future goals does not have this effect. It is not the actual seeing of the view in the future which explains the man's present climbing. It is his present desire for that goal which explains it, or is at least a part of the explanation. This means that the desire is one of the causes of his motion. No doubt among the causes are nervous impulses and muscle contractions. But desires and purposes also appear somewhere in the chain of causes. This amounts to reducing telelogical explanation to a species of mechanical explanation. The teleological explanation of the climbing of the man is part of the mechanical explanation.

There is therefore no reason to say that the two kinds of explanation are inconsistent with one another. And common examples seem to show that they cannot be. It is obviously true that the man climbs because nerve currents and muscles impel him. And it is obviously also true that he climbs because he wants to see the view. These plain facts cannot contradict each other, and if anyone supposes that they do, it must be owing to some mistake. It would be absurd to contend that you have to choose between one or other of the two statements.

It is true that if we admit teleological explanations, difficulties are supposed to arise about the interaction of mind with body. A desire or a purpose is supposed to be a "mental" thing, while a nerve current is a physical thing. What is mental is supposed to be non-physical. And if we admit desires among the causes of human or animal actions, we then seem to be committed to the view that non-material things such as purposes and thoughts have physical effects such as bodily movements. And it is asked how this is possible.

The answer is that there certainly do exist difficult problems of this kind, the solutions of which we do not at present know. There is a problem about the nature of mind and about its relation to the body. There are different views about this, some of which seem plausible; but they are all speculations, not knowledge. And no considerations or theories about matters of which we are ignorant ought ever to cause us to deny plain facts. It is a plain fact that men and animals have desires and are moved by purposes, and that these desires and purposes in many cases explain their actions or are a part of the explanation. It is silly to deny that when I am hungry I desire food, and that when I go out of my office to get lunch my purpose in going out is to satisfy my hunger, and that this is a reasonable and true explanation of my action. This will remain true whether or not I can say what a mind is, or what a desire is, or how a mind is related to a body.

While the motivation of men by purposes is a plain fact, the suggestion that minds and desires and thoughts are "non-material" is not a plain fact. It is a speculative theory which may be true or false. So also is the opposite view that minds and desires and ideas are material things or are in some way reducible to them. If minds are in the end reducible to functions of the physical body, then there is no difficulty in holding that a desire may cause a bodily movement, since this will be no more than a case of one physical phenomenon causing another. But if minds are not reducible to physical functions, then we shall have to admit that a non-physical cause may have a physical effect, no matter what prejudices of ours this may contradict, no matter what modifications we should have to admit in our physical science or in our view of the world.

You may adopt a behavioristic or a materialistic or a dualistic psychology. But in any case it is stupid to deny that desires and purposes exist and that they are among the causes of human behavior. It is unscientific to deny known facts because they seem to conflict with a speculative theory which you hold. And the fact that many psychologists and other scientific men sometimes seem to scout the very word "purpose," and wish to abolish it from their vocabularies, is an example of how very unscientific scientific men sometimes are. The desire to expel teleological explanations from psychology is no more than a prejudice.

We pass on to another consideration having to do with teleology. There is an ambiguity in connection with teleological explanation which, if we are to follow some of the later discussions in this book, must be cleared up. In the example of the man climbing the hill, the purpose which is given as the explanation of the movement is in the moving object itself, that is, in the man. But if we say that a watch has a purpose, namely, that of telling the time, we mean to refer to the purpose in the minds of the people who made, or use, the watch. We do not mean that the watch itself has a mind and that the watch's mind entertains a purpose. This may seem almost irritatingly obvious. Nevertheless if it is not remembered, we may easily become confused. It becomes important if we wish to raise such a question as whether the universe has a purpose. Some philosophers have supposed that, in some sense or other, the universe itself is alive, and may have purposes in itself. But unless we believe this, our question whether the universe has a purpose must be meant as an inquiry whether there is a living being who is related to the universe in some such way as a watchmaker is related to a watch. Hence, if the world has a purpose, either it is itself alive, or there is some living being whose purposes control it and perhaps made it. The former view may be called *immanent* teleology. The latter we will call *external* teleology. Both views have been held, but they have not commonly been distinguished or given separate names. Both have been referred to as teleological explanations of the universe.

The distinction between teleological and mechanical explanation is of very great importance for the understanding of the history of human thought. One of the contrasts between the medieval mind and the modern mind, as we saw, is that the former was dominated by religion, while the latter is dominated by science. We may now add that religion has generally been associated with teleology, science with mechanism. Hence another contrast between the medieval and the modern minds is that by the former teleology was stressed, by the latter mechanism is stressed. It is an important characteristic of the modern mind, which it has derived from science, that its outlook is almost wholly mechanistic, and that it has thrust a teleological view of the world into the background, even if it does not deny teleology altogether. Most biologists are mechanists, and tend to frown upon explanations even of the behavior of living beings by purposes. And in psychology the same dislike of teleology is common, and the introduction of the notion of purpose is often considered unscientific.

It is sometimes said that science has ceased to be mechanistic under the impact of the new physics of relativity and quantum theory. This, however, is a mistake due to a confusion over the meaning of the word "mechanism." It is true that there is a special scientific sense of the word in which science has ceased to be mechanistic. This special meaning of the term will be found explained in books such as Einstein's and Infeld's *The Evolution*

of Physics. It has nothing at all to do with what we are here discussing. For us, as we use the word, any explanation in terms of
causes, or—what comes to the same thing—in terms of natural
laws, any explanation which does not introduce the concept of
purpose, is called mechanical. No physicist dreams of giving
teleological explanations of phenomena. This is not necessarily
because he denies the existence of purposes in events. But they fall
outside his science. His business is to give causal or mechanical
explanations, and his science is therefore wholly mechanistic. He
may sometimes say that a movement, say of an electron, is not
determined by causes. But this is not to say its explanation is teleological. It is to say that it has no explanation. Thus the physicist's
concept of explanation is still entirely mechanical.

Perhaps another point about scientific explanations had better
here be made, lest the absence of explicit reference to it may lead
to misunderstanding. It is sometimes said that the concept of
functional dependence has replaced that of cause and effect in
science. The scientist no longer thinks of the process of nature
as divided up into a series of discrete chunks of which one is
labeled a cause and the succeeding one an effect. Rather he thinks
of a continuous process in which a later part is functionally dependent on an earlier part. This, however, is of no importance
to us. The cause-effect concept and the functional dependence
concept are identically the same idea, except that the former is a
relatively crude and common-sense version of it, while the latter
is more refined and accurate. For our purposes the common-
sense language is quite sufficient, and will not introduce any
errors into our thinking.

Religion as such is perhaps not necessarily bound up with the
belief that there is a cosmic purpose. Buddhism may perhaps be
quoted as an example of a great religion which exists without it.
But it is a characteristic belief of most religions, and certainly of
Christianity, that God made the world for a purpose. Even people
who may have no clear belief in God may sometimes say such
things as "there must be some sort of purpose in things." However vague such a statement may be, it is evidence of some sort

of religious feeling. And a teleological view of the world is in general, I should say, characteristic of a religious attitude to the world, notwithstanding that it may sometimes be found in individuals who entertain no definite theological creed.

That not only the world as a whole has a purpose, but that particular things and events in it are capable of being teleologically explained, has also been characteristic of western religion, and especially of the religion of medieval times. The rainbow is teleologically explained when it is understood as giving man assurance that the human race will not again be destroyed by flood. It is mechanically explained when it is understood in terms of the laws of physics. And that the medieval mind supposed that the ultimate explanations of sun, moon, and stars, of plants, animals, and water, and indeed of all natural phenomena, must be in terms of God's purposes for man, has already been stressed.

But the conception of the world as governed by purpose was not invented by Christianity. It is obvious that ancient Hebrew religion, as set forth in the Old Testament, is permeated by it. And if, instead of going back into the Hebrew origins of our civilization, we trace it backwards into its pagan sources, we find the same thing. The most famous of the ancient Greek philosophers, Socrates, Plato, and Aristotle, developed teleological systems of metaphysics. Plato, in the *Phaedo,* put into the mouth of Socrates, awaiting execution in prison, the following remarkable words:

> I heard someone reading, as he said, from a book of Anaxagoras, that mind was the disposer and cause of all, and I was delighted at this notion . . . and I said to myself: If mind is the disposer, mind will dispose all for the best, and put each particular in the best place. . . . And I rejoiced to think that I had found in Anaxagoras a teacher . . . such as I desired, and I imagined that he would tell me first whether the earth is flat or round; and whichever was true he would proceed to . . . show that this was best; and if he said that the earth was in the centre, he would further explain that this position was best, and I should be satisfied with the explanation given and not want any other sort of cause. And I thought I would then go on and ask him

about the sun and moon and stars, and he would explain to me
their comparative swiftness, and their returnings and various
states, active and passive, and how all of them were for the best.

Thus Socrates is represented as believing that the shape of the
earth, its position in the heavens—whether it is "in the centre"
or not—the orbits, velocities, and states of the heavenly bodies,
could be explained by showing that the facts regarding these
matters were all "for the best," in other words that they served a
good purpose, and he states specifically that he "does not want
any other sort of cause," i.e., any explanation, other than a
teleological one. That he clearly realizes the distinction between
teleological and mechanical explanations, and rejects the latter,
is clear from the fact that he goes on immediately to say that he
became bitterly disappointed with Anaxagoras as soon as he discovered that, after his initial promise of teleological explanations,
Anaxagoras in the end gave only mechanical explanations. He
puts it in these words:

> What expectations I had formed, and how grievously was I
> disappointed! As I proceeded I found my philosopher altogether
> forsaking mind or any other principle of order, but having re-
> course to air, and ether, and water, and other eccentricities. I
> might compare him to a person who began by maintaining gen-
> erally that mind is the cause of the actions of Socrates, but who,
> when he endeavoured to explain the causes of my several actions
> in detail, went on to show that I sit here because my body is
> made up of bones and muscles; and the bones, as he would
> say, are hard and have joints which divide them, and the
> muscles are elastic . . . and as the bones are lifted at their joints
> by the contraction or relaxation of the muscles, I am able to
> bend my limbs, and this is why I am sitting here in a curved
> posture . . . forgetting to mention the true cause, which is, that
> the Athenians have thought fit to condemn me, and accordingly
> I have thought it better and more right to remain here and
> undergo my sentence.

This passage makes clear the distinction between teleological
and mechanical explanation, and brands the latter as inferior
and not the "true" explanation, which is rather to be found in the

purposes of the Athenians and of Socrates himself. The account given in terms of muscles, joints, and bones of why Socrates is "sitting here in a curved posture" is, of course, mechanistic, and is—if we make allowances for the primitive character of the physiology—exactly the kind of explanation considered "scientific" by the physiologists and psychologists of the present day.

Socrates' words exhibit a bias in favor of teleological explanation and a prejudice against mechanism. Our own age, under the influence of science, shows a prejudice in the opposite direction. Since, as has been shown, the two kinds of explanation are not inconsistent with one another, neither bias is justified. Nevertheless what Socrates says seems to me to convey a deserved rebuke to the kind of thought which, in our own day, would try to eliminate the concept of purpose altogether from the sphere of explanation.

We do not know whether the passage just quoted represents the thinking of Socrates himself or that of his biographer, Plato. But in what is generally admitted to be Plato's own philosophy the teleological motif is dominant. If we had the highest kind of knowledge—if we were omniscient, in fact—we should, in his view, understand everything in the universe in terms of what he calls "the form of the good." This may be briefly explained. We accept as brute facts that space has three dimensions; that there are three kinds of angles, acute, right, and obtuse; that there are two kinds of numbers, odd and even; and in general that the nature and structure of the world is as we find it. We take these facts for granted. But *why* should they be as they are? Why should there be three dimensions of space, not two or twenty? (The point is not whether three is the correct number. Suppose it were to be discovered that as a matter of fact there are six dimensions, this would not answer Plato's question. He would still ask: why six, not seven or seventeen? The point is that, however many there are, this is a brute fact for which no *reason* is given.) Why should there be three kinds of angles; why two kinds of numbers? Why, in short, should the world be just the particular sort of world it is, and not some other kind? One might, for instance, ask in the same sense: why should water boil at the temperature at which it does boil and not at some other? These are exactly the kinds of questions which a currently fashionable school of philosophers, the logical positivists, would say are "meaningless." But Plato thought that they could be answered if we could see all things under the "form of the good." There must be some reason why everything is what it is. For if there is no reason at all for the world being the kind of world it is, then the world is irrational. And this he would not admit. The reason of things, however, cannot be mechanical causes. For mechanical causation is always mere irrational brute fact—it just is a fact that such and such a temperature produces boiling, while another temperature does not. The reasons therefore must lie in purposes of some kind. It must be that there are three dimensions, not four, because, in the ultimate scheme or plan of things, which we do not understand, three dimensions is "for the best"—for "the form of the good," as Plato puts it—while four would not be. Every detailed fact of the world, which seems to us irrational in the sense that "it just is so," must have some reason for being what it is, and this ultimate reason must lie in some good purpose which its being so serves. We may give mechanical causes of things, and these may be, so far as they go, interesting, correct, and useful. But in the end they explain nothing. It is true that water boils at a certain temperature. Perhaps a mechanical explanation of this can be given in terms of molecules, atoms, or electrons. But however far we proceed in such a scientific way, we shall only be saying, in greater or less detail, what happens, not why anything happens. The world will still be a brute fact world, which just is what it is, without any rhyme or reason having been given for it. The molecules or electrons behave in this way and not in that way. Only if we could see the ultimate purpose of things, if we could see all things in the light of "the form of the good," should we *understand*. Only then would the world be intelligible. A world seen without this vision of an ultimate plan is nothing but a mass of senseless and unintelligible "facts."

Plato did not, of course, himself profess to be the possessor of any such ultimate explanation of the world. What he calls true "knowledge" is a superhuman ideal which no mortal can attain. Only God himself has such a knowledge. Yet it is the ideal towards which philosophy must strive. And though one cannot actually reach it in its pure state, Plato seems to have thought that a man might glimpse it by means of myths, allegories, and images.

That there is some plan or purpose in things is essentially a part of the religious view of the world, whether or not it is combined with some theistic creed about a God or gods. Wherever we find it we know that the religious vision is at work. Plato was a deeply religious man. The writing of Aristotle strikes us as much colder than that of Plato, as much less permeated by religious or mystical feeling. He is, by comparison with Plato, prosaic and uninspired. Nevertheless he too maintains a teleological view of the world. I shall not here give any detail of Aristotle's teleology. For our point has sufficiently been made, namely, that belief in cosmic purpose was not the invention of Christianity, but stretches far back into antiquity.

There was, it is true, plenty of mechanistic thinking in ancient Greece. The earliest Greek philosophers and scientists from Thales to Empedocles were mechanists. So was the famous Democritus, who was contemporary with Socrates, and who elaborated in some detail an atomic theory of matter. The mechanism of the Greeks influenced modern science, but what the ages chiefly absorbed from Greece was the thought of Plato and Aristotle, not that of Democritus and his mechanistic precursors. Mechanism, always to be found in any advanced human thinking, was nevertheless a recessive strain in western culture until the rise of modern science.

Thus Christianity did not begin, but only continued, the teleological character of the thinking of the western world. Of course the details of the Christian theological scheme are not the same as the details of any Greek philosophy in spite of the great influence of both Plato and Aristotle on Christian theology. But the Platonic vision of a purposive world under the form of the good fitted very well into the Christian scheme of a world created and ruled by the purposes of a good God. And the conclusion which emerges is that the conception of the world as having purpose, of a world in which all apparently unintelligible happenings find meaning in the light of a cosmic purpose, in which all the apparently senseless and irrelevant welter of detail, even all the apparent evil, could—if one could reach the divine vision—be seen as fitting into the one grand scheme of things and finding their meaning in the light of the whole—this, which we may simply call the teleological view of the world, was part of the intellectual and spiritual heritage of western man for over two thousand years, from the time of Socrates in the fifth century B.C. until comparatively recent times. What happened to it in the seventeenth century,. what was the effect on it of the sudden appearance of science with its mechanistic ways of thinking, this question belongs to a later part of our story.

❋ 3 ❋

THE WORLD AS A MORAL ORDER

THERE WERE THREE CENTRAL AND GOVERNING PHILOSOPHICAL ideas which, as we saw, were implicit in the medieval world-picture—God, world-purpose, and the world as a moral order. In the last chapter I discussed the first two. In the present chapter I shall discuss the third. My purpose here, as there, will not be history. It needs no documentation to show that medieval man believed that the world is a moral order. This will be obvious so soon as we understand what the idea means. As before we shall be concerned with discussing what this idea does mean, and what its logical implications and difficulties are. For this is what we have to understand if we are to make any attempt to fathom the per-plexities of our own age.

What does it mean, then, to say that the world is a moral order? The idea, as thus expressed, is certainly extremely vague. Yet it has been of superlative importance in the intellectual and spiritual history of mankind. It is a part of the religious view of the world. It permeates not only Christianity, but all the great religions, at any rate those which are theistic in type.

It will help us at this stage to introduce a little modern philo-sophical jargon. Jargon is to be avoided, if possible, but sometimes it is useful. Some modern philosophers have said that "moral values are objective," while others have said that "moral values are subjective." In this chapter I shall maintain that the assertion that "moral values are objective" is identical in meaning with the assertion that "the world is a moral order." If this is so, then obviously the view that moral values are subjective is the same as the belief that the world is not a moral order. It is not perhaps obvious, and I shall have to prove, that "moral values are objective" means the same thing as "the world is a moral order." But for the moment I propose to take this for granted.

The words "objective" and "subjective" are extremely ambiguous, and have unfortunately been used in different senses by different writers, or by the same writers in different contexts. I shall therefore begin by giving rough definitions of the meanings of the terms as I propose to use them here and throughout this book. I call my definitions "rough," because they do not pretend to very great precision. But they will be sufficiently clear to guide us in our inquiries and to prevent us from falling into fallacies due to ambiguity of language.

Any value will be called subjective if the existence of the value depends, wholly or in part, on any human desires, feelings, opinions, or other mental states. An objective value will, of course, be the opposite of this. It will be a value which does *not* depend on any human desire, feeling, or other mental state.

There are, of course, different kinds of values. We attribute value to anything if we call it, in any sense, good, or use any equivalent term for it. We may be said to attribute a dis-value to it if we call it bad in any sense. We certainly use such words as "good" and "bad" in different senses, of which we may distinguish three of the most important. If we call a picture or a poem good or bad, beautiful or ugly, we are usually speaking of *esthetic* value. If we call a man good or bad, or an action right or wrong, we are usually speaking of *moral* values. If we call a motor car, a house, a pen, or a typewriter, good or bad, we are generally referring to what may be called *utilitarian* or *economic* values.

We can most easily illustrate the meaning of the words "subjective" and "objective" by reference to economic values. For no one, I think, would dispute that economic values are subjective according to the definition I have given. A house or an automobile would have absolutely no economic or utilitarian value if no human beings ever desired such things. Moreover the more human beings desire them, the greater becomes their economic value, the less they are desired the less becomes their economic value. The strength of human desires for an object and the number of people who desire it—what economists call the demand—is one of the factors on which depends the so-called law of supply and demand, the other factor being, of course, the supply. All this makes it evident that economic values depend for their existence on human desires, feelings, or opinions, and are therefore, according to our definition, subjective.

Another value which is plainly subjective—whether we call this too an economic value or give it some other name—is the pleasant or unpleasant taste of foods. A man who says, "Caviar is nice" is not attributing an objective quality to the caviar, as he would be if he described its weight or chemical properties. He means nothing more than "I like caviar," so that his statement really describes his own feelings or preferences, and does not describe any characteristic of the caviar. Clearly, then, caviar is not nice unless someone likes it, so that its niceness depends on human likings or desires, and is accordingly subjective. Another consequence follows from this. If one man says, "Caviar is nice," and another says, "Caviar is nasty," they are not contradicting each other as they would be if they were attributing opposite chemical properties to it. For the first is merely saying, "I like caviar," while the second is saying, "I do not like it," and both these statements may be true.

Since it is admitted that economic values are subjective, it is a very natural suggestion that all kinds of value must be like them in this respect. Let us then raise this question regarding moral and esthetic values. We are not in this book directly concerned with esthetic values, but we shall find that it will be instructive to consider them also to some extent in this chapter. A great many philosophers in the modern period, and at the present day, have thought that both moral and esthetic values must be, like economic values, subjective. Consider the following passage which refers to moral values and was written by the English philosopher Thomas Hobbes, who was born in 1588 and died in 1679, and was a contemporary of Galileo:

> Every man, for his own part, calleth that which pleaseth, and is delightful to himself, good; and that evil which displeaseth him: insomuch that while every man differeth from another in constitution, they differ also from one another concerning the common distinction of good and evil. Nor is there any such thing as absolute goodness, considered without relation. . . . And as we call good and evil the things which please and displease; so we call goodness and badness, the qualities or powers whereby they do it.[1]

This is one of the earliest modern statements of the view that moral values are subjective. For it makes good and evil depend on human feelings of pleasure and displeasure, and is therefore, by our definition, a subjective theory. Such a passage, utterly out of tune with medieval thought, marks a revolutionary change in the climate of European opinion. Moral subjectivism is characteristic of the modern mind, and was, in general, absent from the medieval mind. Something had happened in the interval, say between the thirteenth century and the time of Hobbes, which caused this change, and later on we shall have to discuss what it was. For the present we note only that the opinion expressed by Hobbes, or something essentially like it, has become common in the modern world.

It is true that at the present day almost no one holds the very crude version of subjectivism which is expressed in the above passage. It is crude because it implies that the distinction between good and evil depends on the likes or dislikes of each *individual* man. If this were taken literally, it would follow that if a man liked something he could never call it bad or evil. This, however, is not the case. We do all often admit that something would give us pleasure, which is the same as saying that we like it, but that

[1] Thomas Hobbes, *Works,* ed. Molesworth (London: J. Bohn, 1839-45), vol. IV, p. 32.

nevertheless it would be morally wrong. We may call the view which Hobbes—perhaps carelessly—stated in this passage *individual subjectivism*. According to the most fashionable version of moral subjectivism now current, good and evil, right and wrong, are not relative to single individuals, but to cultures or civilizations or large social groups. Hobbes here writes as if he thought that what "pleaseth" each individual is what that individual considers good. The typical current view is that the standard of right and wrong in any society or culture is rather what "pleaseth" the society or culture as a whole. It is the desires or feelings of the group—and this presumably means the desires or feelings of the majority of the group—which make the standard both of that group as a whole and of the individuals who compose it. We may call this view *group subjectivism,* as distinguished from Hobbes's individual subjectivism. We should note, however, that both views come within our definition of the theory of the subjectivity of moral values. For in both cases moral values are dependent "on human desires, feelings, or opinions."

That a radical change had come over European thought on the subject of moral values by the time of Hobbes has been noted. We also noted that Hobbes was a contemporary of Galileo. Further, the philosophy of Hobbes in general was based upon the new science of his time. It expresses the sort of view of the world which was at that time suggested to philosophers by the work of the scientists. It may be difficult to detect at first sight any connection between the physics of Galileo, Kepler, or Newton and a change of view about the nature of moral values. The seventeenth century scientists confined their inquiries to the properties of matter, to astronomy and mechanics for the most part. What bearing can physics or astronomy possibly have upon morals? What difference can it make to any ethical theory whether the sun goes round the earth or the earth round the sun, whether the planetary orbits are circular or elliptical, whether the laws of motion and of falling bodies are those accepted by Aristotle or those put forward by Galileo? Yet we shall find, when we come to discuss the question, that it was precisely the new science which was the ultimate and basic cause of that radical change of opinion from moral objectivism to moral subjectivism which we are now discussing.

Although moral subjectivism, in one form or another, has become the prevalent opinion of the intellectuals of our time, it is by no means the universally accepted opinion. There have been throughout the modern period, and there still are, some distinguished and many competent thinkers, who repudiate it and accept rather some form of belief in the objectivity of moral values. What does this mean? We may remind ourselves of our definition. Moral objectivism is the view that moral values are *not* dependent upon any human desires, feelings, opinions, or other mental states. This, however, is merely a negative statement. It tells us only what moral values do not depend on. And we may well ask at this stage upon what, according to moral objectivists, they do depend. A preliminary answer might be that any view which holds that moral values are dependent on anything whatever which is not merely a part of the human mind, but is something which we should ordinarily speak of as being *outside* the human mind, would be a form of objectivism. One of the simplest kinds of objectivism would be the opinion that good and evil depend upon "the will of God," that, for example, good is to be defined not, as Hobbes would have it, as that which "pleaseth" a man, but rather as that which "pleaseth" God, and that evil is that which "displeaseth" God. Since the will of God, or that which "pleaseth" God, is independent of any human mental state, this would be, according to our definition, an objectivist view of morals. There are, however, many other possible forms of objectivism which are much more sophisticated and less simpleminded. They may differ from one another in their positive views as to what moral values depend on. But they all agree in the negative condition that, according to them all, moral values do not depend merely upon human psychology.

Let us look at some of the reasons why many philosophers think that moral values cannot be subjective. We saw that economic values are admittedly subjective, and that it therefore seems natural and plausible to suggest that moral and esthetic values are like them in this respect. In fact this is perhaps one of the reasons why people easily think that moral and esthetic values must be subjective. We should, however, note in the first place that this does not at all follow. For there may be important differences between economic values, on the one side, and moral and esthetic values, on the other. For instance, some people would say that moral and esthetic values are in some way "spiritual" in their nature, while economic values are "material," and that the former concern "higher" things, while the latter concern "lower" things. It is very difficult to say what this means, or whether the distinction has any real foundation. But it is at least possible that it indicates some genuine difference. We note at any rate that whereas apparently only men have moral feelings—whether this is also true of esthetic feelings seems a little doubtful—animals may be said in a sense to have or be aware of economic values. They do, that is to say, value such things as food, a shelter, and so on. These vague ideas, of course, prove very little. The utmost that they can be said to show is that *perhaps* there is some important difference between economic values and moral and esthetic values—though we have not been able to show what it is—which should put us on our guard against assuming too hastily that whatever is true of economic values, for instance that they are subjective, must necessarily also be true of moral and esthetic values. We must, however, try to see whether there may not be better arguments than this which have made some philosophers doubt that moral values are subjective. We shall find that there are *better* arguments, but that none of them can be said to be *conclusive*—which is the reason why there are still honest differences of opinion about the matter.

It is pointed out by those who reject subjectivism in moral and esthetic matters that a subjectivist theory implies the following three things, which do not seem to be true of moral and esthetic values. First, if the value of a thing is subjective, this is equivalent to saying that whether it has value or not is no more than a matter of taste. This is especially obvious in the case of individual subjectivism. Whether caviar is nice or nasty is plainly a matter of personal taste. It is nice for one person and nasty for another. And if we take the Hobbesian view of morals, we shall have to say such things as that whether murder is right or wrong is merely a matter of personal taste. It is right if you like it and wrong if you don't. It is true that this is to some extent avoided, or at least mitigated, if we adopt the theory of group subjectivism. Whether murder is right or wrong will not then be a matter of personal taste, but it will still be a matter of the mere tastes of social groups.

Secondly, subjectivism implies that, properly speaking, no value judgment is ever either true or false. That caviar is nice is neither a true statement about the caviar, nor a false one. For it only means "I like caviar." This may be a true statement about *me,* but it is not a statement about the caviar at all, and therefore it does not tell us anything either true or false about the caviar. The same will be true of moral and esthetic value judgments, if these values are subjective. If we say, "Murder is wicked," this is not really a statement about murder at all, and tells us nothing true or false about it, though it may imply something true or false about us or the group to which we belong.

A third implication of subjectivism is that, if it is true, there cannot be any rational discussion about moral or esthetic matters, nor can there be any such things as moral or esthetic education. If we adopt the individual subjectivism of Hobbes, it will be meaningless to discuss whether a thing is good or bad, or whether an action is right or wrong, because which they are is only a matter of the personal tastes of each individual. Not quite the same crude conclusion follows from group subjectivism. There may be, on that theory, a genuine difference of opinion between two individuals about a moral question, and it will be sensible for them to argue it. For if one says, "X is good," and the other says, "X is bad," the first means "our social group likes X," while the second means "our social group dislikes X," and it is possible to discuss rationally which of these two opinions is true. Moreover, on this view there may in a sense be such a thing as moral education, since there will be a necessity to indoctrinate the young with the preferences of the social group. But it will still be the case that *as between social groups* there can be no rational discussion of moral differences, and no such thing as the education of one group by another. For if the group to which I belong disapproves, shall we say, of slavery, this only means that my group dislikes it. And if some other social group approves of slavery, this only means that they like it. Thus the two groups stand to each other in the same way as the two individuals who respectively like and dislike caviar. No discussion between them will then be sensible, for each group is right about its own tastes.

Now the main argument of the moral objectivists has been that, although the three implications of a subjective theory of values— namely, that values are merely matters of taste, that value judgments are neither true nor false, and that no discussion of them is possible—are quite true of economic values and of questions such as whether the taste of a food is nice or not, they are wholly unacceptable if we apply them to moral and esthetic values. We find if we try to apply them to these values that we are forced to conclusions which jar on, or even outrage, our moral and esthetic feelings. And it is urged that a theory of morality which outrages our moral feelings cannot be a true theory; and that the same thing will be true of an esthetic theory.

The case is perhaps rather stronger in the case of moral values than it is in the case of esthetic values. We will take the weaker case first.

Undoubtedly there is, in differing judgments on artistic questions, a large measure of what may be called "mere" personal taste. One competent critic may prefer the poetry of Shelley, while another equally competent critic prefers that of Keats. One music lover may enjoy Beethoven more than Mozart, another Mozart more than Beethoven. In such cases we may be prepared to admit that tastes may legitimately differ. We are not inclined to insist that one opinion, our own, is simply "right," the other simply "wrong," although even here we may suspect that there is some failure of esthetic perception on the part of the critic who differs from us.

We think that he may have a blind spot as a result of which some esthetic quality which we perceive escapes him. But we admit the possibility that we on our side may have a blind spot which renders us incapable of fully appreciating the esthetic quality which he stresses. And so we are not disposed to insist dogmatically on our own opinion, and may be content to say that the difference is a matter of personal taste. But even here there is the suggestion that the question is not really one of personal taste, since we are inclined to suspect failure of perception on one side or the other or both. But since the issue seems undecidable, we are willing to let it go, to drop the argument with the polite or ambiguous phrase that "tastes differ."

But if a man prefers the poetry of Edgar Guest or Mrs. Hemans to that of Milton, the case is different. We are quite sure that he is esthetically blind. We do not usually use such words as "wrong," "incorrect," "untrue," or "mistaken." We are more likely to accuse him of "bad taste." But the word "bad" carries with it the implication of wrongness, the implication of some sort of objective truth in the value judgment which we oppose to his. And the word "taste" does not here have the same meaning as it does in the phrase "merely a matter of personal taste." If anything is merely a matter of personal taste, the implication is that one man's taste is as good as the other's, and that there is no question of a right and a wrong opinion. But to accuse a man of bad taste in art implies that there *is* a right and a wrong opinion, or at least a better and a worse opinion. This implies that the question at issue is *not* "merely a matter of personal taste," but that it is rather a question of true and false values, and in consequence that discussion of it is possible. No sensible person would seriously discuss whether caviar is or is not nicer than oysters. But critics *do* discuss the values of a work of art, and this is evidence that they do regard their disagreements as more than differences of personal taste.

What, it may be asked, is the technique of such a discussion? How does one side hope to convince the other? How can anyone involved in such a dispute ever prove his case? To what observable facts can he appeal? If two men should dispute whether the earth is round or flat, there are definite facts which can be observed which will settle the question. But surely no such procedure is possible when the question is one of the esthetic value of a work of art. And if there is no conceivable way of settling such a dispute, no observable facts which support one side or the other, surely we shall have to admit that the question is one of personal taste regarding which it is senseless to argue, or in other words that the value is subjective.

But critics actually do argue such matters, and their discussions are not regarded, either by themselves or by other people, as merely senseless—as we should regard the argument about caviar and oysters. There must therefore be some method or technique which is in principle capable of settling their disagreements, though it may, of course, fail in particular cases. And it is, I think, usually something like this. Each side thinks that the other has failed to perceive some value or dis-value which is perceivable in the work of art. He assumes, or at least hopes, that his opponent has the esthetic sensitivity required to perceive the value, but that he has somehow missed seeing it. He therefore attempts to point it out. He draws attention to some quality of the work of art which he thinks has escaped notice. He may succeed, in which case the dispute is settled. But if he fails, this may be due to either of two causes. It may be that his opponent does have the required esthetic sensitivity, that he could perceive the value in question, but that the procedure of pointing it out has so far been unsuccessful. Or it may be that he simply does not possess the required sensitivity, or in other words that he has a blind spot. In either case the presupposition of the discussion, the assumption which renders the argument rational and not senseless, is that *there either is or is not some value to be perceived,* and that there is in consequence a right and a wrong opinion about the matter. This is inconsistent with esthetic subjectivism.

The possibility of education in esthetic appreciation points to the same conclusion. A student hopes to learn what are true and what are false values in art. But if all esthetic questions were no more than matters of personal taste, then the opinion of the most uneducated freshman student about a work of art would be just as good as the opinion of the most experienced artist or art critic. Why then should he trouble to go through the arduous process of art education?

Now none of these arguments against esthetic subjectivism is decisive. The instructed subjectivist is well aware of them, and thinks that he has good answers to them. I shall not discuss his possible answers at present, because my aim at the moment is not to solve the problem of the objectivity or subjectivity of esthetic and moral values, but only to present it to the reader as a problem, and to point out how difficult a problem it is. The arguments just put forward against esthetic subjectivism are not conclusive, but on the other hand they are far from negligible. The objectivist has at least an arguable and a tenable case. His opinion may in the end be mistaken, but it cannot be dismissed as foolish. We see at least that we cannot argue that, because economic values are obviously subjective, esthetic values must necessarily be subjective too. We see that there are difficulties in holding that esthetic values are subjective which do not arise in the case of economic values. The truth about the matter, whatever it may be, is certainly not obvious, and is very difficult to discover.

Exactly the same arguments which have just been put forward against esthetic subjectivism apply—but I think with greater force —against moral subjectivism. Are moral questions merely matters of personal or group taste? In order to test this we will take an extreme case, because in an extreme case the principles involved will stand out strongly. Suppose that there is a man who is by nature so cruel, so sadistic, that he enjoys burning children alive. We should, of course, condemn his pleasure as a moral abomination. But should we admit that this judgment was, after all, only a matter of taste? Apparently this is what Hobbes would have to say on the basis of the passage quoted above—though we may be sure that Hobbes would not have said it. If burning children alive pleases a man, then it is, on the basis of the passage from Hobbes, good. If it displeases him, it is evil. And the one opinion is no better or truer than the other. As I pointed out before, individual subjectivism of the Hobbesian type, is not now held, so far as I know, by any philosopher. It is group subjectivism which is nowadays popular. So let us consider the question on that basis. In our culture burning children alive would be universally condemned. But suppose anthropologists discovered some other culture in which such actions were considered highly meritorious. Should we admit that the moral question involved was only a matter of group taste, and that the moral standard of this other culture was not evil or bad or inferior to ours, but was merely *different* from ours? Would not the moral sense of every decent man rebel against such an interpretation? But if so, how can we admit subjectivism?

The fact that the example taken, that of burning children alive for pleasure, is extreme, even absurd, makes no difference to the argument. We should feel the same, only less strongly, if a weaker example were chosen. We cannot admit that stealing or lying are good things merely because some person, or group of persons, likes or approves of them. We cannot admit that moral questions are only matters of taste, that all opinions about them are equally true, and that all discussions of them are senseless.

Again the argument may not be conclusive, for the subjectivist may perhaps have a reply ready, but we can hardly help feel that there must be something wrong with a theory of morals which so outrages our conscience. At least the onus of proof seems to be on the subjectivist, and to be a heavy one.

Suppose we admit, then, that moral objectivism, whether ultimately true or not, is at least a view which has something to be said for it. We may then go on to ask what sort of a theory of the nature of moral values will be consistent with it. The phrase "the nature of" moral values needs explaining. Consider Hobbes again. His theory was that the nature of goodness consists in the fact that the good thing pleases the man who calls it good. This is, in fact, his *definition* of goodness. To give a definition of anything is to state its nature. Hobbes's definition makes moral values subjec-

tive. So we may rephrase our question in the form: what definitions of good and evil could be suggested according to which good
and evil would be objective?

There are many such possible definitions. One example has
already been given. We might suppose that the proper definition
of a morally right action is that it is an action which is in accordance with the will of God. A wrong action will then be defined
as one which is contrary to the will of God. This is a view which
has often been taken, for instance by the theologian Paley in the
eighteenth century. Whether this theory is true or false is not
what I am now discussing. The point is that it is an example of a
theory according to which moral values are objective. For an
objective value is, by definition, one which is independent of any
human desire, feeling, purpose, opinion, or other mental state.
And God's will, if there is such a thing, is plainly independent of
any such human mental states. For instance, if it is God's will
that we love one another, then this will be good whatever any
human being, or set of human beings, thinks or says or feels or
wants. If moral values are fixed by God's will, and not by any
human wills or desires, they are objective.

To give another example of an objectivist definition of morals.
Suppose that someone believes that there is such a thing as a
cosmic purpose. He might believe this without accepting any
theology or any belief in God. He might speak of it as just
"nature's purpose." He might then define good actions as those
which tend to advance the world-purpose, bad actions as those
which tend to thwart it. Moral values would then be objective
because the cosmic purpose is presumably as independent of
human ideas or wishes as is God's will. As we have seen, a non-
theistic teleology of this kind is quite possible. The purpose will
be immanent in the world itself, not a conscious plan in the mind
of a being external to the world. Presumably the world will have
to be in some sense alive, but it does not follow that it must
necessarily be conscious. A tree is a living being, but not a conscious one. We sometimes talk as if a tree, reaching upwards to
the sunlight, or downwards towards the moisture in the soil, were

actuated by purpose. We speak of its "trying" to reach the sunlight or the moisture. It may be said that this is only a metaphor; or that, although it is useful to talk *as if* there were a purpose, we cannot really mean that there is one, because a purpose is necessarily a conscious idea. The Freudian concept of the unconscious renders this doubtful however. It is possible to suppose that the world, or nature, is governed by an immanent purpose or purposes which in some blind unconscious way it has in itself, without this purpose being a conscious plan in the mind of any transcendent personal being. And if any such philosophy is possible, then it will also be possible to suppose that moral values can be defined in terms of the immanent world-purpose, thus making them objective.

A third possible objectivist theory of moral and esthetic values may attempt to define them in terms of the Absolute. The conception of the Absolute was developed by certain German idealistic metaphysicians at the beginning of the nineteenth century, and their thought penetrated into England and America during the latter half of the century. The Absolute was supposed to be a "universal" mind, but not a personal mind like the popular conception of God. This universal mind may then be thought of as the source of all spiritual values, particularly of the so-called trinity of values, goodness, beauty, and truth. Such a philosophy will regard these values as objective, since the Absolute is independent of the human mind.

A more humdrum objectivist theory—which makes no mention of any ultimate reality or absolute being—is that which holds simply that moral and esthetic values are objective *qualities* of things, actions, or situations. By an objective quality of a thing is meant one which it is believed to possess independently of any perceiving mind. The roundness of a penny is such a quality, since it is believed that the penny will continue to be round independently of what any human or other mind either thinks or desires. It does not become square if any human being, or all human beings, should want it to be square or believe it to be square. It is quite possible to suppose that goodness and beauty are objective qualities in the same sense. It could be thought that a picture is beautiful even if no eye is seeing it and no mind thinking of it, in other words that it just has in itself a quality of beauty. In the same way it could be thought that a situation or action has an objective quality of moral goodness.

I do not myself think that this is at all a plausible view, and my purpose in mentioning it is only to illustrate the fact that it is not impossible to hold that moral and esthetic values are objective, since a number of theories of the nature of such values can be suggested any of which will be consistent with their objectivity.

Thus the upshot of our discussion is: first, that there are arguments, drawn from our moral and esthetic feelings, which, though not conclusive, suggest that the corresponding values are objective; and, second, that such a view, since several possible theories of the nature of these values are consistent with it, is a respectable and tenable hypothesis, although we have not yet made up our minds whether it is true.

Medieval men would never have used the language which we have been using in this chapter. They would not have talked of "objective" and "subjective" or even of "values." This is modern jargon. But that the idea which we have expressed by the phrase, "the objectivity of moral values," was implicit in all their thinking there can be no doubt. For as I shall proceed to show this idea is really a necessary part of *any* sort of religious belief about the world.

It is, in the first place, identical with the thought that the world is a moral order. For consider what is implied by the assertion that moral values are subjective. This means that they depend upon the purposes or desires or opinions or other mental states of human beings. Hence if there did not happen to be any human beings in the universe, there would be no moral values in it; nor are there any now, apart from human beings. Nothing in the universe is, in itself, either good or bad. There are no values— economic, esthetic, or moral—in the non-human universe. Values are purely human things. Such a view is common enough nowadays. The universe, it is sometimes said, is "indifferent" to our values, whether of beauty or goodness. Nature has no preference for good over bad things. Its mills turn out any kind of grist indifferently. This is the view that the world is *not* a moral order.

The view that it is a moral order—in other words that moral values are objective—was not only implicit in medieval thought, but is held, consciously or unconsciously, by religious men everywhere. It is an essential part of the religious attitude. It still finds expression in many things which plain people, who do not profess to be either philosophers or theologians, often say. Often enough those who give expression to it do not profess belief in any religious creed, and would perhaps deny that they are religious. The thoughts of the majority of plain men on such matters are apt to be vague and incoherent. But they may yield strong evidence of the persistence among us of ideas which intellectuals are doing their best to obliterate.

For instance, many people seem to believe such propositions as that "the good must triumph in the end"; or that truth has some inherent power which will enable it ultimately to win out over falsehood; or that there is some "force" in things making for goodness, a drive towards goodness immanent in the world. During the blackest period of World War II, when Britain was fighting alone after the fall of France, and when many people in America believed that Britain was about to collapse before a barbarian assault, a correspondent in England wrote to me with complete confidence that Britain would win the war even if the United States did not intervene. When I inquired what basis he had for this belief he replied that "it is impossible for a system based on lies, such as Hitler's, to prevail." He was an agnostic. The empirical or historical evidence for his belief is wholly inadequate. Such a belief stems rather from a vague feeling that the world is a moral order.

In the last chapter I remarked that belief in the teleological character of the world was not invented by Christianity, but has been characteristic of the thinking of the western world since at least the time of Plato and Socrates. The same is true of the view that the world is a moral order. According to Plato the world is moved not only by purpose, but by good purpose. It moves everywhere in the direction of the "form of the good."

It may be relevant to add that this belief is not confined to the western world. The idea of a world-purpose can be traced in Hinduism, which is in some sense theistic, but not perhaps in Buddhism. But the idea of the world as a moral order appears in both religions in the conception of "karma." The essence of the doctrine of karma is that every living being receives at some time —if not in his present life then in some later reincarnation—exact justice in the way of punishment or reward for his good or evil deeds. Thus at least the ethical quality of absolute justice is attributed to the world-order.

The truth is that the ultimately moral character of the universe, whether it is personified in the form of a righteous and transcendent God or is conceived as immanent in the world-process itself, has been a part of all advanced religious cultures. It has been, until recent times in the West, a universal belief of civilized humanity. The opposite conception, that of a blind universe which is perfectly indifferent to good or evil—though it appears occasionally in the ancient world, as in Lucretius—is characteristic only of the western world during the last three centuries, and is the product of the seventeenth century scientific revolution. That values are subjective and relative, that the world is not a moral order, is the fashionable belief of the intellectuals of our time. And this view of the world has seeped down to the masses. But since the older religious view persists under the surface, this gives rise to perplexities and contradictions in men's minds in contrast to the monolithic clarity and simplicity of the medieval mind.

Part II

The Modern World-Picture

※ 4 ※

THE RISE OF MODERN SCIENCE

THE FAMOUS CONFLICT BETWEEN SCIENCE AND RELIGION IS commonly thought of in terms of supposed contradictions between particular dogmas of religion and particular discoveries of science. Thus the discoveries of geology shattered the belief that the world was created in six days a few thousand years ago. The Darwinian theory of evolution showed that man is not a special creation unrelated to the animal kingdom. The application of scientific techniques of historical and literary criticism to the Bible proved that that book is not a literal record of facts dictated by God. A long history of scientific discoveries of this kind produced a series of shocks in the domain of Christian belief.

While it cannot be doubted that these shocks have had a powerful effect in the way of undermining religious faith, it must be pointed out that this is on the whole a very superficial account of the conflict between religion and science. The real antagonism lies much deeper. It is not between particular discoveries of science and particular dogmas of religion at all. It is rather that certain very general assumptions which are implicit in the scientific view of the world conflict with basic assumptions of the religious view—any religious view, not merely the Christian view —of the world. For instance, it is part of the religious view that the world is a moral order. Now the denial of this, the assertion that the world is not a moral order, is not, of course, a "discovery" of any particular science. It does not belong to physics or astronomy or botany. It is not even part of the general body of science, and no scientific man would be thought "unscientific" for denying it. It is not a scientific problem at all. It is a philosophical problem. How then can it be in any way fathered upon science? We are not yet ready to answer this question. That there is some connection is certain. But before we can say what it is we must have before us some account of the origins of modern science and its implications.

If we were concerned with the difficulties raised for religion by particular scientific discoveries, we should have to concentrate on comparatively recent science, particularly that of the nineteenth century. It was then that the new geology and the theory of evolution broke upon the world. But the general scientific attitude, the basic assumptions of the scientific view of the world —which have been the real enemies of religious faith—were rather the work of men such as Kepler and Galileo. The program of the whole scientific movement of the modern world, the presuppositions upon which it has been built, were complete by the time Newton had done his work. In so far as we are to consider science as the builder of the modern mind, it is the early scientists whom we have to study, not Lyell or Darwin, much less Einstein or Niels Böhr. It was the founders of science in the seventeenth century who produced the violent change from the climate of opinion of the medieval period to the climate of opinion of the modern period, some of the characteristics of which we have already examined. Those special discoveries of science which have seemed to conflict with special Christian dogmas came mostly in the nineteenth century. Yet the great age of religious skepticism was the eighteenth century, immediately following the birth of modern science. The nineteenth century was by comparison almost a return to an age of faith. For the romanticism which dominated it was essentially a religious reaction against skepticism. The modern mind is the product of seventeenth century science, not of that of the nineteenth century much less of twentieth century science. For this reason I shall devote the present chapter to a brief factual account of the seventeenth century scientific revolution.

Copernicus (1473-1543) lived a full century before the period which is properly denominated the seventeenth century scientific revolution. Yet that revolution would have been impossible without him, and it built upon his theories. Extracts from his book, *De revolutionibus orbium coelestium,* were published as early as 1530, but the full text did not appear until 1543, the year in which he died.

His great achievement, as everyone knows, was to replace the geocentric by the heliocentric theory of astronomy. In crude terms this means that the earth goes round the sun, not the sun round the earth. The geocentric theory, which had been taken for granted since ancient times, had been elaborated into a mathematical system by the Alexandrian astronomer Ptolemy in the second century of our era. The Ptolemaic system was built upon three basic assumptions: first, that the earth rests immovable at the center of the universe; second, that all the heavenly bodies revolve around it; third that their orbits round the earth are circular.

While the first two of these assumptions caused no difficulties, the third conflicts with plain facts which were well known even to the ancients. It had been known from ancient times that the planets "wander" in the sky. For instance, if Jupiter is watched throughout the year it will be observed that, in addition to its daily revolution round the earth along with the stars, it has an annual movement relative to the stars which is a kind of loop, roughly like this:

Diagram I: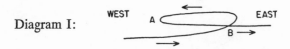

That is, it moves among the stars from west to east, turns backwards in a "retrograde" movement from B to A, and then resumes its eastward march. It traverses the loop in a period of some months. In the following year it loops the loop again, but not in the same region of the sky. The loops themselves move round the sky returning to roughly the same region after about twelve years. Thus the movement among the stars over the period of twelve years looks something like this:

Diagram II:

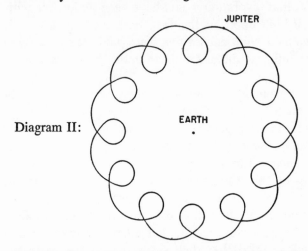

How is this complicated motion—something like which occurs in all the planets, and not only Jupiter—to be made consistent with the view that they move in circles round the earth as center?

The explanation of this was the great feat of Ptolemy's astronomy. He accounted for it by an ingenious theory of "epicycles." Suppose that on the rim of a wheel another wheel, which we will call an epicycle, is centered, as in the diagram:

Diagram III:

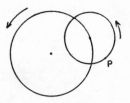

Then if both wheels rotate round their centers, a point on the rim of the epicycle, such as P, will perform an evolution similar to that of Jupiter as shown in Diagram II.

But suppose that the observed motions of a planet cannot be exactly explained by a circle and one epicycle, it may be that a circle and two epicycles, or even more, can be arranged so that the movement of the point P will exactly correspond to the movement of the planet, as thus:

Diagram IV: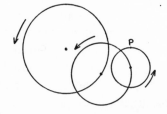

There is no end to the possible detailed elaborations of such an idea, and it is obvious that, with sufficient mathematical ingenuity, almost any wandering movement in the sky, provided it returns upon itself, can be explained in terms of nothing but circles. Great care will have to be taken to get the diameters of each of the circles right, and also the velocities of their rotations. But this is what the Ptolemaic system achieved for each of the heavenly bodies. It was done with sufficient accuracy to enable astronomers to make at least rough predictions about their positions in the heavens at future dates.

The great disadvantage of the system was its cumbersome and complicated character. No less than seven circles and eighty epicycles were found necessary to explain the movements of the known bodies of the solar system.

An interesting sidelight on the history and characteristics of human thought appears in connection with the question why the Ptolemaic astronomers thought it necessary to construct the actually non-circular observed motions of the planets out of fictitious circles. Why were they obsessed with the idea of the circle? Why did not Ptolemy simply say that Jupiter in fact moved round the earth in the eccentric course shown in Diagram II? Why should it not? Why must it be pretended that only circles are involved?

The question is complicated by the fact that the ancients believed that the heavenly bodies are fixed on to solid revolving spheres. If this were so, then the epicycles might be real. But if there were no such revolving spheres, if the planets moved in empty space, then the epicycles would be mere fictions, imaginary circles out of which the actually eccentric motions of the planets were constructed. They would be no more than mathematical dodges. Ptolemaic writers appear to have held both views. But whatever was the truth about the solid spheres, there is no doubt that this was not the only explanation why the Ptolemaic astronomers thought that all planetary paths must be somehow made out to be circular. There was another cause at work.

The Greeks, including Plato, supposed that the heavenly bodies are divine beings. They also thought that the circle is the only "perfect" figure. Therefore, since the heavenly bodies are divine, their motions must be perfect, that is to say, circular. It is not to be supposed that the Ptolemaic astronomers believed exactly this. But this belief of the Greeks produced in the western world a reverence for circles which obstructed astronomy for about two thousand years.

What exactly did Copernicus accomplish? The essence of his contribution to science lay in the brilliant insight that the looplike motions of the planets could be explained, in a much simpler manner than that employed by Ptolemy, if the assumption were made that the planets revolve round the sun, and that the earth itself is a planet which revolves round the sun while at the same time it rotates daily on its axis. Copernicus proved that if this assumption were made, he could dispense with most of Ptolemy's epicycles, and thus greatly simplify astronomical calculations. The exact point will be made clear by looking at the diagram:

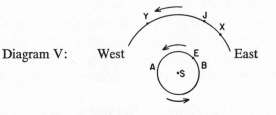

Diagram V: West   East

Suppose that the earth revolves around the sun in one year as shown by the arrows, and that Jupiter moves round the sun in a little over twelve years. In one year, then, Jupiter will move through an arc of a circle, say XY. Then when the earth is moving on the lower half of its circle from west to east, Jupiter will appear from the earth to be travelling rapidly from east to west. But when the earth is moving on the upper half of its circle from east to west, it will catch up and pass Jupiter, so that Jupiter will appear to an observer on the earth to have reversed its direction and to be travelling backwards from west to east. It will appear to be travelling backwards for the same reason as a train moving west at thirty miles an hour will, as seen by an observer on another train which passes the first on a parallel track at sixty miles an hour, appear to be travelling backwards. This explains why Jupiter is seen to be moving from east to west during part of the year, and then appears to reverse itself into a retrograde movement from west to east during the rest of the year. Thus we can get rid of the epicycles and explain the observed facts by merely having two circles, one for Jupiter and one for the earth. The same principle can be applied to the other planets.

One might naturally suppose that in this way Copernicus could have got rid of all Ptolemy's epicycles and be left with nothing but the sun in the middle and one circle for each planet. As a matter of fact he could not do this. But he greatly reduced the number of epicycles. Ptolemy had to assume eighty epicycles. Copernicus got rid of forty-six, but was left with thirty-four. The reasons for this are complicated. But one reason was that Copernicus still assumed that the orbits of the planets must be at least roughly circular. They are, in fact, elliptical, as Kepler afterwards showed. Hence the actual ellipses had still to be explained by Copernicus in terms of epicycles. But he did get rid of those epicycles by which Ptolemy had explained the loop-like motions of the planets.

By reducing the number of epicycles from eighty to thirty-four, Copernicus greatly simplified the calculations necessary in the astronomy of the solar system. This greater simplicity is the only way in which the Copernican system is superior to the Ptolemaic. It is not any "truer." It is only more convenient, because simpler. Copernicus did not discover a single new fact about the universe. He made no observations on the nature or movements of the heavenly bodies which had not been made before. He did not, for instance, observe a new planet or a new comet. He thus discovered no new facts. What he did was to arrange the already known facts in a new and simpler way. That the heliocentric theory is not truer, but only more convenient, than the geocentric theory, follows at once from the principle of the relativity of motion. Suppose that there were only two bodies, A and B, in the universe, and that they were, at a given time, ten miles apart; and that five minutes later they were observed to be only five miles apart. Motion has taken place. But which of the two bodies has moved, or have they both moved? There is obviously no possible way in which this question could be answered. No measurement or observation could throw any light on it. Thus it would make no difference at all which body you say has moved. You could assume, if you like, that A has remained at rest, and that B has moved towards it at a velocity of a mile a minute. Or you could assume that B was at rest and that A moved at a velocity of a mile a minute. Or you could assume that they both moved, A at twenty miles an hour and B at forty miles an hour; or A at fifty miles an hour and B at ten miles an hour; and so on. Since there would be no facts against which you could check these assumptions so as to say which is correct, it follows that no one of them is more "true" than the others. But it is possible that one might be more convenient than the others. For instance, it might be easier to assume that only one of the bodies had moved, and not both. But any of the different hypotheses would equally well explain the observed fact, namely, the diminution of the distance between A and B. Exactly the same principle will hold if the number of bodies in the universe is three, or thirty, or a billion, instead of two. You can take any one body as your center of reference, consider it at rest, and suppose that all the other bodies are moving relatively to it. Thus it is no truer to say that the sun is at rest and that the earth goes round it than it is to say the opposite. But

Copernicus proved that it is mathematically much simpler to take the sun as the center, since it gets rid of a lot of complicated calculations about epicycles. Hence if anyone today likes to be an eccentric individualist and to assert that he still believes that the sun goes round the motionless earth, there will be nobody who can prove him wrong—a way of defending the medieval view which unfortunately did not occur to the Pope and the Inquisition who condemned Galileo as heretical for accepting the heliocentric theory.

It is sometimes said that although Copernicus did not prove his theory to be true, this was later proved by Newton, and further confirmed by later discoveries such as that of stellar parallaxes. This is not strictly correct. All it means is that Newton found it convenient to base his law of gravitation on the Copernican view, and that this procedure proved enormously successful. But it would still be logically possible to assume the Ptolemaic view, and to account on the basis of it for all the facts of astronomy and physics known up to date. One can go further and say that no fact which could be observed in the future could ever conceivably contradict it. The only trouble is that if we were now to assume the truth of the Ptolemaic view, we should have to rewrite the whole of science to fit the assumption, including of course Newton's law of gravitation, not to mention Einstein's; that this new version of science would be almost inconceivably complicated; that this would be very inconvenient; and that it seems therefore better on the whole to "believe in" the Copernican theory.

It must not be supposed that the heliocentric theory, as soon as it was proposed by Copernicus, gained ascendancy. It took over a century before it came to be generally accepted even by men of science. It was still in doubt even in Galileo's time a hundred years later. The great Danish astronomer Tycho Brahe, who flourished roughly half a century after Copernicus, still insisted that the earth is at rest with the sun moving around it, although he followed the new theory to the extent of believing that some of the planets move round the sun—a curious compromise between the Ptolemaic and the Copernican hypotheses which found considerable favor at the time. It will be noted, of course, that this compromise theory is, in view of the principle of the relativity of motion, a perfectly defensible hypothesis, as "true" as either of the two hypotheses between which it mediates. Even Galileo accepted the heliocentric theory only after hesitation. It then became a matter of furious controversy between science and the Church. Galileo finally put it on the scientific map, though he suffered imprisonment at the hands of the Inquisition for doing so.

Tycho Brahe (1546-1601) is a transitional figure. His contribution to science does not lie in his compromise between the two theories of astronomy, or in any other theoretical advance— his gifts were not those of the theoretician—but in the practical business of observation. He built the first astronomical observatory. He invented the quadrant for measuring the altitudes of the heavenly bodies above the horizon, and the sextant for measuring the angular distances between them. The telescope not having been invented, his observations were made with the naked eye. He spent his life making and recording in tables the positions of the planets in the sky at specific dates and times—that is to say, in plotting their paths. He did this with a degree of accuracy previously unknown. He reduced the previous margin of error from ten minutes of arc to half a minute, i.e., to one one-hundred-and-twentieth of a degree. His tables and observations constituted the data on which Kepler and Newton afterwards built their theoretical constructions, and their work could not have been done without his prior spadework. He may be called the father of accurate measurement in astronomy.

Kepler (1571-1630) brought to science gifts which were the opposite of Tycho's. He was not a skilled observer, but a great theoretician. He made use of Tycho's observations. His great discovery was that the planets move in ellipses, not in circles. He established three laws of planetary motion. The first was that the planets move in elliptical orbits with the sun in one focus, the other focus being empty. The second law, that each planet sweeps out equal areas in equal times, established a mathematical formula which correlated the velocity of a planet at a given point in its orbit with its distance from the sun at that point. The third law stated that the square of the time of a planet's revolution in its orbit is proportional to the cube of its mean distance from the sun. Given these three laws, the position of a planet in the sky at any time can be predicted without recourse to any theory of epicycles. What enabled Kepler to get rid of the epicycles which were still left in the astronomy of Copernicus was his substitution of ellipses for circles. Thus he completed the simplification of astronomical theory which had begun with Copernicus.

Kepler's work is revolutionary in that he broke finally with the superstitious awe in which the circle as the perfect figure had been held. And his work is marked also by one of the outstanding characteristics by which modern science is distinguished from medieval and Greek science. Whereas the ancients and the medieval writers tended to argue *a priori* from assumed first principles that the truth *must* be so and so, modern science is based upon the belief that the only way to discover truth is to look at the facts. If you want to know whether there are oak trees in the Congo, you cannot find this out by sitting in an armchair in New York and arguing from some *a priori* axiom that there must be oak trees there, or that there cannot be any. You have to look at the facts, which in this case would mean going to the Congo to see. This seems obvious to us now, but it is only modern science which has made it obvious. The argument that the planets must move in circles because that is the perfect figure was an example of the opposite procedure. But Kepler, by looking at the facts (as observed by Tycho Brahe)—which in this case meant observing the actual paths of the planets in the sky—discovered that the planets move in elliptical orbits.

Galileo (1564-1642) is famous for so many discoveries that we must here pass over most of them with a bare mention in order to concentrate on the one which is most important to our story—which concerned the laws of motion.

He constructed the first astronomical telescope. Turning it upon the moon, he discovered that that body is not a perfect sphere, but is wrinkled by mountains and valleys. This was a nail in the coffin of the medieval view of the world because it had always been supposed that the heavenly bodies must be perfect spheres for the same reason as their orbits must be perfect circles; the sphere being the only perfect solid figure. The existence of mountains and valleys on the moon also made it probable that the moon is composed of the same sort of gross matter as the earth, whereas the medieval view was that the earth alone is made of crude matter, while the heavenly bodies, being nearer the divine, are composed of a special ethereal or semi-divine substance.

Galileo observed with his telescope many new stars invisible to the naked eye. He made the famous discovery of four of the satellites of Jupiter. This raised a storm because it suggested that the earth with its moon might very likely be a planet moving round the sun, like Jupiter. Accordingly learned men refused Galileo's invitation to look through his telescope and see Jupiter's satellites for themselves, lest their faith in religion should be corrupted. One critic made the comment that these satellites are invisible to the naked eye, and can exert no influence on the earth, and that they are therefore useless, and consequently cannot exist. This remark is not merely funny, as it may seem to us. It brings to a sharp focus a fundamental contrast between the medieval mind and the modern mind. For it is based upon the premise that *what is not useful for some purpose cannot exist,* which expresses in a sentence the assumption of the teleological character of the universe. If it seems funny to us, this is because we no longer believe that whatever exists must serve some purpose, because, in fact, we have lost faith in a world-purpose. The incident also illustrates the medieval habit of arguing from *a priori* principles that the truth must be so and so, whereas Galileo, embodying the spirit of modern science, looked at the facts. The whole clash of the medieval and the modern thus appears in this incident.

But the great discovery of Galileo on which attention should here be concentrated was the first law of motion. This was not indeed very clearly stated by Galileo. It received explicit formulation in the work of Newton. Nevertheless Galileo was the first to understand it. If you push a cart along a rough road, and then stop pushing, the cart soon slows down and stops. If your automobile is running at fifty miles an hour, and you turn off the engine, the automobile likewise slows down and comes to a stand-still. To keep the cart or the automobile running at a uniform speed, you have to keep on applying a force to it. All ordinary observations of moving bodies seem to prove the rule that a force of some kind is required to keep a body moving. This was sup-posed by Aristotle to be a law of nature, and was accepted as such throughout the middle ages until the time of Galileo. The same law was applied to the planets and stars. They are in continual motion in the sky. Therefore some force must be pushing or pull-ing them. A popular belief was that spirits or angels carry them along. Even scientific men made the same assumption that a moving force is required. Thus Descartes suggested that space is full of whirlpools of ether which carry the planets round and round, as the force of the water in an eddy will carry floating objects round with it.

The first law of motion tells us, to the contrary, that no force is required to keep an object moving with a uniform velocity. It states that a body continues indefinitely in its state of rest, or of uniform motion in a straight line, unless some force acts upon it. So far as the condition of a body at rest is concerned, this agrees with common sense. If a body is at rest, it will remain at rest indefinitely unless some force pushes or pulls it from its place. This is what everybody would suppose. But what the law states about a body in motion is revolutionary, and seems contrary to all experience. It says that if an automobile is travelling at sixty miles an hour, with the engine turned off, it will continue travel-ling in a straight line at sixty miles an hour *forever,* unless some force is applied to it to stop it. The force which stops it is, of course, friction. If there were no friction, the car would never stop.

How did Galileo know, or "prove" this? How do we prove it now? The answer is that nobody can prove it. We have absolutely no experience of bodies moving without any force acting upon them. On the earth friction of some kind acts on all moving bodies. It is true that if a stone is thrown along a sheet of ice it will travel much further than if it is thrown along a rough surface. This is sufficient to *suggest* Galileo's law, since it tends to show that the less friction there is the further the body will keep on moving before it comes to a stop. But it is a bold and vast leap from this to the statement that with no friction at all it would keep on moving forever. No one could ever have any positive and decisive evidence of the truth of this because bodies moving without forces of some kind acting on them are unknown in our experience, and probably do not exist in the universe. For even the stars and planets are acted on by the force of gravitation.

Thus the law cannot be proved, but it is the simplest assumption we can make if we want, in a convenient manner, to predict physical motions. The case is the same here as with the "discovery" of Copernicus that the sun is the center of the solar system. There are various other assumptions about motion which you *could* make, and on the basis of which you could successfully explain all the observed phenomena of motion. You could make the common-sense assumption that bodies slow down and stop if no force acts upon them. Or you could assume that bodies acted on by no force will go on moving forever, but that their paths will be circular. You would then have to make suitable assumptions about the forces, for instance, that if a body is moving in a straight line a force must be acting on it to pull it out of its circular path. But if you make any assumption other than Galileo's, you will have to rewrite the science of mechanics in very elaborate and troublesome ways.

The special way in which the first law of motion became important in astronomy is that it enabled scientists to explain planetary and other celestial motions without assuming either the spirits or angels of popular thought or the whirlpools of Descartes.

This brings us to Newton (1642-1727). Newton was the great genius who completed the work of the foundation of modern science. He stood on the shoulders of Copernicus, Tycho Brahe, Kepler, and Galileo, and he could not have done his great work without them. But he brought to a conclusion the revolution in scientific outlook which they began. His contributions to science, apart from his discovery of the law of gravitation, were enormous. But here we shall have to ignore everything except the law of gravitation.

The point to note is that the assumption of the first law of motion abolished the necessity of supposing that there must be a tangential force pushing or pulling the planets along their paths. Newton began his work by trying to explain the revolution of the moon around the earth, and only later applied the same explanation to the revolution of the planets round the sun.

Diagram VI:

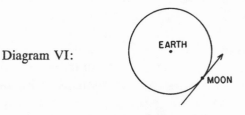

The theory that spirits push the planets and their satellites, and Descartes' theory of whirlpools, however we may consider the former more superstitious and the latter more scientific in spirit, were exactly alike so far as their mechanics were concerned. Both the spirits and the whirlpools exert forces acting along the tangent. The direction of the force must of course keep changing from point to point on the orbit in order to push the planets around instead of in a straight line, but it will always be along the tangent. But now if we assume, as the first law of motion does, that the moon would, if no force at all acted on it, go on moving forever at the same speed in the straight line represented by the arrow in the above figure, then we see that the only thing required to make it move round and round the earth will be a force acting along the radius from the moon to the center of its orbit, the earth.

Diagram VII:

No tangential force is necessary, since the moon's everlasting motion is explained without any forces, and the only thing which requires a force to explain it is the change of direction from the straight line.

Newton, perceiving this, could dispense with all tangential forces, and look for a radial force. That this force was gravitation was by no means at once obvious, and to identify it as gravitation required great imaginative genius. It was not that the idea of gravitation was wholly new. Gilbert had already suggested that the earth is a magnet. Kepler had believed that the planets are moved by some power emanating from the sun. In any case gravitation was already known as a force acting towards the center of the earth. Apples fall from trees. But how far out into space does the gravitational force of the earth extend? If you ascend a mile in a balloon, you know that it is still exerting its influence, because if you throw something out of the balloon it falls to the ground. And bodies carried to the top of a mountain are still heavy. But as a matter of fact, as you ascend higher, the force of gravitation grows less and less, as is shown by the fact that a body at the top of a mountain weighs less than it does at sea-level. How can you be sure that the force does not fade out altogether at some point between the earth and the moon? How can you be sure that the moon, like the apple, tends to fall to the earth, and is only prevented from doing so by the outward pull of its own centrifugal force as it whirls round in its orbit?

There can be no direct evidence of this since no one can travel to a point halfway to the moon to see whether objects at that distance still tend to fall back to the earth. Newton therefore could not prove it, nor can anyone now. He just took it as an hypothesis and endeavored to see whether by this hypothesis he could explain the facts of the moon's motion. He made another guess. If the moon tends to fall to the earth, the only thing which keeps it from doing so must be its centrifugal force. And in order to keep it in its orbit the earth's attractive force must be equal and opposite to the centrifugal force. Some work had already been done on centrifugal forces by Huyghens, and Newton made use of this. Putting everything together he tried out the hypothesis—which subsequently, when it was found to work, was named the law of gravitation—that the gravitational force between any two bodies is directly proportional to the product of their masses and inversely proportional to the square of the distance between them. For the sake of shortness we may call this the law of the inverse square. In order to try this formula on the moon, he had to know its distance from the earth and the masses of the earth and the moon. He made use here of estimates which had already been made. His problem was to see whether, on these assumptions, he could mathematically calculate the motions of the moon so that the calculated motions would agree with the observed motions. To his great disgust he found that his attempt was a failure to the extent that there was a twelve per cent difference between the calculated motions and the actual motions. Newton, whether for this reason or some other, abandoned the problem for a long period. But when later it was found that the estimate of the distance of the moon from the earth which he had used in his calculations was in error, and a more accurate estimate was made, he took up the problem again. Using again the law of the inverse square, and the new estimate of the moon's distance, he recalculated the moon's motions, and this time his calculations agreed with the observed facts.

The rest of the story is brief in retrospect, though it involved immense labors. Newton found that he could explain the motions of the planets round the sun by the same law as explained the motion of the moon round the earth. Subsequent work showed that the law can successfully explain vast numbers of other phenomena, for instance, those perturbations of the planets which are due to their gravitational forces acting on each other, and the phenomena of ocean tides. It was also found that the law can be extended beyond the solar system, and applies throughout space to all the stars. It thus became the universal law of gravitation. As is well known, Einstein has now substituted for it a more all-embracing law of gravitation. But that part of the story of science does not concern us in this book.

A further important point is that Kepler's three laws of planetary motion were shown to be consequences of the one law of gravitation. That is to say, if you assume the law of gravitation, mathematical calculation will show that Kepler's three laws follow from it. They are not now "ultimate" laws as they seemed to be in Kepler's time. They have been "explained" by the law of gravitation. This throws light on the scientific concept of explanation. To explain a particular fact, such as the position of Jupiter in the sky at a given moment, means to show that it is a particular instance of some general principle or law, such as Kepler's laws. To explain the law itself means to show that it is a particular instance of some more general law. Thus Kepler's laws were proved to be particular cases of Newton's law, and Newton's law has now been shown to be a particular case of Einstein's law. How far explanation can go in this way we do not know. The ideal would be to show that everything which happens in the universe of whatever kind is finally to be explained in terms of one single ultimate law. No one knows whether this is even theoretically possible. And whether, if it were, one would have to say that the one ultimate law is itself "inexplicable" is a question which I leave to the reader to ponder.

A point of importance in regard to the relations between religion and science must here be noted. It was known to Newton that there are certain "irregularities" in the observed motions of the planets which he could not explain in terms of his law of gravitation. In other words, their actual motions diverged very slightly from what they should be as calculated by his law. Moreover if these irregularities were cumulative, they would in the course of time pile up to such great deviations that they would upset the whole balance of the solar system. The planets would either dive into the sun or break loose from its control and rush off into outer space. Why is it that this does not happen? Newton could think of only one explanation. It must be that from time to time God intervenes and puts the errant planets back on their proper paths. This is noteworthy as being, so far as I know, the last historical occasion on which a great scientist was willing to give supernatural intervention as a cause of an observed phenomenon. The German philosopher Leibniz observed that Newton's God was a mechanic, and a poor one at that, since he could only make a machine which could be kept going right by frequent subsequent tinkering.[1]

There is one other scientist whom I wish to mention here. Laplace (1749-1827) is not one of the founding fathers of science, and does not belong in the movement of thought which is commonly called the seventeenth century scientific revolution. He lived a century after Newton. Nor was he a scientific genius of the stature of Galileo or Newton. But he is of some importance in our story for reasons which will become evident in the next chapter.

Laplace showed that the irregularities in the movements of the planets which Newton was unable to explain by his law of gravitation are not cumulative, as Newton had supposed, but are self-correcting. Over a long enough period they cancel each other out. *Therefore it is not necessary to introduce God to correct them.*

Laplace was also one of the originators—Immanuel Kant being the other—of the famous nebular hypothesis for explaining the origin of the solar system. This was very influential in its time, although it is no longer accepted by astronomers. According to this hypothesis, the solar system was the offspring of a whirling nebula of incandescent gases. As the nebula cooled down, it contracted towards its center which became the sun. But in the dwindling process concentric rings of gas were left behind, and these rings, further cooling down, contracted into solid lumps which became the planets.

Now Newton had supposed that God created the solar system and set the planets and their satellites revolving round the sun with their proper speeds and motions in their proper orbits. The masses, distances, and velocities must all have been perfectly calculated by a mind "very well skilled in mechanics and geometry" so as to keep the machine running perfectly. If the earth had moved much more slowly than it does, it would have followed an orbit so eccentric that life on it would have been impossible; and if it had moved sufficiently slowly it would have collided with

[1] Leibniz' correspondence with Clarke: letters 1.4, 2.8, and 3.13.

the sun. If it had moved much faster than its present speed, it would have rushed off into outer space. If the distance between the earth and the sun had been much greater or less than it is, similar results would have ensued. The same things would be true of the other planets and satellites. The distances and velocities of all these bodies must all have been calculated so as to keep the celestial machine in perfect balance—except for the unfortunate and unaccountable "irregularities." Laplace gleefully pointed out that just as God was not necessary to correct the irregularities, so he was not necessary to create the solar system, since its origin was now explained by the nebular hypothesis. It is related that Napoleon said to him: "I understand, M. Laplace, that you have written a great book on the system of the universe, and have never even mentioned its Creator"; and that Laplace replied: "I have no need of that hypothesis."

The comment of a theist will be, of course, that even if the nebular hypothesis were true, it would in no way do away with the necessity for God as a creator. It only pushes the necessity back a step. Presumably God created the nebula which caused the solar system. Or perhaps he created something which caused the nebula which caused the solar system. If a creating mind is necessary at the beginning, it does not matter how many phases of the universe have intervened between the creation and the present time. That criticism of Laplace, however, makes another story. I am not now discussing the reasonableness of his views, but stating what they were. We shall see that they were to play an important part in the development of the modern mind—a topic which we shall have to leave to the next chapter.

5

THE CONSEQUENCES FOR RELIGION

NEWTON WAS A VERY DEVOUT CHRISTIAN. HE TOOK HIS theology even more seriously than his science. He would have been horrified if he had thought that his lifework would result in a general undermining of religious faith. And his own opinion was that it should have exactly the opposite effect. He even supposed that his system of celestial mechanics provided a proof of the existence of God. He wrote:

> The motions which the planets now have could not spring from any natural cause alone, but were impressed by an intelligent agent. . . . There is no natural cause which could determine all the planets, both primary and secondary, [this means the planets and their satellites] to move the same way in the same plane, without any considerable variation: this must have been the effect of counsel (i.e., planning). . . . Had the planets been as swift as comets . . . or had the distances from the centres about which they move been greater or less . . . or had the quantity of matter (i.e., mass) in the sun, or in Saturn, Jupiter, or the earth, and by consequence their gravitating power, been greater or less than it is; the primary planets would not have revolved round the sun, nor the secondary ones about Saturn, Jupiter, and the earth, in concentric circles as they do, but would have moved in hyperbolas or parabolas, or in ellipses very eccentric. To make this system, therefore, with all its motions, required a cause which understood and compared together the

quantities of matter in the several bodies of the sun and planets, and the gravitating powers resulting from thence; the several distances of the primary planets from the sun, and of the secondary ones from Saturn, Jupiter, and the earth; and the velocities with which these planets could revolve . . . ; and to compare and adjust these together in so great a variety of bodies, argues that cause to be not blind or fortuitous but very well skilled in mechanics and geometry.[1]

If the velocity of a planet were much greater than it is, or if its distance from the sun were greater, the planet would fly off by centrifugal force into outer space. If the planet moved at a slower speed than it does, or if its distance from the sun were less than it is, the planet would pass so near the sun that, if its speed or distance were sufficiently reduced, it would fall into the sun. Hence the velocity and the distance had to be exactly calculated for each and every one of the numerous bodies which compose the solar system, and each had to be adjusted to all the others, to ensure the continuance of the system in a balanced state. Obviously dead matter could not itself make these calculations. The cause of this could not be "blind or fortuitous." A mind, and moreover a mind "very well skilled in mechanics and geometry" was therefore required to account for the facts. This all-governing mind could only be God.

Newton's argument is only a particular version, or example, of what philosophers call the "argument from design" for the existence of God. The essence of the argument is that nature shows examples of the adaptation of means to ends, in other words, of planning, and that this implies a planner. In Newton's example the end is the balanced running of the solar system, and the means are adjustments of the velocities and distances of the planets to one another. Thinkers, including Newton himself, have given many other instances of such apparent design in the universe. The human or animal eye is a favorite example, although any other organ of the body, or the body as a whole, would do as well. The eye is a mechanism composed of a great number of

[1] Quoted, A. E. Burtt, *Metaphysical Foundations of Modern Physical Science* (New York: Harcourt, Brace & Co., 1925), p. 286.

parts, such as the iris, the lens, the cornea, the retina. Each of these parts again has parts. All of these parts, great and small, have to be exactly adjusted to one another to produce vision. Vision is evidently the end aimed at, and the means are the elaborate and complicated adjustments of part to part. The argument is exactly the same as Newton's. If the lens were at a greater or less distance from the retina; if it were opaque, not transparent; if the pupil were much larger or smaller than it is; if any of the parts were not adjusted as they are to the other parts; in any such case the result would have been, not vision, but blindness, or vision too dim or blurred to be useful. This co-operation of part with part, this delicate adjustment of each part to every other, it is argued, shows design, the adaptation of the parts to the end of enabling the animal to see.

Thousands of other examples have been suggested. Thus the pollination of flowers by bees and other insects is often quoted. The bee carries pollen from flower to flower. Chance cannot account for this. Evidently there is a purpose in nature to produce flowers. That is the end, and nature has adopted a singularly ingenious set of means. The purpose, it is evident, is not in the mind of the bee. The only explanation is the purpose of a mind which controls nature.

A Belgian scientist, Lecomte du Noüy, recently produced a book called *Human Destiny*. In this he argues that the protein molecule, which is necessary for life, could not have been produced by chance, but must have been the result of design. For its chemical structure is so enormously complicated that even if chance should have produced one such molecule on the earth, it is inconceivable that it should have produced, during the relatively short astronomical period of the earth's existence, the millions of such molecules which were necessary for the existence of races of living beings. Life, then, was the end; the adjustments of atom to atom in the molecule the means.

It is evident that all the cases cited—the solar system, the production of the eye, the pollination of flowers, the protein molecule —are merely different examples of one and the same argument, and that they all depend on the same logic. The logical examination of the argument as it appears in one example will therefore apply to all the others. I shall accordingly analyze Newton's argument from the solar system to see what, if anything, it actually proves.

Lest there should be any misunderstanding about the motive which leads me into this analysis, I will state it. I shall show that Newton's argument is entirely worthless, and therefore that the argument from design—whatever example is chosen—is worthless. The aim is not to produce skepticism regarding the existence of God. The problem of the truth of religion will in the end come up for discussion, but not now. The immediate aim is to show that no scientific argument—by which I mean an argument drawn from the phenomena of nature—can ever have the slightest tendency either to prove or to disprove the existence of God, in short that science is irrelevant to religion. This aim evidently has two parts, first, to show that no argument from nature—such as the argument from design—has the slightest tendency to prove the existence of God; and second, that no argument from nature can disprove it. At present I am concerned with the first half of this argument.

It has to be admitted as a fact that the various masses, velocities, and distances of the planets, being what they are, have produced the *effect* that the planets move as they do round the sun; and that any other combination of masses, velocities, and distances, would have produced some other effect. But how does this show that this effect, which was actually produced, was not merely an *effect*, but also an *end?* An end, in the sense in which the word is used here, means something which is aimed at, planned, or purposed, by a mind. And how does the argument show that the effect was an end in this sense?

The same question arises in regard to any alleged instance of design. In every case we have a certain set of causes which produces a certain set of effects. Various mechanisms in the eye produce vision. The peculiar anatomies of the bee and the flower, the search of the bee for honey, and other circumstances, produce pollination. A variey of forces and movements of atoms produces the protein molecule. The whole point of the argument lies in the assertion that these effects, the balance of the solar system, vision, pollination, the protein molecule, are not only effects produced by causes, but also ends aimed at. How is this known? That they are effects can be established by observation. But if something is an end, this can never be directly observed, and must accordingly be an inference of some kind. For we can observe only successions of events and things; we can observe colors, weights, shapes, measurements, and the like, but never the fact of a thing being purposed as an end. For instance, I receive a letter with my name on it. All I can *observe* is the paper and the ink. The fact that my receiving the letter was an end aimed at by a person who wrote the letter is inferred. Hence our question is: from what facts is it inferred in the argument from design that the various effects—solar system, pollination, etc.—were ends aimed at by a mind? Why is it said that they could not have been produced by "chance," that is to say, by the mere operation of the "blind" forces and laws of nature without any design?

We shall find that there are two grounds on which the inference is based. The first is the extreme complexity of the causes, the fact that a vast variety of causes have had to work together to produce the effect. Thus it is an essential part of Newton's argument that the solar system is enormously complicated. There are a very large number of bodies in it. There are a large number of different masses, velocities, and distances to be adjusted to one another. The wonderful thing is that so many different things co-operate with one another to produce the balanced solar system. "To compare and adjust these together *in so great a variety of bodies* [italics mine] argues that cause to be not blind or fortuitous, but . . ." If there had been only two bodies in the solar system, the argument would not have been so impressive. There are in the sky examples of two bodies—binary stars—which revolve around one another. Does this show design? Might it not have been the result of chance? In all the examples of supposed design in nature, the fact that very great numbers of things have co-operated to produce the effect is stressed. The eye is a vastly complicated mechanism. How could all these thousands of parts have been exactly adjusted to one another to produce this one result, vision, unless by design? The complicated character of the protein molecule—the alleged fact that such a complicated structure of atoms could not have been produced by chance—is the very nerve of Lecomte du Noüy's argument.

How does complexity of co-operating causes prove design? Newton does not say, but Lecomte du Noüy does. If chance alone had operated, any arrangement of atoms might have occurred. Their actual arrangement in the protein molecule is only one out of thousands of billions of possible arrangements which might have occurred. Therefore the chances against this particular ar-rangement occurring, rather than any other, had thousands of billions of chances against it, and was almost infinitely improb-able. We must therefore suppose that it was designed. Applying this line of thought to Newton's instance of the solar system we see that, in addition to the one pattern of paths which the planets actually do take, there is a practically infinite number of other patterns of paths which might have been taken if the masses, distances, and velocities had been different. The earth might have followed any one of millions of more or less eccentric elliptical orbits, or any one of millions of parabolic or hyperbolic orbits. Therefore the chances against the one orbit it does take were billions to one. Hence it was almost infinitely improbable that it should take its present path, if the matter had been left to chance. Therefore a special cause, a divine mind, must be postulated to account for its actual orbit.

In order to test this argument, let us suppose that the earth had actually taken some other path, for instance:

Diagram VIII: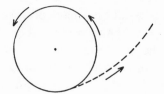

The circle in the diagram represents the actual orbit of the earth. The dotted line represents some other path which it might have taken if, for example, it had been heavier and flown off by centrifugal force into outer space. Now what were the chances against the earth taking *that* particular path (the dotted line)? *They were exactly the same as the chances against its present orbit.* For there were exactly the same number of other paths which it might have taken. The same would be true whatever path the earth took, whether it had flown off into space or spiraled into the sun. Whatever path the planet had taken would have been equally improbable. Therefore the fact that it took the path it did is no argument in favor of its having been planned.

We now see what may at first appear to be a very curious fact. *Whatever happens in the world is almost infinitely improbable,* for there are always an infinite number of other things which could have happened instead. A man walking along a street is killed by a tile blown off a roof by the wind. We attribute this to chance—that is, to the operation of blind natural laws and forces, without any special design on the part of anyone. Yet the chances against that event happening were almost infinite. The man might have been, at the moment the tile fell, a foot away from the spot on the sidewalk on which the tile fell, or two feet away, or twenty feet away, or a mile away. He might have been at a million other places on the surface of the earth. Or the tile might have fallen at a million other moments than the moment in which it did fall. Yet in spite of the almost infinite improbability of that happening, we do not find it necessary to suppose that someone threw the tile down from the roof on purpose. We are quite satisfied to attribute the event to chance, that is, to the operation of natural forces.

The complexity of the causes which had to co-operate to produce the death of the man from the falling tile was incalculably great. The movements of all the molecules of air in the world were involved, for if the meteorological state of the atmosphere anywhere had been different, that gust of wind might not have come at that moment. One of the causes of the man's being killed was the discovery of America by Columbus. For if America had not been discovered, neither the man nor the tile would have been where they were. Indeed the whole complexity of the world's history was involved in that event. And this is true of every event which happens in nature. Whatever happens in the world, the complexity of the causes which must co-operate to produce that exact event is beyond all possible reckoning. Plainly therefore the argument that the extreme complexity of co-operating causes is evidence of design is wholly fallacious.

We must not, of course, be misled by the use which the argument makes of such words as "adjust" and "co-operate." The parts of the eye, and the masses, distances, and velocities in the solar system, are said to be adjusted to one another and to co-operate. If "adjusted" is understood to mean "consciously fitted together to produce an end," and if "co-operate" is understood to mean "consciously work together," then of course the words are question-begging. For whether the complex causes are adjusted to one another and co-operate to produce an end in this sense is the very question to be decided. But if the words are not used in this question-begging way, then they mean nothing except that as a matter of fact the many causes combine to produce the effects which they do produce. Whenever any complex combination of causes produces a certain effect they may be said to co-operate and be adjusted to one another. Thus billions of molecules of air may be said to co-operate to produce the whirlwind which wrecks the city. And co-operation in this sense is clearly no evidence of design.

Why then does the argument from design seem so persuasive? This is due, I believe, to the fact that there is a second ground— the first ground being the co-operation of a complexity of causes —on which the argument, secretly as it were, relies. It is usually hidden, or at least not explicitly stated. It will be noticed that the things or events which are chosen as instances of the adaptation of means to ends are never the kind of things which human beings consider bad, evil, ignoble, ugly, or disadvantageous to human beings. They are always things which human beings consider good, or beautiful, or noble, or advantageous to themselves. Let us class all such things together under the label "valuable things." In order to show design the argument selects the balance of the solar system, which is advantageous to us because it renders life on the planet possible; or the pollination of flowers, because flowers are beautiful things; or the protein molecule which is necessary for life—and life is something which we consider good; or vision, which we think good for obvious reasons. The argument never selects as proving design those complicated trains of causes which produce blindness in some persons or animals; or the causes which produce, not life, but death. If a city is wrecked by a tidal wave and thousands of its inhabitants are drowned, or any other train of events produces a human disaster, such cases are never chosen as instances which prove design.

But it is obvious that the causes in such cases are just as complex as are the causes which produce valuable things, and that they co-operate with one another and are adjusted to one another to produce the effects which they do produce. Millions of causal conditions co-operate to produce the wreck of a city, just as millions of causes co-operate to produce the balanced solar system or the eye. Why then are not the evil things chosen as showing design as well as the valuable things?

The answer is obvious. Valuable things are the kind of things which we, assuming that we are virtuous persons, would aim at producing if we were creating a world. We therefore think that, if there are valuable things in the world, they have probably been produced by a mind with purposes similar to our own. If we put this train of thought in its briefest form it amounts to this: in our experience virtuous minds produce, or tend to produce, valuable things; therefore the valuable things in the world must have been produced by a virtuous mind.

But if this is taken seriously as an argument, it will be seen that it has a fatal logical defect. Because X causes Y you cannot argue in reverse that Y must be caused by X. Lightning often causes houses to be set on fire. But if you see a house on fire, you cannot argue that the fire must have been caused by lightning.

For there are many other causes which might have produced it—
arson, a cigarette end carelessly dropped, and a thousand others.
And just as you cannot argue from the fact that lightning causes
fires to the conclusion that all fires are caused by lightning, so
you cannot argue from the fact that minds, especially virtuous
minds, produce valuable things, to the conclusion that valuable
things must have been produced by a mind. Why should not natural causes produce them?

It may be suggested that although the existence of valuable
things in the world does not *prove* the existence of God, yet the
existence of God is at any rate an hypothesis which at least explains the existence of valuable things; and that this is some reason for believing it. This is true. But unfortunately if God is taken
as an hypothesis in this way, although the hypothesis explains the
existence of good things in the world, it does not explain the existence of bad things. In fact bad things conflict with and contradict
the hypothesis. Also, although this may be a good hypothesis in
so far as it explains some of the facts, namely, the valuable things,
it is not so good as the hypothesis that "chance," i.e., the laws of
nature operating without design, produces all the events and
things in the world. For chance explains *both* the good and the
bad things. For if the world is *not* ruled by a designing mind, but
only by the blind laws of nature, then that the world would be an
indiscriminate mixture of good and bad things—as it is—is precisely what we should expect. Thus if, as a matter of logic, we
treat God as an hypothesis, we find that chance is a better hypothesis than God.

Thus from whatever point of view we regard it the argument
from design turns out to be worthless.

We must now turn to the other side of the picture. If Newton's
celestial mechanics did not prove the existence of God, they
certainly did not disprove it. Not only this. It is very important
to realize that, in the whole history of the seventeenth century
scientific revolution, no single discovery was made, no idea was
put forward which, from the point of view of logic, should have

had the slightest effect in the way of destroying belief in God. And yet the scientific revolution actually did have such an effect. This is something which we have to try to understand. First, let us make sure that none of the discoveries of early science have any tendency to prove the non-existence of God. We may set the matter out in this way. Ignoring details, the essential discoveries were:

That the earth moves round the sun, not the sun round the earth (Copernicus).

That the planets move in ellipses, not circles (Kepler).

That moving bodies will continue moving at a uniform speed in a straight line, unless some force acts on them. They will not stop (Galileo).

The law of gravitation (Newton).

Now how can any of these physical truths have any bearing at all on the problem of the existence of God? How can they possibly provide any argument against it? Surely God can as well exist with the earth going round the sun as with the sun going round the earth? Or is the existence of God consistent with circles, but not with ellipses? Or can he not exist in a universe which follows Galileo's law of motion, but only in one which follows Aristotle's? Finally, is the law of gravitation atheistic or incompatible with belief in a divine being? What then was there in the scientific revolution which could be inimical to religion?

It is true that the Copernican system is inconsistent with the astronomy which the Christian Church at that time erroneously considered to be a necessary part of Christian faith; and that it produced, for that reason, a devastating shock in the theological system. Not only in the literal physical sense, but in a metaphorical sense too, the universe had been believed to revolve round man and his home on this earth. Man was at the physical center of the universe, and also at the center of God's care and attention. In some way or other the whole creation centered round man. The sun, moon, and stars, the waters, the herbs, and the animals, had all been created for the sake of man. But this belief in the cosmic importance of man is much more difficult to hold if the earth is merely a speck of dust revolving, with other similar specks, round one out of billions of stars. Doubts began to haunt the minds of men, even of fervently religious men. Might there not be beings like men on millions of other little rotating bodies in the universe? Might they too not have sinned? And was one to suppose that God had sent his son to be crucified again and again on all these millions of centers of life? Was not the incarnation of God in Christ credible only if one believed that man is at the center of the cosmic drama?

All this is well known, and it is unnecessary to repeat here how in these ways the Copernican theory shook the Christian world. This was the first of the great clashes between particular discoveries of science and particular beliefs of the Church which were to occur in the modern world. But the real conflict between science and religion lay elsewhere. For the particular beliefs which the Church had thus to abandon one after another were none of them *necessary* to religion. What was necessary was a certain attitude, which I have called the religious view of the world. This has expressed itself in the western world in the form of three central beliefs—that there exists a divine being who created the universe, that there is a cosmic plan or purpose, and that the world is a moral order. And neither the Copernican astronomy nor any of the other discoveries of the early scientists—nor, for the matter of that, any discoveries of later science—are inconsistent with these religious beliefs. As for the particular beliefs which the Church has had to abandon, these could all be left behind without loss to the essential core of religion. Or at least they could be given an allegorical meaning when they could no longer be accepted in their literal interpretation. In this way religion could easily accommodate itself to the new discoveries of science. But if the three central beliefs should be lost, religion itself would be destroyed. Or so it would seem, at least on a first survey. Hence it is the effect of science on the central beliefs of religion that we have to study. And the conclusion which we have reached so far is that the discoveries of the scientific revolution neither supported nor tended to disprove them.

Certainly they had no bearing on the question of the existence of God. And yet—the scientific revolution did, actually and historically, profoundly undermine faith in God. It is a fact that the rise of science was immediately followed by a great wave of religious skepticism. On the heels of the seventeenth century came the most skeptical age of the modern world, the eighteenth century. This was the age in which an English king could complain that half his bishops were atheists. This was the age which produced Hume, Gibbon, Voltaire. It is true that there is a sense in which it may be said that these men may have "believed in the existence of God." But they were religious skeptics nonetheless. They did not believe in anything like the medieval Christian God. And whatever belief in God they had was no more than a cold and dead intellectual abstraction utterly chilling to the religious mind. For religion, though it may always be accompanied by beliefs, is not itself a mere matter of the intellect.

This historical succession, the birth of science followed immediately by a century of skepticism, is no mere coincidence. There is a connection. Our business is to discover this connection. And this may be thought to constitute something of a problem. For if seventeenth century science has no logical tendency at all to disprove the central beliefs of religion, how can it have produced the devastating effect upon them which it actually did?

The key to the solution of this problem lies in the consideration that men's minds do not usually work in the way that logicians say they should. Logic has very little to do with what men believe. Suppose that a man, holding a certain idea or belief, A, comes, as a result of it, to hold another idea or belief, B. There has been a transition of thought from A to B. It is possible that the passage from A to B may have been due to a logical connection between the two ideas; in other words it may be the case that B follows logically from A, and this may account for the fact that the man who believed A afterwards came to believe B. But logical transitions of this sort are the exception rather than the rule. More

often the transitions are due to quite non-logical connections between ideas by way of association or suggestion. In the stream of
human consciousness there are transitions from thought to
thought continually going on. In this complex flow from idea to
idea there are here and there tenuous threads of logical connection. But they tend to be far outnumbered by the non-logical
transitions due to suggestion and association. We may use the
label "psychological transitions" to describe these non-logical
sequences and to distinguish them from logical sequences of
ideas.

The solution of our problem why the scientific revolution produced an age of skepticism, when there was no logical reason why
it should, is that there were profound psychological causes at
work. This matter is, of course, very complicated, and from the
skein of human thoughts in such a case we cannot hope to do
more than pick out a few of the more obvious threads.

First of all, then, Newtonian science produced in men's minds
an ever-growing sense, or feeling, of *the remoteness of God*. Any
sort of living religion requires a God who is near us, who is all
around us in the world *now*. In superstitious ages this sense of
present nearness was produced by belief in miracles. God worked
immediately in our lives by causing fire out of heaven to fall on
our enemies, by sending food to us by ravens if we were hungry,
or by sending manna down out of the sky for us to eat. These
things did not of course happen to everyone. But they did happen
to those men who, more conspicuously than others, followed
God's commands. And this was sufficient to show that God is
near at hand and is always helping those who love him and whom
he loves. He is working in the world all the time. In an age which
no longer hopes for divine interventions in the workings of outward nature a living religion at least requires a sense that God
still works inwardly in the hearts of men, for instance when we
pray. God, it is thought, may not now intervene in the physical
world, but he does intervene in the psychological workings of the
inward world of our minds. If he does not send us physical food
by ravens, he does send us spiritual food by the sacraments and

the means of grace. In one way or another religion—if it is not to be a mere intellectual abstraction—requires the sense of a God who is close to us and works in our lives.

But Newtonian science tended to dry up the springs of a living religion by pushing God back in time to the beginning of the world. Whether this was thousands, or millions, of years ago makes little difference. God created the world, and he also, in doing so, created the natural laws—for instance, the laws of motion and gravitation—by which it was to be run. God was thus the "first cause" of the world, but after he had once created it, natural law, which he had also created, took over the job of running it. After the original creation God did nothing. Gravitation and the laws of motion did everything. God was like a watch-maker who, having once made and wound up his machine, left it to be moved by its own internal mechanism. God differed from the human mechanic only in that he had invented a perpetual motion machine which would go on working for ever by itself without any intervention on his part. Was not this precisely what Galileo's first law of motion implied?

Thus, so far as we are concerned, God is "far away and long ago," at the beginning of things, not acting now, remote from the actual happenings of our daily lives. But such an imaginative picture of a God far away and long ago is death to a living religion. God becomes then a mere intellectual belief, necessary perhaps as an "hypothesis" for explaining how the world originated, but of no importance in the daily affairs of our lives. This is what he actually became for the eighteenth century deists. And this consequence of Newtonian science—and the consequence is of course still with us—is only partly mitigated by the continuing belief that God can still work in the internal psychological world of our minds. We need not at this point comment on the obvious thought which presents itself here—that only our relative ignorance of the workings of that inner world allows us still to suppose that it is not wholly governed by law and that divine interventions are still possible in it. The historical fact is that the sense of the nearness of God all about us was once and for all destroyed by Newtonian science, and has departed from the modern world in general, though it remains doubtless for individual men.

There is evidence that Newton himself was worried by these thoughts. God, of course, created the world, but what is there left for him to do in it *now?* And Newton answered absurdly that God, after all, has still the function of intervening from time to time to correct the irregularities of the planets and of putting them back in their proper orbits when they have deviated from them.

In the *Reader's Digest* of January 1949 there appeared an article entitled *God and the American People*. It recorded the results of a nation-wide poll on religious questions. Asked whether they believed in the existence of God, ninety-five per cent answered yes. But asked why they tried to lead good lives, only twenty-five per cent gave religion as one of the considerations which counted with them. Asked whether religion in any way affected their politics or their business, fifty-four per cent said no. Analyzing the polls, the Reverend Dr. Greenberg observed: "People do not apparently associate God directly with their own behavior."

Why should they when, while subscribing to the conventional belief in the existence of God, they also believe that he has nothing whatever to do with the actual events going on all round them in their daily lives, all of which are fully explained by "natural causes"—including, of course, their own actions? This belief that all events are due to natural causes, and that God has nothing to do with them—whether we acknowledge it or not, and even if with our lips we deny it—is simply a part of what is taken for granted by the modern mind. It is a part of our imaginative world-picture, and is a heritage which we owe to seventeenth century science. We are accustomed to say that while the medieval period was an age of faith, our time is not. No doubt ninety-five per cent of the people say they believe in God. But this is not an evidence of religion. Such a belief is either a mere intellectual abstraction, inoperative in our behavior, or it is a conventional and barren verbal formula which people out of habit keep repeating because they are too unthinking or too lazy to change their habits. A God who "exists" but does nothing in the world, who in no way affects the outcome of events, is simply a God who does not matter. Of course most people do not *say* things like this, do not even think them in their minds. But this modern world-picture, consciously envisaged only by a few intellectuals, is nevertheless the unconscious background of modern life. And we see now that when we speak of Newtonian science as having undermined or even destroyed belief in God, it is not meant that it has resulted in people saying "there is no God," but in the draining of all life out of the assertion that there is.

This too is the significance of the work of Laplace which I mentioned in the last chapter. Newton had pushed God back to the beginning of the solar system. But Laplace pushed him back to the beginning of a pre-solar nebula. How far in terms of measurable time this may be does not matter. Imaginatively it is further and further away. And we see now too how irrelevant it is for the believer to answer Laplace by saying that all he did was to push the necessity of a creator one step back in time, and that this makes no difference to the necessity of postulating God as the first cause of the universe. Logically no doubt it makes no difference, but psychologically the difference is that it vastly increases the sense of God's remoteness. If God created the sun and the moon and the earth, and man on the earth, perhaps about six thousand years ago as suggested by Genesis, the period which has elapsed since God did anything is no doubt very great. But still it is at least within the human period, recorded in human documents. The memory of the race in some sense goes back to that time. That God personally and directly created our ancestor Adam means that he was interested in man, and this gives a glimmer of warmth even to our present relations with him. Perhaps this God, though he does not act now, is still looking at us and thinking of us. But if the race of men is only a by-product of natural laws set going millions of years ago, then—even if God created the natural laws—what can man be to God, or God to man? And if we push God back through astronomical aeons to the beginning of a nebula which evolved into a solar system—the terrible gulfs of time which have elapsed since God made himself manifest in the world chill our minds and numb our hearts. This train of thought, of course, is not logic. But logic has little to do with human thinking.

Such was the imaginative importance of Laplace's nebula. The effect of his discovery that the irregularities of the planets are self-correcting and not cumulative is, of course, similar. Newton had thought that God does still, after all, act in the world by correcting the deviations of the planets. But Laplace showed that they correct themselves. Thus even the small corner which Newton had left for God's action in the world was eliminated and his place was taken by the laws of nature. Hence Laplace's remark that he had no need for God as an hypothesis.

We have spoken of the sense of the remoteness of God as the first of the psychological effects of Newtonian science which have tended to destroy the force of religion in men's minds. The second, to which we now turn, is perhaps no more than another way of expressing the same thing. Science has everywhere substituted natural causes of phenomena for the supernatural causes in which men formerly believed. Since the seventeenth century it has become a fixed maxim of science that no supernatural causes are to be admitted in the universe; that even if a natural phenomenon is at present unexplained, it must never be taken as a case of divine action, but always a natural cause must be assumed to exist and must be sought for. This, it will be noted, is not a particular discovery of any particular science—like the Copernican hypothesis, the Darwinian theory of evolution, or the geological discovery of the immense age of the earth. It is a basic assumption of science as a whole. It is part of the scientific view of the world. And it is this general scientific view of the world, and not any particular discovery, which has worked havoc with religion.

No doubt in pre-scientific times there was belief in a general regularity of nature, the recurrence of cycles of events in accordance with a reign of law. The sun rises regularly every day. The seasons return regularly every year. But within these general cycles there was still plenty of room left for divine intervention in details. Hence the possibility of miracles which could very well be fitted into the picture of a world which was, in its larger features, regular and orderly. The thought which was born into the world with the new science of the seventeenth century, and which has become a part of the world-picture of the modern mind, is that every small detail of the world's happenings is completely determined by inflexible laws of nature—that if a grain of sand, or a single molecule of a grain of sand, moves a thousandth of a millimetre, this movement is wholly a predictable effect of pre-existent natural causes. This basic assumption of science has become, since the seventeenth century, a part of the unconscious mentality of the modern man. And it leaves no room for divine action in the world.

Nor has the recent discovery that electrons and other basic particles of matter are "indeterminate" in their movements in any way altered the picture. For in the first place a habit of mind has been created which cannot be thus airily waved aside by some sudden new pronouncement of the physicists. And apart from this, it would surely be absurd to suggest that belief in the indeterminacy of the electron is a return to belief in the supernatural, or that the apparently unaccountable and irregular jumps which the electrons make are cases of divine intervention. Either there are natural causes of these movements which have not yet been discovered or, as physicists seem to think is the case, there are no causes at all. If the latter is true, then causal laws do not operate in the smallest parts of nature. But nature still remains nature, and does not become supernatural by being non-causal. It would be thought just as "unscientific" to attribute the movements of electrons to the immediate action of God, because they are at present unexplained, as it would be to suppose that, because the origin of cosmic rays is unknown, they must be emitted by God.

If one admits the scientific maxim that every event in nature has a natural cause, it is still, of course, possible to bring in God at the beginning as a first cause. But this leads to the conception of a God who, since he does nothing in the world now, is of no practical importance in our lives.

By a little logical ingenuity one can, no doubt, avoid this result. One can suppose that God is operating all the time, but that he operates only through and by means of natural laws. The force of gravitation does not act by itself. It is God who is acting in this force at every moment. And so with all other natural laws. If he were not continually thus working in nature, gravitation and the other forces of nature would cease to act and nature would collapse. God is, as it were, continually creating and re-creating nature. This hypothesis did in fact suggest itself to a few philosophic minds, but it had no influence with the masses of men who continued to feel that God could only have acted at the beginning.

It must not be thought, of course, that these thoughts and difficulties have been explicitly realized in the minds of the masses of men. Intellectuals have realized them, and their influence has, through devious channels, seeped down to the masses. The concept of a world wholly governed by natural forces forms in their minds a vague background unconsciously assumed. And they instinctively sense, rather than argue, that this excludes the supernatural.

It is instructive to note that the influence of the new world-picture has been steadily and progressively increasing since Newton's time. We see this if we look first at Newton himself, then at Berkeley, an eighteenth century philosopher intermediate between Newton's time and ours, and then finally at our own age. In spite of the fact that Newton was the creator of the modern world-view, its hold on his own mind was comparatively weak. This is shown by his way of dealing with the problem of the irregularities of the planetary motions. The concept of a world completely ruled by natural laws, admitting no capricious interventions of the Deity, was the basis of his own science. His celestial mechanics would not have worked if he had not assumed that the planets move under the influence of the law of gravitation alone. They would not have worked if unexpected interventions of God at any moment had been admitted. Nevertheless he was prepared to admit an exception in the matter of the irregularities of the planets.

Berkeley in the eighteenth century introduced into his philosophy the notion of the complete regularity of the order of nature. Although he accepted the conventional belief in miracles, Newton's idea of exceptions to the natural order plays no part in his system. To that extent, it may be said, the new world-picture has a greater hold on him than it had on Newton. Nevertheless, in a curious manner which is characteristic of him, he introduces God to fill up a gap which would otherwise have existed in his philosophy. Berkeley was the author of the famous idealistic theory according to which material objects can only exist when they are being perceived by a mind. Their existence *consists in* their being perceived. For what is a material object except a collection of qualities, such as color, hardness or softness, hotness or coldness, roughness or smoothness, scent, taste, sound, etc.? There is nothing else in the object beyond these qualities. If you say there is something else, point it out. Try the experiment. Take any material thing you like, say this piece of paper. It is white, smooth, soft, cool, oblong, etc. These are its qualities. Can you find anything else in it? You can cut it up into small pieces, atoms if you like, and you can say that it consists of these atoms. But the atoms themselves will be nothing but collections of qualities, hardness, weight, roundness, etc. But these qualities which make up all objects turn out to be, when you examine them, nothing but sensations. The hardness of a thing is perceived, say, by pressing it with the finger or some other part of the body. What is it but a sensation in the finger or other part of the body? And this sensation, though, in one sense, we locate it in our finger, is, in another sense, in our mind, in our consciousness. For a sensation could not exist unless we were conscious of it. An unconscious man does not have sensations. The same is true of hotness and coldness. What is hotness except a sensation which we feel when we come near a fire? So, too, color is a visual sensation. It is perceived by the eye, no doubt. But it can only exist in a mind which is conscious of it. Thus all qualities are sensations which can exist only in minds when those minds perceive them. Therefore a material object, since it consists only of qualities, and these qualities are sensations in minds, can only exist when some mind perceives it. The whole world consists only of minds and the sensations which those minds have.

But there seems to be one obvious difficulty here. If the piece of paper exists only when it is being perceived, what happens to it when no one is perceiving it? While I am typing this page there is no one in the room except myself, and I am at this moment perceiving it. It exists accordingly as a set of sensations in my mind. But what happens to it when I turn my back and no longer look at it? Or what happens to it if I go out of the room and leave it here? Must it not, on Berkeley's theory, cease to exist because it is no longer perceived? Of course when I turn round again or come back into the room I see it again. Am I then to suppose that, after ceasing to exist when I ceased to perceive it, it comes back into existence when I begin to perceive it again? Does not all this follow from Berkeley's theory that the existence of material objects consists in their being perceived, so that they do not exist except when they are being perceived? And are not these consequences plainly absurd?

But Berkeley has a ready answer. He never said that the existence of the object consists in *our* perceiving it. He said only that its existence consists in its being perceived by *some* mind. Thus when I am looking at the paper it exists as a collection of sensations in my mind. When you are looking at it, it still exists, even though I have turned my back, because there are the sensations of it in your mind. What then happens to it when no human mind is perceiving it? Is there not in the universe, asks Berkeley, a being, a mind, which never sleeps, which never turns its back, which, being omniscient, is always conscious of everything, the mind of God? Material objects then do not cease to exist when human beings cease to perceive them. They continue to exist as ideas or sensations in the mind of God. Thus Berkeley, though he does not introduce God into the world-scheme to explain any irregular motions of the planets, introduces him to explain the continued existence of objects when men do not perceive them. And there is no reason to suppose that his eighteenth century readers, whether they happened to accept his idealistic philosophy or not, saw anything specially wrong with the way in which he introduced God into his system. Thus the exclusion of the supernatural by the concept of a world wholly governed by natural laws had not completely dominated the mentality of that time. We have in Berkeley a halfway house between Newton and the present day.

If we look, finally, at the present time, we note two things. First, Newton's way of explaining the planetary deviations would utterly scandalize even the most religious scientist today. The scientific dogma that no phenomenon whatever, however mysterious it may seem, is to be explained by supernatural causes, has hardened into an "absolute" since Newton's time. There must be no exceptions to natural law anywhere. It is the settled procedure of science that if there is a phenomenon which we are at present unable to explain by natural causes, such causes must nevertheless exist and must be sought for. And even if a phenomenon is found for which it is believed that no cause can be assigned, such as the indeterminate movement of the electron, this is not then set down as caused by God, but rather as showing that the law of causation does not apply in the sub-atomic world.

The second thing to note is that the exclusion of God as a philosophical principle of explanation has also hardened since Berkeley's time. One must not have a *deux ex machina* in one's philosophy. If there is a gap or a hole in a system of philosophy, it must not be filled up by the "arbitrary" introduction of God. Why not? The only reason which can be given is that it is assumed, following the example of science, that the whole universe must be explained solely by natural causes, and that the introduction of a supernatural concept is illegitimate.

A curious piece of evidence can be given to show that this thought is not confined to professional philosophers or other intellectuals, but has also come to govern the minds of quite unlearned persons. Anyone who has had the experience of introducing Berkeley's philosophy to a miscellaneous group of freshman or sophomore students taking their first course in philosophy will know that, when they are told how Berkeley answered the objection that on his principles the piece of paper ought to cease to exist when we cease to perceive it, they instinctively revolt. They regard the fact that he could not explain this without introducing God to keep the universe going as a glaring weakness in his system. They say that his philosophy would plainly fall to the ground unless it were "bolstered up" in this way.

What, however, is wrong with God as an hypothesis? Scientific procedure simply consists in introducing hypotheses (for which there is often no direct evidence) in order to "bolster up" the system of thought which science has developed. If the physicist finds that electrons and protons are insufficient to explain observed phenomena, he plugs the hole with new hypotheses, positrons, neutrons, mesons, etc. If it can be said that Berkeley "drags in" God to make his system work, then it may equally be said that the physicists of the nineteenth century "dragged in" the ether of space, and that the physicists of today "drag in" neutrons and mesons for the same reason—to make their systems work. It cannot be said that there is a difference because scientists always have independent evidence of the existence of the entities which they postulate. For this is simply not the case. For instance, there is no evidence of waves of any kind in space except that the supposition of their existence helps to explain the observed facts about light, heat, etc. No one has ever seen the waves themselves. Men have only observed the effects of which the waves are supposed to be the causes. What then is the difference between waves as an hypothesis and God as an hypothesis? From a logical point of view there is none at all. And if the one hypothesis is logically respectable, so is the other.

Why then do students, why does the modern mind in general, object to Berkeley's procedure? Why is it plastered with smear phrases like "drag in," "bolster up," "*deux ex machina*"? Because, although it does not conflict with any principles of logic, it conflicts with the scientific maxim that all facts are to be accounted for by natural causes, and that God is never to be introduced as an explanation of anything. Beginning students do not, of course, argue the matter out. If you ask them *why* they revolt against Berkeley's hypothesis, they do not know. They simply *feel* that it is objectionable. And this shows that the scientific world-picture has penetrated the marrow of our minds. It has become an unconscious background of all human thinking. It is no longer the mere abstract theory of intellectuals. It has sunk into the depths of human personality.

We have studied so far the effects of the scientific revolution on the idea of God. This was the first of the three ideas which we saw to be essential parts of the pre-scientific world-view. The second idea, to which we now turn, is that of the teleological character of the world. The third, the belief that the world is a moral order, will form the subject of the next chapter.

What was the effect of the rise of science on the belief that there is a world plan or purpose? It goes without saying that diminution of effective belief in God will be accompanied by diminution of effective belief in a world-purpose. For the two ideas are, of course, intimately connected. A divine being and a divine purpose seem to imply each other. Nevertheless they are two distinct ideas which it is better to keep separate. As we have seen, it is quite possible to believe, in some vague way, in a purpose of nature without any theistic implications.

Belief in a world-purpose was, we saw, a part of the intellectual heritage of the western world for two thousand years, from the time of Socrates until the seventeenth century. What happened to it as a result of the birth of the scientific spirit?

The comparison between Newton's solar system and a clock is an obvious one. The point about the clock is that once it has been wound up it runs itself because it is provided with its own force in the spring. The spring which runs the solar system is the force of gravitation. The planets too resemble wheels. The solar system not only resembles a clock; it is one, for it keeps perfect time.

Thus arose the idea of "Newton's world-machine." The thought that the universe is a machine spread like wildfire through Europe. Not only is the world as a whole a machine, but everything in it is mechanical. Hobbes compared the human body to a machine. "What," he wrote, "is the heart but a spring, and the nerves but so many strings, and the joints but so many wheels, giving motion to the whole body?" Hobbes lived before Newton's discovery of gravitation, but the mechanical view of nature was already in the air, and Newton's solar clock merely clinched it. Hume in the eighteenth century wrote: "Look around the world. You will find it to be nothing but one great machine, sub-divided into an infinite number of lesser machines."

Now if everything in the world is a machine, then everything that happens in it can be explained mechanically, and teleological explanation is excluded, or at least becomes unnecessary. I have already shown that mechanical explanation does not really exclude teleology. That the man's climbing the hill is caused by nerve currents and muscle contractions does not render it untrue that he climbs in order to see the view from the top. That a watch's movements can all be explained as caused by its spring does not alter the fact that the watch exists for the purpose of telling the time. In the same way the world may be a machine, but it does not follow that it has no purpose.

This means that the jump from the mechanical conception of nature, which science has introduced, to a view of the world as having no purpose, is not a logical transition. It also means that however mechanistic science may be, the denial of a world-purpose does not follow from it. Science is logically irrelevant to the question of teleology. Nevertheless the modern mind has made the illogical jump. The conviction of the utter purposelessness of things is one of its main characteristics. I shall present some evidence of this in a moment. But first let us consider how the rise of science, by a process of psychological suggestion and not by logic, could have brought about such a result.

Scientific explanation and mechanical explanation are one and the same thing. A fact is explained scientifically when its cause is given. It comes to the same thing to say that it is explained by being shown to be a particular case of a general principle or law. Science is thus wholly mechanistic. And this has not been altered by recent scientific advances. For any explanation is mechanical which is in terms of causes or laws and not in terms of purposes. And recent physics does not explain events by means of purposes.

We can see at once, then, one of the trains of thought which has led to the fading out of teleology from the modern mind. Any explanation, to be scientific, must be mechanical. For seventeenth century science, as we have seen, excluded teleology and decided to include in science only mechanical causation. Therefore a teleological explanation is "unscientific." Therefore it is bad, and not worthy of the modern mind. The absurdity of such a line of thought is, of course, obvious. Why should it be supposed that science has the key to everything? May there not be aspects of existence which lie outside science? But science is the idol of the modern world, blindly worshipped by the gaping hordes of the unscientific. This, one might say, is the general cause of the disrepute into which teleology has fallen. But there are more particular causes to which we must draw attention.

The tremendous importance given by the science of the seventeenth century to the concept of mechanism simply crowded out the concept of teleology from men's minds, caused it to be obliterated and forgotten. The enormous success of Newtonian science dazzled western man. Throughout the middle ages men talked of purposes, gave teleological explanations of eclipses, rainbows, and earthquakes, and got, scientifically, nowhere. Medieval science stagnated, or was practically non-existent. For a thousand years no scientific discoveries of importance were made. Why? Because men looked for God's purposes in things instead of for their causes. The new science came with its mechanical explanations, and all became luminous and clear. Knowledge leapt forward. The sheer success of mechanical explanation from Newton's time to the present day has been spectacular. Why? Because scientists stopped thinking about purposes and concentrated on causes. Has not the whole of modern "progress" been due to this one fact alone? Is it any wonder then that the world abandoned teleology?

Another point deserves attention. We see that a mechanical explanation of a phenomenon is a *complete* explanation. It is not as if mechanism partly prevails in the world but there are gaps left in its explanations which have to be filled in by teleology. There are no gaps. The movements of the planets, for example, are *entirely* explained by gravitation and the laws of motion. To predict an eclipse of the sun, one does not need to know the purpose of eclipses in the plan of nature—if they have any. Indeed, to know the purpose would be useless. To predict a phenomenon, what one needs to know is its causes—that and nothing else. But if mechanical explanations are in this way complete explanations, what is the necessity or use of seeking some other kind of explanation as well? Thus teleological explanations, even if they exist, naturally fall into the background and are forgotten. And if this is true of the particular happenings, such as eclipses, which make up the world, will it not be true of the world as a whole? The very idea of a world-purpose ceases to be operative in an age dominated by the scientific spirit.

These then seem to be the basic psychological transitions which have led the modern mind to forget the concept of a world-purpose. Thus it came about that for the old imaginative picture of a world governed by divine purposes there gradually came to be substituted the imaginative picture of a purposeless world.

But has this really happened? Does the modern mind deny that there is any plan or purpose in things? Who denies it?

There are certainly plenty of intellectuals who deny it, or who would, if pressed, at least take up an agnostic position as regards it. For instance, Bertrand Russell, after giving some account of science, wrote in a famous passage: "Such, in outline, but even more purposeless, more void of meaning, is the world which science presents for our belief."[2] The important question, however, is how far this conception of a purposeless world has passed down from the intellectuals to the masses of plain men. Regarding this, it is in the nature of the case difficult to find much positive evidence. Very few people, of course, make such explicit statements as "The world has no purpose," just as they do not make such statements as "There is no God." No poll has been taken, so far as I know, in which people were asked: "Do you believe that the world has a purpose?" If such a poll were taken it would be surprising if at least ninety-five per cent did not reply yes. And no doubt vague thoughts of a purpose in things flit through almost everyone's mind at times. There must be very few people who have not at some time stood out under the stars at night and wondered what is the purpose of all these wheeling orbs. Thus the idea of a world-purpose has not been eradicated wholly from the human mind. But how effective is it?

I suggest that current literature and art, which presumably reflect the general *Weltanschauung* of the age, are impregnated with a sense of the futility and senselessness of things. If the world as a whole is meaningless and purposeless, so also is human life, and that human life is thus meaningless seems to be the main message of much modern literature. There is a contrast here between the present and the past. To the great dramatists of all time human life has always appeared tragic. But some pattern— if only a pattern of Fate—could be traced in it. It has been left for the modern age to find life literally senseless. And does not the discordant character of modern music tell the same tale? Is it too far-fetched to suggest that the older more harmonious music reflected the idea of a world made harmonious by its obedience to a divine plan, while current music by its jarring discords suggests the uselessness of all things and all life?

Of course, other explanations can be given of these facts. Two world wars caused widespread disillusionment and despair. For this reason alone the system of things seems senseless to many.

---

[2] "A Free Man's Worship," in *Mysticism and Logic* (New York: Longmans, Green & Co.).

It cannot be doubted that this diagnosis is true. Yet I cannot believe that there is not a deeper cause as well. And I find it in the scientific picture of a mechanical world. Certainly the idea of a purposeless world had infected philosophers before the First World War. Witness Bertrand Russell's remark which I quoted above. It was first printed in 1903.

Much of the darkness, perplexity, and loss of sanity in the modern world, perhaps even the vast increase in the number of neurotic individuals and nervous breakdowns in our time, can be traced back ultimately to that loss of faith in the existence of any purpose or plan in the world-process which has been one of the major results of the work of the mainly devout and pious men who were the founders of modern science. Sensitive scientific men may protest that not science, but misunderstandings of science, have been the source of the modern *Weltanschauung*. This is quite true. We have been at pains to insist that the conclusions which men have drawn from science do not follow from it by any correct logic. That many of those who have drawn these conclusions have themselves been men of science makes no difference. It is childish to ask whose fault it is. We are not concerned either with blaming science or with relieving it from blame. We have been concerned only with trying to describe what has happened.

✻ 6 ✻

THE CONSEQUENCES FOR MORALS

WE HAVE NOW TO TRACE ANOTHER SET OF CONSEQUENCES WHICH flowed from the seventeenth century scientific revolution. This time our question is: what has been the effect of that revolution, and of the consequent domination of the modern mind by science, on our moral ideas?

The first thing to see, as in the case of the effects of science on religion, is that there is no logical connection at all between the discoveries of the founders of science and any moral question. What difference can it make to any such question whether the earth goes round the sun or the sun goes round the earth? Does it alter the nature of our duties if the planets move in ellipses rather than circles? Is it any less our duty to be honest, sober, truthful and just, if Galileo's law of motion rather than Aristotle's holds; or if Newton's force of gravitation rather than Descartes' whirlpools controls the heavenly bodies? How, we may well ask, can these scientific discoveries possibly have anything to do with our moral problems?

It is the old story. There is indeed no logical connection. Yet in fact these scientific concepts have had a profound and unfortunate effect on moral ideas. *They have brought about the collapse of the belief that the world is a moral order.*

We may briefly remind the reader of the implications of this belief. It meant that the final government of the world is in some way a righteous government. There is a drive towards moral goodness in the world-process. This may be personified in the concept of a righteous God who rules the world. It may be vaguely conceived as a force in nature making for goodness. It expresses itself often enough in the mere feeling that somehow or other the good must triumph in the end and the evil be defeated.

It is the same as the conception which philosophers have expressed in their own jargon by saying that moral values are objective. And the belief that the world is not a moral order is the same as the conception that moral values are subjective. For a value is subjective if it depends on human desires, feelings, or opinions. It is objective if it does not depend on any such human mental states. And if moral values depend on human psychology, then they do not exist in the universe apart from the existence and the thoughts of human beings. There was no good or evil in the world before there were any men, and there will be none after men cease to exist. The non-human universe which is our dwelling place has in itself nothing either moral or immoral. It is indifferent to our human values. It is a non-moral world.

Finally, the belief that the world is a moral order is a part of the intellectual or cultural heritage of all highly civilized peoples. Not only is it a part of Christianity—finding expression therein in the concept of a righteous God—but in ancient Greece it expressed itself in different ways in such philosophies as those of Socrates, Plato, and Aristotle. It permeates the Hebrew scriptures. In Indian religions, in Buddhism and Hinduism, it shows itself, somewhat dimly perhaps, in the law of karma.

Confining ourselves to the western world since the birth of Christ, we may say that one of the major contrasts between the medieval mind and the modern mind is that the former believed that the world is a moral order while the latter believes that it is not. Of course this is to state the matter too strongly, for the sake of emphasis. It is not meant that *everybody* in medieval times believed that the world is a moral order, while *nobody* in the modern world believes this. The former statement might be true, or very nearly true. But the latter statement needs much qualification. Throughout the modern period there has been a continuing series of powerful protests against the doctrine of the subjectivity of morals. To this aspect of the matter I hope to do justice in a later chapter. For the moment let us put the matter thus. In spite of frequent protests, it is characteristic of the modern *Weltanschauung* to hold that the world is not a moral order. This is the prevailing, if not the universal, opinion. And it would appear— at least to the present writer—to be the opinion which is winning out. The drift of the modern mind since the rise of science has set steadily more and more in that direction. And we have to ask how this has come about.

The key to the answer lies in the consideration that the concept of value—value of any kind, economic, esthetic, or moral—is intimately bound up with the concept of purpose, and that therefore those causes which operated to destroy or diminish belief in the existence of a world-purpose also operated to destroy or diminish belief that value is a factor in the universe. If there is purpose in the world, then there will be values in the world; values will be objective. But if there is no purpose in the world, but only in human minds, then there will be no values in the world, but only in human minds; values will be subjective.

We have to make clear the connection between the concept of value and that of purpose. It lies in the fact that, if anything is in any way valuable, it must presumably be valuable for some purpose. If we say that something is valuable, it is natural to ask: valuable for what purpose? It is also natural to ask: valuable to whom? And if we should say, "Such and such a thing is valuable, but it is not valuable for any purpose, or to anybody, it is just valuable," this would appear to be nonsense.

It is no doubt possible to dispute the statement that whatever is valuable must be valuable for some purpose. There may be ingenious philosophical theories of value which would deny this. But if so I shall have to point out that this does not really in the end concern us. For we are not in fact concerned with the theories of philosophers, or even with logic or truth, but with the psychology of the ages, with what men actually think and have thought. And even if a clever philosopher could construct a rational theory which made value wholly independent of purpose, it would still nevertheless be true that plain men always connect value with purpose. It is at least natural to think that if anything is valuable, this must be because it is valuable to somebody and for some purpose. Even if there is no logical transition from the concept of value to that of purpose, there certainly is a psychological transition. Men have supposed, rightly or wrongly, that there is a connection. And in terms of this psychological transition we can explain how men in the modern age came to believe that moral values are subjective.

For to say that something is morally good is to say that it has value of a certain kind. And if what is valuable must be valuable to some person and for some purpose, it is natural to ask to whom and for what purpose the thing which is morally good is valuable. Now so long as men believed in a world-purpose, whether existing in the mind of God or immanent in the world itself, what is morally good could be connected with that purpose and defined in terms of it. Either what is good is defined as that which is in accordance with God's purposes; or it is defined as that which is in accordance with the immanent world-purpose. I do not mean that common men would consciously articulate any such definitions. They doubtless did not consciously articulate any definitions at all. But some such definitions they would have had to give if they had been capable of thinking out clearly the implications of their own ideas. We may perhaps say that in pre-scientific times these theories of the nature of moral value unconsciously controlled men's thinking.

As has been pointed out already, any such theory of the nature of moral value makes that value objective. For the purposes of God, and the immanent world-purpose, are independent of the human mind.

Now suppose that men lose their effective beliefs in God or a world-purpose. What will be the consequences for their conceptions of moral good and evil? They can no longer define them in terms of divine or cosmic purposes. But in terms of some purpose they have to be defined because of the principle that everything of value must be of value for some purpose. Men must therefore find some purposes other than divine or cosmic purposes on which to base moral values. What other purposes are there? None except human purposes. It therefore follows that men will be compelled to believe in some view of the nature of good and evil according to which they are dependent on human purposes. But this, by definition, is subjectivism. And it is the view that the world is not a moral order.

Thus the train of thought which has led from the pre-scientific belief that the world is a moral order to the modern belief that it is not may be summarized thus:

If morality is grounded in divine or cosmic purpose, it is objective. The world is a moral order.

Newtonian science caused a loss of effective belief in divine or cosmic purpose in the manner explained in the last chapter.

Hence morality could no longer be grounded in divine or cosmic purpose.

But values have to be connected with, and defined in terms of, some purpose.

If divine and cosmic purposes are eliminated, the only remaining alternative is human purpose.

Therefore moral values must now be made dependent on human purposes.

But this, by definition, is subjectivism, and is the view that the world is not a moral order.

This is the bald outline of the train of thought by which the moral objectivism of the medieval mind passed into the moral subjectivism of the modern mind. Of course it is not meant that this exact argument was ever laid out by thinkers in this exact way. This is no more than a schema, a naked skeleton of human thought, not the full flesh and body of any actual human thinking.

Nobody, so far as I know, in the transitional period between medieval and modern times, ever actually argued precisely in these terms. Yet this does represent the compulsive force which must have lain behind human thinking. However men argued or expressed their thoughts this, or something like it, must have been what caused them to think and argue in the way they did. If men's belief in God or in a world-purpose ceased to be effective, it was inevitable, for the reasons given in the skeleton summary, that they should come to think of moral values in human terms and not in divine or cosmic terms. Loss of religious faith necessitates the substitution of a secular ethics based on human purposes for an ethics grounded in religious conceptions.

It does not matter what men say they believe. It does not even matter much what they think they believe. Ninety-five per cent of Americans may say they believe in God, and it is not of course suggested that they are saying what is not true. No doubt they are quite sincere. The important question, however, concerns the effectiveness of the belief. If a belief has no influence, or extremely little influence, on action, then it is not an effective belief. Only if men base their mode of living on it can it be called effective. No doubt there are many people now alive who do base their lives on their religion. They are the truly religious souls. But they are few in number. No doubt in a sense this has always been true, even in the middle ages. Then, too, a majority may have been apathetic in religious matters. Yet it is commonly admitted that there was then in the world an "age of faith" which is now gone. It is impossible to measure such matters in terms of percentages. But there is certainly a truth in the contrast between the medieval and the modern ages in this respect.

We cannot say then that before the rise of science men believed in God and in cosmic purpose and that now they do not; and that therefore they then believed that the world is a moral order but now they do not. This would be plainly over-simple. But perhaps we can say something like this—that as the depth and effectiveness of religious belief has waned in the modern age, so belief that the world is a moral order has waned; that whereas the typical ethical thinking of the medieval period was objectivist, so the typical ethical thinking of the modern period is subjectivist; that this change-over began to appear precisely at that juncture in history which coincided with the birth of science; and that this was not a coincidence but a case of cause and effect. And how this cause, science, produced this effect, subjectivism, is what I have been trying to explain.

That subjectivism did appear first at the time of the rise of the new science is evidenced by the words of Hobbes already quoted.[1] Hobbes was not a great philosopher. But he was the philosophical mirror of the new science of his time. His philosophy is simply the generalization of the tendencies of the new science. Whatever appears in Galileo as a truth limited to the particular area of physics reappears in Hobbes as a universal truth about the whole cosmos. For instance, the new science is atomistic, which means that, according to it, matter is composed of atoms. Hobbes applies this to the whole universe. Nothing exists which is not made of atoms. Even the human soul is made of atoms. Everything which exists is material, and there are no non-material things. Thus the physical science of Galileo is translated by Hobbes into philosophical materialism. Again, the new science is based upon the principle that everything which happens in the physical world is rigidly determined by causes. This is universalized by Hobbes, and therefore applied to human actions. Either there is no free will, or free will has somehow to be understood within a framework of determinism. The world-view which Hobbes teaches is the world-view which he thought followed from science. And this fact makes him for us—in spite of his crudeness—a sensitive instrument for recording the influences of seventeenth century science on the more general trends of human thought. And thus it is too that Hobbes at once records the influence of that science upon moral ideas. He records the change from medieval objectivism to modern subjectivism.

The moral subjectivism which first becomes apparent in Hobbes runs, as a major theme of the modern *Weltanschauung,* through

1 P. 35.

through all those philosophers who, from his day to our own, have preached in one form of words or another that the world is not a moral order. I shall record some of the detail of this history in a later chapter. We may note now that John Dewey, who is generally admitted to be the mouthpiece of the most characteristic American thought of our day, is perpetually insisting that morality is a human thing, having its roots in human nature. This is saying the same thing as Hobbes said, notwithstanding that Hobbes's version of subjectivism is crude, while Dewey's version is subtle and sophisticated. The same thing is true of the subjectivism of the currently fashionable philosophic school of the logical positivists. According to them an ethical statement, such as "Murder is wicked," is no more than an expression of a human emotion or a human attitude. They have their own way of using the term "subjectivistic," according to which their theory is not subjectivism. But we must not be misled by words. Of course whether a theory is subjectivistic or not depends on your definition of subjectivism. The positivists have a definition which is different from mine. By my definition any view is subjectivistic in which moral values are dependent on human psychology. And by this definition the positivistic theory that moral statements are expressions of our emotions or attitudes is a version of subjectivism. And the subjectivism of the present day has its roots in the same causes which led Hobbes to his subjectivism, the science of the seventeenth century and the general domination of the modern mind by science which dates from that time.

We must now take another step forward. The scientific revolution was the ultimate cause of modern moral subjectivism. But that moral subjectivism led at once to moral relativism, the theory that all moral values and standards are relative either to individual persons—individual relativism—or to cultures or societies—group relativism. We must describe both what this idea means and how it has seemed to men to be a necessary corollary of subjectivism.

The latter point is easy to understand. Subjectivism means that moral values have their source in human purposes or desires. But what things do men desire, and what are their purposes? The first thing that occurs to one is that this differs from man to man. What one man likes is exactly what another dislikes. To see how moral relativism has been supposed to follow from moral subjectivism, we have simply to point to the vast variety of human purposes. If what is good or right is simply what suits the purposes of a man, then, since the purposes of one man or set of men differ from those of another, what is good for one man or set of men will not be good for another. It may be indifferent or it may be positively bad. As usual Hobbes records at once the view which he thinks follows from science. "Every man," he writes, "calleth that which pleaseth, and is delightful to himself, good." This is subjectivism. He goes on immediately: "while every man differeth from another in constitution, they differ also from one another concerning the common distinction of good and evil. Nor is there any such thing as absolute goodness, considered without relation." This is relativism.

Thus the skeleton framework of another part of the modern *Weltanschauung* is exposed naked:

Science leads to subjectivism.
Subjectivism leads to relativism.

The reason given by Hobbes—the differing constitutions of men, the differences of their desires and purposes—has always been, from his time to the present day, the fundamental reason for believing that morals are relative. We may ask whether the transition from subjectivism to relativism is a valid logical transition. I hold that it is not, or at least that there is in it only a partial validity leading to conclusions differing widely from the chaotic relativism which is characteristic of our time. But I must reserve consideration of the logic of the question to a later chapter. At present I am describing only what has happened in the modern world. And what has happened is given, in essence, in the transition exhibited above. It is for the reason there stated that the modern *Weltanschauung* is relativistic in regard to its moral theory.

We must of course make the usual qualifications. Not everyone living in our day accepts a relativistic view of morals. There have been, and there still are, important protests in the modern period. We are describing only the most characteristic and dominant trends of the modern age. The protests will be considered in their proper place.

The contrast of the modern view with the medieval view is obvious. In the "age of faith," before faith had been undermined by science, it was taken as a matter of course that the moral law is absolute and is the same for all men. There is but one God, the father of all men, and his commands for all his children are the same. The same moral law is in reality the law alike for the Christian and for the most benighted heathen. The difference is that the heathen has not learned and does not know the law. Hence he may develop different views as to what is right and wrong. Where these views coincide with the one true moral law they are correct, where they diverge from it they are mistaken. This belief in a single absolute moral law is not in the least inconsistent with the fact that in different countries, ages and civilizations, moral ideas vary. The fact that the same thing is thought good in one culture and bad in another does not show that morals are relative in the sense that the same thing *is* good in one culture and *is* bad in another. For one belief or the other may be mistaken, and those who hold it may be ignorant of the true moral law. If stealing is wrong it is wrong, everywhere and always. If some uncivilized tribe should be found which thinks stealing a duty, this does not mean that stealing is in fact a duty for them. It means that they are ignorant of the true conception of duty.

This is not merely the view which was common in Christendom. Anyone who believes that the world is a moral order must necessarily hold it if he is to be consistent. For if moral values are objective they are independent of the beliefs or opinions of men, so that something is not made good by the mere fact that some men or some cultures think it good. If what is good or bad is determined by any sort of cosmic purpose, or by the nature of the universe, it will be quite independent of the special idiosyncrasies of particular societies. What is right will be what is in harmony with the cosmic order. Men's beliefs about this will naturally vary, as they vary about other facts in the universe. But there can be only one truth about the facts. Thus any kind of moral objectivism implies the existence of a single universal morality. It is only subjectivism which leads to the contrary view. And it is very important to realize that ethical relativism is in conflict not only with Christianity but with any genuinely religious view of the world. For the belief that the world is a moral order is a part of the religious view of things, and it implies a single universal morality.

That relativism is characteristic of the modern mind can hardly, I think, be doubted. The most "advanced" philosophers of our time, the logical positivists, proclaim it. So do numerous philosophers of other schools. The only contemporary philosophers who tend to deny it are the so-called idealists, and they are commonly regarded as "out of date." Anthropologists and sociologists generally support it. Nor is it only the learned who teach it. It has become a part of the mental outfit of common men. Anyone who has much to do with students in their freshman and sophomore years—and these perhaps constitute something like a cross-section of the upper layers of our society—will know that if a moral question is under discussion, some student is almost sure to say, "But of course morals are all relative," and this will generally pass without any comment from his fellow students. The "of course" tells its own tale as to the general opinion. The very same people, students or more adult members of the population, who say that "of course" morals are relative may at the same time profess belief in some form of Christianity. They are unaware that there is a contradiction in their views.

The genealogy of moral relativism has now been traced. Its source is in seventeenth century science. That science led to subjectivism, and subjectivism led to relativism. There seems to be a popular belief that it is the anthropologists of the present day who originated relativism, or at least "proved" it. I do not know whether the anthropologists themselves would make any such claim. It is, at any rate, absurd. Relativism was born into the world long before the rise of the new science of anthropology, as a mere glance at Hobbes would be sufficient to show. The anthropologists and sociologists are merely carried more or less helplessly along on the tidal wave of modern thought propagated by the scientific earthquake of three hundred years ago.

The claim that recent anthropology has proved relativism is even more absurd than the claim that it originated that tendency of thought. All it has done is to discover a large number of new instances of the fact that moral beliefs vary from society to society. Anthropologists study the customs of Melanesian islanders or American Indians, and they discover among these peoples widely varying ideas of what is good or bad, right or wrong. But the general fact that moral ideas vary from society to society has been known at least since the time of the Greek historian Herodotus, who travelled widely and recorded in his book many differing sets of moral beliefs among the different peoples among whom he dwelt. Plato knew quite well that the moral standards of "barbarians" were different from those of the Hellenes. Christian writers throughout the ages must have known that moral beliefs vary, otherwise they could not have protested against the false moral ideas of the heathen. And recent anthropology, for all its interesting revelations about primitive peoples, has contributed nothing whatever to the solution of the problem whether morals are relative. It has only underlined the already well-known truth that moral beliefs vary.

This brings us to the all-important question of the *meaning* of the doctrine of ethical relativity. The sentence, "Morals are relative," might no doubt be understood in a variety of ways. But there are two meanings which must be carefully distinguished, because the failure to keep them separate is the root cause of much muddled thinking on this subject.

First, the sentence, "Morals are relative," may be intended to mean only that moral beliefs, ideas, and standards vary from society to society, from age to age, from culture to culture, and are therefore in this sense relative to the cultures in which they make their appearance. This is indisputable, and anyone who denied it would be ignorant. This is what Herodotus and Plato knew. This is what most educated men have always known. And this is what the anthropologists have more abundantly proved.

The second meaning of relativism includes this, but goes much further. The sentence, "Morals are relative," is in this case taken to mean that the moral ideas of any society are *true* for that society. It is one thing to say that a man believes an idea, and quite another thing to say that the idea is true. According to this second meaning of relativism, it is not only the case that two different cultures may have two differing beliefs about some moral question, but it is also the case that each of these beliefs is true in the culture which accepts it. It is one thing to say that the Greeks *thought* that slavery was right, another thing to say that in ancient Greece slavery *was* right. There is exactly the same difference as there would be between saying that men in a certain age *thought* that the earth is flat and saying that in that age the earth *was* flat.

We may put this second meaning of relativism in another way. According to those who hold it there is no single universal moral truth which is the standard by which all varying moral beliefs are to be judged. There exist only the varying moral beliefs of the different cultures. Each of these is therefore its own standard of moral truth. This comes to the same thing as saying that there is no objective moral standard. There are only the varying subjective standards of different cultures. Therefore, if any question arises as to what is right or good, one can only look to these varying cultural standards to find the answer. According to one such standard a certain thing will be good. According to another such standard the very same thing will be bad. There is no sense in asking whether the thing is "really" good or bad. For this implies some objective standard by reference to which the answer is to be given. And no such standard exists. What alone exists is the varying subjective opinions about good and evil. Therefore if one insists on asking the question whether a certain thing actually *is* good or not—which is really, on the relativist view, a meaningless question—the only possible answer is that it is good in one Society and bad in another.

It is this second meaning of relativism—and not only the first—which is characteristic of the modern mind. For if the philosophers, anthropologists, and sociologists who assert relativism meant only that moral beliefs vary from society to society, they would merely be asserting a platitude, the truth of which has always been known by educated people.

And it is important to see that it is this second meaning of relativism which follows from—or has been thought to follow from—subjectivism. One can see this simply by looking again at Hobbes. Good is by him defined as "that which pleaseth a man," and evil as "that which displeaseth a man." There is, on this view, no objective standard of what is good or bad. The standard is only the subjective pleasure of the individual. Accordingly, if a thing pleases me, that thing *is* good—for me. And if the same thing displeases you, that thing *is* bad—for you. There is no external or objective standard by reference to which it is possible to say that one of the two opinions is right, the other wrong.

Exactly the same thing holds if we substitute group relativism for the individual relativism asserted in the sentences quoted from Hobbes. Good will then be defined as that which pleases the group, evil as that which displeases it. The same conclusion follows that there is no objective standard, and that if the same thing pleases one group and displeases another, then the same thing is good for one and bad for the other, and that neither of the two opinions is more right or correct or true than the other. Each is right according to its own standard, and there is no other standard to judge by. Modern relativists do not usually define good and evil, as Hobbes did, in terms of pleasure and displeasure. They speak of differing feelings, emotions, or attitudes. But this obviously makes no difference to what I am saying. Feelings, emotions, and attitudes are just as subjective as pleasures and displeasures, and just as variable. And if good and evil are defined in terms of them, we shall have varying subjective moral standards with no objective standard to decide between them.

I said that it is very important to keep the two meanings of the sentence, "Morals are relative," distinct; and that much of the muddled thinking in our age results from confusing the two. This is because, if one supposes that the first meaning, namely, "moral ideas and beliefs vary from culture to culture," is equivalent to the second meaning, namely, "there is no objective moral standard, and the moral beliefs of each culture are true in that culture," then of course one also supposes that if the first meaning is true the second meaning must be true too. And since the first meaning obviously is true, it will seem to follow that the second meaning must be true. But if the two meanings are kept distinct, it will be seen that relativism in the second sense does not follow from relativism in the first sense.

There is very good reason to believe that a vast number of people, including, I regret to say, both anthropologists and philosophers, do fall into this trap and commit this fallacy, and this is one of the main reasons why moral relativism—in the second sense—is so easily and uncritically swallowed by the multitude. They point to the fact that moral beliefs vary from culture to culture. They quote the discoveries about primitive peoples made by the anthropologists. And they think that these facts "prove" the truth of relativism. Obviously all they actually prove is that "morals are relative" in the first of the two meanings of that sentence. They have no tendency at all to prove the second and important meaning of relativism, unless one wrongly supposes that the two meanings are the same, or that the second follows from the first.

One can perhaps make the essentially fallacious character of this common thinking clear by pointing out that men differ in their opinions, not only about moral matters, but about almost everything; and that, in matters other than moral, nobody supposes that the existence of conflicting opinions shows that there is no objective standard of truth. For instance, suppose someone should argue in this way:

> We believe that the earth is globular, but there was an age and a culture in which it was believed that the earth is flat.
> Therefore the earth is globular now in our culture, but it was flat in that age and that culture.

Everyone would recognize that this argument is ridiculous. But the logic of it is exactly the same as that of the argument:

> We believe that head hunting is a moral evil, but there is a culture in the South Seas in which it is believed that it is a very fine thing.
> Therefore head hunting is bad in our culture and good in that other culture.

In both of the arguments the premise states that beliefs are variable. In both the conclusion is drawn that no objective standard of truth exists, and that consequently any and every opinion must be admitted to be true in and for the age or the culture which believes it. But if the logic is bad in the one case, it is bad in the other. Therefore it is a complete fallacy to think that the great variety of moral codes in the world in any way tends to show that morals are relative in the sense in which that phrase is commonly understood in our day. Yet there is no doubt that this absurd *non sequitur* influences the popular mind. And I cannot help suspecting that the same logical naïveté characterizes the thinking of some social scientists and some philosophers. Of course they do not state the argument as I stated it. If they did, they would see its absurdity. But they are influenced by it in the sense that they vaguely suppose, without thinking it out, that in some way the great variety of moral beliefs is an evidence of relativism.

That this argument for relativism is a bad one does not prove, of course, that relativism is false. For true conclusions are often supported by bad arguments. And there might be other arguments for relativism which are valid. For instance, *if* it were proved that subjectivism is true, i.e., that the world is not a moral order; and *if* it were shown that relativism follows (as most modern thinkers have supposed that it does) from subjectivism; then this would be a good, in fact a conclusive, argument for relativism. And this is the argument on which those philosophers, as distinct from social scientists, who believe in relativism, have always relied. It is the argument, or at least the train of thought, which has actually produced the characteristic relativism of the modern age. And if the modern discoveries about the moral ideas of primitive peoples have exerted an influence, it has been only on a superficial level. Seventeenth century science caused the trend towards relativism, brought relativism into existence, and the work of the anthropologists is merely seized on by an age which already believes in relativism as a support for its conclusions.

What all this amounts to is that the older religious foundations of morality have disappeared owing to our "scientific" ways of thinking, that no other foundation has been discovered, and that in consequence the theory of morality is bankrupt and is collapsing. For to say that the moral beliefs of every society, however primitive it may be, are for it the only possible standards, and that in consequence the moral ideas of one culture are not any better than, but only different from, those of another, is really to say that morality has no foundation at all and moral beliefs no truth.

What influence, if any, the collapse of moral theory has had, or will have, upon actual moral behavior, is a difficult question to discuss. People, of course, go on being moral up to a point out of mere habit. Without a minimum of moral behavior a society cannot flourish, or even survive. Common decency, apart from any conviction, impels most men to treat their fellow beings with a certain amount of fairness and even kindness. Generous impulses are strong in many people. Such considerations, though they are insufficient to be motives for any exalted nobility of action, will always ensure that good behavior does not entirely disappear within any given society.

But if we turn from the internal relations between individuals in the same society to the relations between societies, the picture seems to be different. It is difficult to resist the conclusion that the present breakdown of international morals is, at least in part, due to the relativism of the modern age. We cannot, of course, ignore economic and other purely material causes. But spiritual and intellectual conditions are not without effect. And it cannot be denied that the present moral chaos of international relations is the perfect reflection in the practical world of the theory of ethical relativity. It is not without significance that Mussolini described the ethical theory on which he based his state as "political relativism." We are inclined, at the moment, to ascribe the breakdown of international morals to communism. But a little while ago we were blaming fascism. Mussolini was right. For suppose we apply moral relativism to the relations between societies. According to the group relativism now popular among social scientists and philosophers, the moral standards of a given society are, within that society, binding upon the individuals who compose it. (Whether there is any logical basis for this contention or not is another question. I should hold that there is not.) But as between societies or cultures, there can be no moral code which is binding. On the view stated by Hobbes, good is what pleases the individual, evil is what displeases him. This is now given up. Group relativism is the view that what pleases (or evokes an attitude of approval, or some other subjective emotional state, in) a society is good *within* that society and for that society, but not outside it. Translated into practice, what this means is that what Germany likes is morally right for Germany, and what Russia likes is morally right for Russia. This is "political relativism," and it is equivalent to the total absence of any morality as between nations, and this is exactly what we see in practice.

The relativistic spirit of the age is, of course, rampant in western Europe and America. Indeed, it was in western Europe that it originated, and not in Germany or Russia. And if the western democracies do not follow its lead in international affairs, if they still believe in international justice and try to establish it, this can only be because we in the west are muddled in our thinking. We keep murmuring, "Of course morals are only relative," and our intellectuals argue for ethical relativity. But fortunately we do not yet act on these beliefs. We act as if we still believed that there is a law of justice valid for all men, valid between nations as between individuals. This is inconsistent with modern "enlightenment." But our actions seem to be better than our theory.

We must now briefly trace another line of thought which had its source in the scientific revolution, and which has had at least a measure of influence on men's moral ideas. This concerns the so-called "problem of free will." To say that a man has free will is to say that he has the power to choose between alternative courses of action. I am presumably free to choose whether I shall drink tea or coffee for my breakfast. Nothing normally compels me to drink either the one or the other. This is not what we call a moral choice, because whether I drink tea or coffee is morally indifferent. But we do make moral choices, and these may be profoundly important. I may have a choice between murdering my mother to get her life insurance and not murdering her. There may be cases in which it is very difficult to say whether an action was done as a result of a man's free choice or as a result of compulsion. For instance, whether a man who steals a loaf of bread under the urge of intense hunger, which he could not satisfy in any other way, can be said to act freely or under compulsion, may be a matter of dispute. But it cannot be doubted that there are frequently situations in which we seem to be quite free to choose whether we shall do what is right or what is wrong. In these cases at least we commonly believe in the existence of free will.

The connection of free will with the theory of morality lies in the fact that it has usually been held by philosophers that, unless there is free will, nobody can rightly be held morally responsible for what they do. Suppose we disbelieved in free will. Suppose we believed that everybody, in everything they do, from the most important to the most trivial actions, acts under unavoidable compulsion, we should doubt whether we ought to hold anybody morally responsible for their actions. How would it be just to punish, or even to blame, a man for doing something which he could not help doing? For the same reason we should very likely feel that no one really deserves the reward, or the praise, which he gets for his good actions since he could not help doing them. Thus free will seems to be essential if there is to be any moral responsibility. And if no one can be held morally responsible for what they do, how can there be any morality?

All normal people instinctively believe in free will. Nothing seems more obvious than that I am free to choose whether I will drink tea or coffee. I have no doubt myself that the obvious view is the true view, and that we do have free will. Nevertheless this can be doubted, and has been doubted, by many very clever and learned men. They have used arguments to show that free will, however strongly we may feel that we have it, is in fact a delusion. And the reason why this becomes a part of our story is that these arguments are based upon ideas which have been derived from the scientific revolution. I do not mean to say that science invented the problem of free will, or that the difficulties which are inherent in the conception of it were discovered by modern science. There may be said to have been a problem about free will ever since men began to think. It was discussed in the middle ages by Thomas Aquinas, and in ancient times by Aristotle. What science did was to make the problem acute in the modern period by providing a new argument for disbelieving in free will. And modern disbelief in it—maintained, it should be said, only by a few intellectuals and not by the man in the street, who is usually unaware that there is any problem—is the immediate result of the scientific view of things.

Newtonian science gave rise to the assumption that every event is completely determined by a chain of causes which could, if we knew enough, be traced back indefinitely far into the past. Whatever happens, therefore, has been certain and pre-determined from the beginning of time. This general thesis is called determinism. It was well expressed by Laplace who wrote:

> An intelligence knowing, at a given instant of time, all forces acting in nature, as well as the momentary positions of all things of which the universe consists, would be able to comprehend the motions of the largest bodies of the world and those of the smallest atoms in one single formula, provided it were sufficiently powerful to subject all data to analysis; to it nothing would be uncertain, both future and past would be present before its eyes.[2]

Recent physics has shown reasons for doubting the complete truth of this view. But it was the view which seemed to follow from Newtonian science, and it was Newtonian science which became influential in the making of the modern mind. Moreover —in spite of the assertions of some physicists—the indeterminism of recent science does nothing to relieve the difficulties of the problem of free will, as will be shown in due course.

The postulate of determinism provided the modern argument against free will. Every event is completely determined by causes. A human action is just as much an event in nature as is a whirlwind or an eclipse of the sun. Therefore a human action is wholly determined by its past causes. Therefore it could not possibly be other than it is. If you know all the causes which produce an event, you can predict the event. The eclipse of the sun which occurred yesterday could have been predicted a million years ago if there had been astronomers alive then who knew all the causes which operate in the solar system. Apply this thought to the actions of human beings, which are, after all, nothing but motions of their physical bodies. Everything which men do could be predicted beforehand by anyone who knew enough about the causes, and the chains of causes stretching back into the past, which produced their actions. This means that whatever you do you were certain to do. You could not have done otherwise. You had no choice. You told a lie yesterday. It was certain thousands

---

[2] Quoted, *Foundations of Physics,* R. B. Lindsay and H. Margenau (New York: Wiley, 1936), p. 517.

of years ago, nay, millions of years ago, that you would tell that lie; and the intelligence imagined by Laplace—the Laplacean calculator, as it is sometimes called—could have foreseen it. But if this is so, what sense is there in saying that, when your life came to the moment of time in which you told that lie, you could have chosen whether you would tell it or not?

The general argument then is simply that all human actions must be wholly determined by causes of some kind, and that this is inconsistent with belief in free will. But if it is asked what kind of causes determine human actions, the answer is not so clear. Different answers have been given to this question, and these differing answers have given rise to different versions of the denial of free will. In general there have been two versions which may be called respectively the materialistic and the dualistic view.

The materialistic view holds that a human being is simply a material object and nothing more. What is called mind, soul, or spirit is not a non-material thing, but is material or a function of matter. In that case a human being—body and soul as we say —is entirely composed of atoms. Human actions are motions of the body, and these are ultimately reducible to the motions of swarms of atoms. The motions of each atom, and therefore the motions of the whole body, are entirely controlled by physical laws and physical causes. Therefore human actions are no more free than are the motions of the individual atoms which compose the human body.

The dualistic view depends on the belief that what we call mind cannot be reduced in this way to material atoms. Thoughts, emotions, and mental states generally, are not physical existences. (We need not specify, for our purposes, what they are supposed to be.) It may be thought that any dualistic view of the nature of mind will free us from the dilemma into which we have fallen about free will. For it cannot be said, if we hold a dualistic view, that all our actions are the results of the physical forces which control atoms. May not our minds, then, be free?

But it has not usually been thought possible to adopt this way out. For the general theory of determinism has been held to apply to minds, even if they are not material. Dualism only leads to another version of the denial of free will. Dualistic determinism usually says that our actions, or many of them, are caused by motives, or desires, or volitions. These in turn must have had their causes; and their causes must have had causes; and so on back indefinitely. In other words, it makes no difference whether we regard the universe as made of only one kind of thing, matter, or whether we think that there are in it two distinct kinds of thing, matter and mind. The principle of determinism, that whatever happens, is wholly determined by causes, and is theoretically predictable and therefore certain beforehand, applies to everything which exists, mind as well as matter. Therefore on either view human actions are not free.

It may be said that although physical determinism may be true, there is no reason to suppose that determinism applies to minds as well as to matter. But this suggestion seems to be groundless. Whatever kind of psychology you accept, materialistic or dualistic, it would appear that desires, motives, emotions, thoughts, and other mental states have causes, and that these causes have causes, and so on indefinitely back into the past. Hunger, or the desire for food, is caused by well-known physiological states of the body. Desires for drink and sex obviously also have bodily causes. These simple desires are easily explained. Even the more complex desires plainly have causes, though it is often very difficult to trace them in detail. Environment, heredity, social pressures, education, all play their part. And it would seem that if one knew all the causes of a man's mental condition at any time, one could predict his actions with certainty.

The fact that the causes which determine actions are often unknown, or are so complicated that it is impossible to determine them in detail, is nothing to the point. For the same is true in the physical world. Who can set out all the conditions which bring about a certain rainstorm? For this reason the weather is notoriously unpredictable. And if human actions often seem unpredictable, it is for the same reason. Theoretically, if one knew all the relevant meteorological conditions, one could predict every detail of the rainstorm. It will be the same with human actions. And just as the weather is in some degree predictable, so are human actions. The more you know of a human being, and of his psychology, and of the forces, social, environmental, or spiritual, which act on him, the more nearly you can say beforehand what he will do.

Thus there is every reason to think that the law of causal determinism is universal, that it applies in the internal world of mind as well as in the external world of matter. Whether we adopt a materialistic or a dualistic theory of human personality, in either case free will seems to be impossible. However you look at it, Newtonian science implies determinism, and determinism has seemed to most people to imply the denial of free will. Whether it really does so, whether there is any escape from this impasse, will be discussed in a later chapter. For the moment we have been concerned only with the story of how the modern mind came to its denial of free will.

Admitting that belief in free will is necessary to belief in moral responsibility, it is an open question whether the modern denial of free will has had any noticeable effect on morals. I shall later show that the whole line of thought which led to the denial of free will is a logical muddle, that there is nothing either in recent or in Newtonian science which need have caused it. But this would not prevent it from influencing human thoughts and actions. Nothing in Newtonian science need have caused a breakdown of religious faith. But the modern mind has supposed that it must. Nothing in it excludes belief in a cosmic purpose. But the modern mind has supposed that it does. Nothing in it has any tendency to prove that the world is not a moral order. Yet the world has drawn from it that conclusion. All these fancied implications of science are logical muddles. But the history of human thought is the history of muddles. And the question now before us is whether this particular muddle about free will has had any practical influence in the way of undermining morality.

The main reason which can be given for doubting whether it has is that the denial of free will has been practically confined to intellectuals, and does not seem to have seeped down, in any noticeable degree, to the unlearned. In this it differs from the loss of effective belief in God or a world-purpose, which have infected popular thought. The picture of a meaningless and sense-less world, and therefore of the futility of human life, is mirrored in the popular art and literature of our time. It does not seem that the denial of free will is so mirrored—unless perhaps the sort of fatalistic view of human life to be found in some of the writings of Thomas Hardy could be given as an example. The reason for this difference is, I think, plain. God and world-purpose, whether in fact they exist or not, are not at any rate obvious in our daily lives, whereas the existence of free will is obvious every time we decide to eat or drink or go for a walk. And as a rule only very learned and clever men deny what is obviously true. Common men have less brains, but more sense.

But on the question of the actual influence of the denial of free will there is a certain amount to be said on the other side. The notions of historical determinism, economic determinism, and cultural determinism, although they are primarily intellectualist ideas have become fairly widely popular. The thoughts that we are all engulfed in "the wave of the future," that nothing that any individual can do will affect the course of history, that even great men are the products of historical movements and are not, except in a negligible degree, the causes of these movements, exert their influence. In the conduct of our private lives also determinism may be thought to be apparent. Whereas even fifty or a hundred years ago people were in general believed to be responsible for their evil actions, these are now more generally attributed to causes beyond their control. Crime is not really a moral lapse but a disease which, like measles, should not be punished but cured. Men, on any view, do wrong. But former generations urged moral endeavor as the preventive of wrongdoing. Now we think that pills and injections should be substituted for the prescriptions of the saints. It may be that all this is an improvement in our thinking. But it may also be that men and women who could, with a little effort, control their tempers, their lusts, or their folly, may think themselves excused from such effort by laying the blame for their ill behavior on their glands, their livers, their environment, their heredity, the social system—on anything, in fact, except themselves. It may be the case that the more humane treatment of criminals, the benefits which can be derived from the work of psychiatrists, the greater tolerance which may now be extended to certain forms of behavior which were formerly treated with brutal lack of understanding, outweigh the disadvantages which attach to a weakened sense of moral responsibility. But the latter should not be ignored, and is fraught with obvious dangers.

7

THE CONSEQUENCES FOR PHILOSOPHY

PHILOSOPHY IS NOT A POPULAR SUBJECT. I ONCE OFFERED THE manuscript of a book to a publisher. The word "philosophy" appeared in the title. The publisher accepted the book, but said that the word "philosophy" must be expunged from the name of it. This, he said, must be done in order "to take the curse off it." If, on the other hand, I could introduce the word "science" into the title, the book might sell like hot cakes. For everyone knows that whatever science says is both true and wonderful, whereas the thoughts of philosophers, besides being dull, are idle speculations. If, in an average class of students any question is being discussed and someone says "but science says so and so," that is thought at once to settle the matter finally.

There are many causes of the unpopularity of philosophy. Only one of them is relevant to our inquiries in this book. Philosophy in the original sense of the word, as it was understood for example by Socrates and Plato, had a direct relevance to life. Socrates and Plato were both concerned with discovering what the good life is and how to lead it. But—according to the current accusations— the academic philosophers of today do not concern themselves with the question of a way of life. Indeed many of them despise such a question—at any rate if it is thought to be a part of the kind of philosophy which should be taught in a university. Is it not the business of preachers rather than of scholars? Academic philosophers—so the accusation goes on—nowadays discuss only a variety of intellectual puzzles which have no importance at all. They may be interesting or amusing to a certain type of mind which is fortunately not very common, in the same way as cross-word puzzles are interesting or amusing to certain people. But the typical so-called philosophical problem of the textbooks is like the cross-word puzzle in the respect that its solution does not really matter to anybody.

It will be relevant to our purposes to give one or two examples. A philosopher will assert that it is impossible to prove by any logical argument that the sun will rise tomorrow. Everyone, including the philosopher, knows that it will rise. That is not the question which the philosopher proposes to discuss. The question is whether it can be "proved" that the sun will rise. Hume in the eighteenth century thought that he had proved that this cannot be proved. A large number of philosophers during the last two centuries have spent major portions of their lives trying to discover a proof of it, so as to refute Hume. Other philosophers since his time have agreed with him. The dispute is still going on in philosophy lecture halls all over the world.

Again, a philosopher will assert that it cannot be proved by any logic that a stone or any other material object continues to exist when no one is actually looking at it or perceiving it with any of his senses. Everyone knows that it does. That is not the question. The question is whether it can be proved. And this dispute, like the one about the rising of the sun, has been going on for centuries, and philosophers still range themselves on one side or other of the question.

Another famous philosophical problem is whether anyone can know that any person other than himself "has a mind." I know that I have a mind because I am conscious. But how can I know that my mother is conscious or has a mind? She might be an automaton cleverly constructed by nature to behave *as if* she had a consciousness inside her. It might be the case that I am the only conscious mind in the universe. This view—that I am the only mind in existence—has even been dignified by philosophers with a special label—solipsism. No philosopher, so far as I know, has ever gone to the length of believing in solipsism. They all know that other people have minds, just as everyone else knows it. That is not the question. The question is how, or whether, it can be proved.

At the present moment there is a highly influential school of philosophers who hold that the only business of philosophy is to discuss the different meanings which common words have, and that philosophy is, or should be, only concerned with verbal questions. They discuss, for example, whether seeing a color ought to be called having a visual "sensation," or whether only things like headaches or being tickled by a feather ought to be called sensations.

The general public is inclined to turn with disgust from such questions, which they regard as nothing but trifling, although they have now been given by academic minds the august name which was once reserved for the profound thoughts of genuinely wise men.

In these accusations against the philosophy of the university lecture halls there is a measure of truth. Nevertheless they do not tell the whole story, and in my opinion they seriously misrepresent the truth. I shall begin this chapter by trying to present a conception of philosophy which will exhibit both the truth and the untruth of these criticisms. I shall do this, not for the purpose —itself rather academic—of giving a correct definition, or description, of what philosophy is, but because in my opinion it is impossible to understand how the modern mind has grown to be what it is without understanding the part which philosophy has played in it. And we cannot understand this unless we have a just conception of the nature of philosophy. In my view the philosophy of a people or an age is an integral part of its culture and its spiritual life. Therefore if one does not understand its philosophy one can have but a maimed view of its culture. No one would deny that religious and moral ideas are of vital importance in a culture. I shall try to show that philosophical ideas are just as important. If you want to understand an age you have to understand its philosophy just as much as you have to understand its art, its literature, its science. Indeed its philosophy is perhaps a better key for unlocking the secrets of its *Weltanschauung* than either its art or its literature. But this could not be the case if philosophy were nothing but a collection of curious verbal puzzles which have no bearing on life. There must therefore be something wrong with the conception of philosophy which has given rise to the sort of criticisms referred to above. We have to substitute a juster conception.

It is true that, on the surface, philosophy may look like a collection of unimportant puzzles, the mere acrobatics of agile minds. It is true that philosophers themselves sometimes view it in this light. It is true that some philosophers spend their whole lives in attempting to solve such puzzles. But if you look below the surface you will find that something different is going on— and I think that many philosophers themselves do not see it— which is what I want to display.

Each age, each culture, has its own peculiar imaginative world-picture, its *Weltanschauung*. Let us first consider what a *Weltanschauung* is, and how it expresses itself. As it exists in the minds of the majority of the people who are the bearers of the culture it may be said to consist in a welter of essentially vague ideas and feelings about the nature of the world, man's relation to the world, his place in the scheme of things, his destiny, his attitudes towards himself and his cosmic environment, his feeling of what he ought to do, what part he ought to play, in this cosmic environment. As it exists in the minds of the majority, it is a sort of formless and chaotic mass. But in the minds and the work of a few individuals it takes on definite forms. And it, that is to say one and the same *Weltanschauung,* takes *different* forms for different kinds of mind. It manifests itself differently in the main cultural activities of the age or culture, that is to say in its art, its literature, its religion, and finally its philosophy. Thus the art, literature, religion, and philosophy of an age are like the branches of a single tree, springing from a single root and trunk. It is the same life, the same sap, which is in them all.

The art, literature, religion, and philosophy of a period are, of course, all different from one another. The differences lie in the media through which the content of the *Weltanschauung* is expressed. For instance, the contrast between the art and literature, on the one hand, and the philosophy, on the other, may be roughly described by saying that the same ideas appear in a sensuous form, in colors, and sounds, in images, myths, or stories, in art and literature, while they appear in the form of abstract thought in philosophy. Philosophy is the crystallization into abstract intellectual propositions of the same ideas which are the lifeblood of art and literature, but which in them appear in non-abstract, that is to say, in concrete and sensuous shapes. In a novel an idea may be exemplified by a story. In philosophy it may appear as a theory. For instance, a philosopher may put forward the proposition that the universe is not governed by any purpose. The same idea may appear in a novel in the frustrations and feelings of futility of its characters. Or the philosophical theory of determinism may appear in a drama in a sense of helplessness in the face of some overmastering fate which is felt by the dramatis personae or illustrated by the denouement. Something of this sort may be the meaning of some of the great tragedies of the world's literature. Man feels helpless before some power. His struggles avail nothing. The power may be envisaged as Fate, as chance, as necessity, or even as God. In the philosophy of the modern age it tends to be a determinist theory of the world.

This is why I suggested that the philosophy of a period may be a better key to the understanding of its *Weltanschauung* than its art or literature is. For in the latter it takes the form of feelings and images which are still relatively vague and confused. But in philosophy it takes, or at least attempts to take, the form of clear statements. The philosopher's effort is thus seen as an attempt to analyze and make clear the vague floating ideas of his age. Not that he usually consciously intends to do this. He may very well deny that he is doing it, and may put forward some quite different conception of his function and of the nature of philosophy. But we must be cultural determinists at least to the extent of believing that the spirit of an age overrules the conscious intentions of the philosopher and forces itself into his intellectual constructions.

It is not meant, of course, to deny that the philosopher may be highly original. Nor is it meant to assert that all the philosophers of a period are saying identically the same thing. Each has his own contributions to make. Each expresses the spirit of his time in his own individual way. The case is here the same as it is in the world of art. We may recognize that the different artists of a school, a period, a culture, all breathe a similar spirit, have a certain over-all resemblance. Yet each may have his own peculiar vision. So too it is in the sphere of poetry. Wordsworth, Coleridge, Shelley, and Keats, are all very different from one another, and each is highly original. Yet they are all romantic poets, and romanticism is, or expresses—as we shall see later—a specific world-view which they all share. Among the philosophers of the modern period Hobbes is very different from Hume, Hume from Comte, Comte from Vaihinger, Vaihinger from the pragmatists, the pragmatists from the positivists. One and all have original viewpoints. Yet there is a sense in which they are all saying the same thing, all expressing the same world-view, each in his own terms. If we take a rapid survey of the philosophy of the modern period, from Descartes to the present day, we seem at first sight to have before us a chaos of conflicting opinions about everything. Indeed this is often made a reproach against philosophy. But if we look below the surface, we shall find that there is a pattern; and I hope in the following pages to show this pattern.

But if it is true that philosophy is thus an integral part of culture, and that the philosophy of an age expresses and contributes to the solution which the age gives to the great questions about the nature of the world and of human life, how does it come about that philosophy, at any rate in the modern period, appears on the surface as nothing but a collection of unimportant logical puzzles and conundrums such as those which were illustrated at the beginning of this chapter? How does it come about that to many philosophers themselves it seems to be only concerned with the meanings of words? They probably would not refer to their verbal puzzles as "unimportant," because they would say that the problems which they discuss are of interest, and therefore of importance, to them, just as some mathematical abstraction which has no known practical application may be considered important by the mathematician. But they do very frequently apply the word "puzzle" to their special problems. I have not chosen this word myself as a means of belittling their efforts. I have selected it because it is a favorite word which many philosophers of the present day themselves use for the problems on which they are engaged. And they would insist that whether their puzzles have any reference to life or not does not concern them. They are like some of those "pure" mathematicians who take delight in the fact that the world of abstractions in which they live seems to be wholly cut off from practical affairs. How has this state of affairs in philosophy come about, and how is it consistent with the view of the nature and function of philosophy which I have expressed?

There are two points to be considered. The first concerns the application of philosophical ideas to life. Ought we always to insist that these ideas, and the studies which philosophers make of them, must have relevance to life? The second question concerns the alleged triviality of many of their inquiries, for instance those which are admittedly concerned only with the meanings of words, or with what are called "verbal questions."

In regard to the first question, the practical applications of an idea—whether it is a philosophical, a mathematical, or a scientific idea—are not the only proper reasons for studying it. There is such a thing as knowledge for its own sake, and it is a perfectly legitimate human motive. Knowledge for its own sake means, of course, knowledge which is sought regardless of whether it has any practical applications or not. And if there did not exist men in whom it is the chief, or even the sole, motive for research and study, science and philosophy alike would dry up at their sources. And even those who value knowledge only for its practical uses ought to recognize that the very knowledge which they thus value was for the most part originally obtained by the kind of man who does not care whether it has any practical uses or not. Nearly all the great discoveries of science have been made by men whose only motive was a great hunger for knowledge, a vast wonder and curiosity about the workings of nature, which they desired to satisfy for its own sake. Witness the importance of what is called "basic research" in science. This is nearly all done by men who are not much interested in practical applications, or at least by men who do not regard the practical applications as being part of their business.

It may also be urged that even if the knowledge which they acquire had not, and never could have, any practical utility at all, yet to seek it is a noble end which belongs to man's spiritual life, and is one of the things which set human beings above animals. Bertrand Russell has written: "We must free our minds from the prejudices of what are wrongly called 'practical men.' The 'practical' man, as the word is often used, is one who recognizes only material needs, who realizes that men must have food for the body, but is oblivious of the necessity of providing food for the mind."[1] Knowledge, apart from its practical uses, is—like art, literature, poetry, religion—one of the things which set men free from the narrow and confining life of the senses, and from the feverish pursuit of selfish personal ends.

There is therefore a place, in philosophy as well as in science, for the man who devotes his whole life to the examination and discussion of questions which may seem useless to men whose interests lie in more practical spheres. And even if one thinks—as I do—that the ultimate justification of philosophy lies in the contributions it can make to the good life, it is narrow and intolerant to be impatient with such men. And if something of their spirit is imparted in philosophy courses to students who, when they leave the university, will be engaged in practical activities,

[1] *The Problems of Philosophy* (Home University Library Series; New York: Henry Holt & Co.), chapter 15.

this is all to the good. It will act as a leaven in lives which might otherwise become wholly absorbed in material things.

It may be said that the verbal or logical puzzles which so many philosophers discuss cannot be compared to the great questions regarding the nature of the universe which scientists seek to solve. Both may no doubt be studied for their own sakes with no regard to practical applications. But the problems of the pure scientist are at least great questions. The study of galactic systems other than our own can hardly have any practical use; or at least none is visible at present. But there is something about the contemplation of such matters which is great and ennobling. The same is true in greater or less degree of the studies of the chemist, the physicist, the geologist. They at least open up vistas to the human mind. But the "puzzles" characteristic of the philosopher may seem by comparison utterly trivial. How can the question whether seeing a color ought to be called a sensation, or whether that word properly applies only to headaches and ticklings, enlarge the mind? This brings us to the second question we were to discuss, the alleged triviality of many philosophical problems.

The answer to this is—in my view—as follows. It has been found, over and over again, that the solutions of the Big Questions—whether the world has a plan or purpose, whether it is run by an overruling Mind, what is the destiny of man in the universe —turn upon points which may seem to those who are not trained in philosophy to have no bearing upon them at all, points which, if taken by themselves, may seem trivial and picayune. I will give one or two notable illustrations of this.

The question whether seeing a color is properly called a sensation or not is relevant to, and has a powerful bearing upon, the problem whether the universe is ultimately governed by an over-ruling Mind or is entirely controlled by blind physical forces. This comes about in the following way. Berkeley tried to defend religion against materialism by showing that there are no such things as dead substances, but that the universe is really composed of nothing but minds, including the mind of God, and their "ideas" or sensations. If this is true, then it is mind, not matter, which rules the world. And anyone can see how such a philosophy tends to support the religious view of things. A part, indeed the greater part, of Berkeley's argument consisted in trying to prove that what we call dead things, gross material objects, are ideas or sensations in the minds of men and ultimately in the mind of God. To show this he argued that all the qualities of material objects, such as their color, taste, smell, shape, hardness or softness, hotness or coldness, are sensations. For sensations, it seemed obvious to him, can only exist in conscious minds. We should all admit that headaches, itchings, tickling sensations, and pains could not exist unless there were a consciousness to feel them. Tickling, as Galileo observed, is not in the feather which tickles us. It is in us. Hence if colors, shapes, heat and cold, hardness and softness, are sensations in the same sense as ticklings and itchings are, this will go a long way to show that something like Berkeley's idealistic philosophy might be near the truth. And this in turn would tend to support the religious view of the world. This enables us to see at once how important this verbal "puzzle" about sensations really is.

Another outstanding example of how what seems a mere barren conundrum may affect the Big Questions is found in the philosophy of Kant. Kant, like Berkeley—though through quite a different train of thought—sought to find a place for religion and morality in a world from which science seemed to be banishing them. He sought to defend the ideas of God, freedom, and immortality, against a non-religious, deterministic philosophy which he saw was developing as a result of Newtonian science. He found that, in order to give a logical foundation to his own philosophy, in which room was to be found for these religious and moral ideas, it was necessary for him to discuss the nature of a simple arithmetical equation such as $7 + 5 = 12$. The question he raised about arithmetic was this. Of course we know that $7 + 5 = 12$. Nobody, least of all Kant, doubts this. But *how* do we know it? Do we know it merely as a result of knowing the meanings of the words used in the equation? If you know what the words "seven" and "five" and "twelve" and "plus" mean, can you, without having any other source of knowledge, thereby know that the phrase "seven plus five" means the same thing as the word "twelve"? Put in another way the question is: does the knowledge that the equation is true follow from the definitions of the terms used in it?

Kant argued that we cannot know the truth of the equation merely by knowing the definitions or meanings of the words which are employed in it. For neither the meaning of the word "seven," nor that of "plus," nor that of "five," nor that of the combination of all three words, contains or implies the meaning of the word "twelve." He said that in order to know that $7 + 5 = 12$, there must exist a special power in the mind which does not consist merely in understanding the meanings of words. This led him to believe that he had discovered—by means of a line of thought which is too complicated to reproduce here—something very important about the nature of mind, namely, that it is mind which, in some sense, *makes,* or at least helps to make, the world we live in—a conclusion not wholly unlike that of Berkeley, though it would be a mistake to press very far the resemblance between two philosophers who are in most respects very unlike one another.

Most philosophers now think, perhaps rightly, that Kant was mistaken in his view about how we know the truth of arithmetical propositions. The point, however, is this. How we know that $7 + 5 = 12$ seems a question which is utterly trivial and academic. We certainly do know it, just as we know that material objects exist when no one is perceiving them, or that the sun will rise tomorrow. What difference, then, can it make *how* we know it? The answer is that Kant uses his solution of this question as an entering wedge for his whole theory of the nature of the universe. This is one of the hinges on which his philosophy turns. If he is wrong about arithmetic, this does not of course show that God, freedom, and immortality, are not real. But it does show that at least one avenue to belief in them—the avenue which Kant thought he had opened up—is a false trail. In this way the problem how we know the truth of arithmetic achieved enormous importance in the history of human thought.

This partly answers our question about the alleged triviality of many of the problems which philosophers discuss. But not entirely. For if they always discussed these little conundrums only as a means towards the solution of the Big Questions—as Kant did—they would be fully justified by what has just been said. But this is not the case. What they seem to be doing for the most part is to detach the little conundrums from the Big Questions, and to discuss them as ends in themselves. Their original importance is forgotten, and they sink to the level of professional disputes. For instance, to this day the question how we know that $7 + 5 = 12$ is debated in philosophy lecture rooms. Practically never is its original connection with God, freedom, and immortality pointed out or remembered. The professor treats it as an interesting puzzle. In the discussion of it he becomes involved in a maze of logical refinements, semantics, and verbal distinctions. Each separate maze becomes a new puzzle, which in turn generates more puzzles. The whole question becomes a game played for its own sake.

This is no doubt regrettable. It is one of the causes why philosophy, once regarded as the crown of knowledge, gains few students in the universities, and is practically ignored by the general public. Yet we must remember that even the exploration of logical puzzles has a certain right to be pursued as a part of the search for pure truth. Philosophy, like any other human enterprise, is subject to the principle of the division of labor. In the manufacture of automobiles there are men who spend their whole lives in the construction of single minute parts, and have but little conception of the relation of these parts to the whole machine. The over-all plan is the work of a few superior minds. Ought we not to expect the same thing in the construction of great world-philosophies? Of these the great engineers are the Platos, the Aristotles, the Kants. But the work of the little logical puzzlers contributes in the end to their great designs.

The conception of philosophy which I have here suggested sees it as ultimately concerned with the great questions of the nature of the world, the nature of man, the place of man in the universe, the good life. And if this is correct, then the *Weltanschauung* of an age, its beliefs about these ultimate problems, will find expression in the art, the literature, the science, the religion, and the philosophy of the age. Philosophy will be the abstract expression, in the form of intellectual propositions, of ideas which appear elsewhere in the form of myths, stories, images, feelings, and picture-thinking. This view finds room for the technical disputes of the professionals, but it regards them as means to greater ends, not as ends in themselves.

Armed with this view, let us begin our attempt to see how the philosophy of the modern period reflects that period's essential beliefs about the nature of the world, about God, about world-purpose, about man, his ideals and aspirations. We shall then see what its place in the development of the modern mind has been.

In the preceding pages I have emphasized that the typical characteristics of the modern mind are its loss of effective belief in God, the practical disappearance of the teleological view of the world, its denial that the world is a moral order, and its consequent ethical relativism. This is quite correct, but nevertheless the picture drawn has been one sided. It has exhibited only the main current of modern thought. There have been, of course, other currents, running sometimes in an opposite direction. There have always been, and still are, religious men, or men whose fundamental attitudes to the world are religious, whether or not they happened to profess any particular creed or brand of theology. This observation refers primarily to the masses of men to whom philosophy, in the technical sense of the term, is a sealed book. But the same is true of technical philosophers. Though the most typical representatives of philosophy in the modern world have been inspired by the world-view derived from science, there have been, among philosophers, many protests and reactions against that view. And we have to exhibit both sides of the picture if we are really to understand what has been, and is, going on.

If we are to succeed in our attempt, we must have first an over-all picture of modern culture as a whole. We must then fit into this the particular developments of philosophy, so as to show them as integral parts of the whole picture. And in my view, modern culture as a whole, whether we think of it in terms of art, literature, or philosophy, is the arena of a vast struggle between two radically opposed views of the world, two opposite imaginative world-pictures. The history of this struggle is the history of modern thought. The two sides stem respectively from religion and science. The religious view of the world is the older, going back through the middle ages into long pre-Christian times— from which it will be seen that by "the religious view of the world" I do not mean any particular religion or creed, but something much wider and deeper, of which perhaps different creeds are varying expressions. It still lives in the modern world, but it is increasingly challenged by the other view, which is quite recent, and which is the product, in fact, of the seventeenth century scientific revolution. For this reason I shall call the latter the scientific view of the world. The conflict between the two views is the essential conflict between science and religion, which does not therefore consist in disputes about particular dogmas of Christianity and particular discoveries of science.

It may be thought that the label "the scientific view of the world" does injustice to science, since it is not necessarily the view held by scientists themselves. But it is not meant to imply that it is actually held by all scientists, or even by a majority. The question what proportion of scientists believe in some kind of religion, what proportion disbelieve in it, and what proportion are indifferent, is irrelevant to anything except the personal biographies of scientists. Neither does our label imply that the scientific view of the world is the official view of science. Science has no official view, because the question whether the religious or the scientific view of the world is true is not a scientific, but a philosophic, question. The views of scientists on it have no more importance or authority than their views on politics, nor are they in any way competent to decide it. Nor, finally, does our label imply that the scientific view of the world follows logically from, or is a necessary logical consequence of, anything in science. Indeed I have labored to show that this is not the case. To call it the scientific view means only that its derivation is in science, that science has been the cause of it in the manner explained in the preceding pages, that it is the set of ideas which has *seeemed* to the most typical minds of the modern period to represent the scientific spirit, whether in fact it does so or not. If, however, "the scientific view of the world" is thought to be an objectionable title, we may call it instead, if we like, "the naturalistic view of the world," or simply "naturalism." And I shall often use these synonyms for it in the following chapters.

Let us set out the essential ideas of the two world-pictures in tabular form so as to see their flat contradiction of one another at a glance.

The Religious View of the World	*The Scientific View of the World, or Naturalism*
The world is ultimately governed• by spiritual forces.	The world is wholly governed by blind physical forces, such as gravitation, the laws of motion, the laws of chemical combination, etc.
The world has a purpose.	The world has no purpose. It is entirely senseless and meaningless.
The world is a moral order.	The world is not a moral order. The universe is "indifferent to" values of any kind.

These propositions are not often stated, in literature, in art, or even in philosophy, in this bald and naked way. Hence we may often fail to recognize them when they appear dressed up in other guises. But my purpose is precisely to strip them naked.

It will be noticed that, in the statement of the first religious proposition, the phrase "spiritual forces," and not the word "God," has been used. I have used the wider and vaguer phrase intentionally, because I wish to include here, not the Christian interpretation of things only, but any religious interpretation. The religious view of the world extends far beyond the confines of Christendom. This needs emphasis. The Christian peoples have no monopoly of religion. Christianity is only one particular version of the religious view of the world. And I should wish to emphasize that that view is a part of man's universal spiritual heritage, belonging to all ages and all cultures, although just recently denied in one part of the world, the West. Seeing that belief in God is central not only to Christianity, but also to Judaism, Islam, and Hinduism, though not to Buddhism, I might perhaps have used the word "God" in my formulation of the religious view of the world without any very great disadvantage. But it is apt to carry with it, in Christian countries, the suggestion that what is being talked about is the special doctrines of Christianity. Hence I have avoided it here.

The contrast between the two opposing world-views has also been made by William James, although his terminology is somewhat different from mine. He does not express it in the three pairs of contradicting statements which I have given. And he does not bring out the idea that the struggle between the two philosophies is the key to the understanding of the modern period. As to terminology, what I call "the religious view of the world" he calls "theism"—which I think has too narrow and precise a connotation. What I call "the scientific view of the world" he calls "materialism." It is worth while to quote some passages from James so that we may come to recognize the same essential sets of ideas in different forms. To be a materialist means, he says,

> . . . explaining higher phenomena by lower ones and leaving the destinies of the world at the mercy of its blinder parts and forces. . . . The laws of physical nature are what run things materialism says. . . . Over against it stands theism [which]

says that mind not only witnesses and records things, but also runs and operates them: the world being thus guided not by its lower, but by its higher element. . . .

[According to materialism] in Mr. Balfour's words: "The energies of our system will decay, the glory of the sun will be dimmed, and the earth, tideless and inert, will no longer tolerate the race which has for a moment disturbed its solitude. Man will go down into the pit, and all his thoughts will perish. . . . Imperishable monuments and immortal deeds, death itself, and love stronger than death, will be as if they had not been. Nor will anything that is be better or worse for all that the labor, genius, devotion and suffering of man have striven through countless ages to effect."

This utter and final wreck and tragedy are of the essence of materialism. . . . It is . . . not a permanent warrant for our more ideal interests, not a fulfiller of our remotest hopes.

The notion of God, on the other hand . . . guarantees an ideal order that shall be permanently preserved. A world with a God in it to say the last word may indeed burn up or freeze; but then we think of him as still mindful of the old ideals and sure to bring them elsewhere to fruition. So that where he is, tragedy is only provisional . . . and shipwreck and dissolution not the absolutely final things. . . .

This need of an eternal moral order is one of the deepest needs of our breast.

Materialism means simply the denial that the moral order is eternal, and the cutting off of ultimate hopes; . . . [Theism] means the affirmation of an eternal moral order and the letting loose of hope.[2]

I have said that the history of the modern period is the history of the struggle between these two points of view. I should now repeat that the scientific view is in some sense the typical or dominant view of the modern world. It is what is characteristic of the modern mind, what marks it off from all other periods of history. Moreover, although no one can predict the future, it appears—to the present writer at least—to be gradually winning out over its antagonist. It has, on the whole, steadily increased its hold on the

[2] William James, *Pragmatism* (New York: Longmans, Green & Co., 1928), chapter III. Quoted by permission of Longmans, Green & Co., Inc. Copyright 1907.

modern mind during the last three hundred years. It has not indeed registered a continuous and uninterrupted advance. The battle lines have wavered. The seventeenth century saw its birth. The eighteenth century was the age of its triumph. The nineteenth century was mostly a time of reaction against it, taking the form of romanticism in art, music, literature, and philosophy. The twentieth century has witnessed the decline of romanticism, the strong resurgence of the scientific view of the world. We are now once more in its grip. There are still reactions and protests, but their authors seem to be fighting a losing battle. This is not meant as a value judgment. It is not intended to imply that the scientific view, because it is winning, is therefore right or true. I make at present no implications one way or the other about this. I make only what seems to me to be a correct interpretation of historical events. In spite of the nineteenth century reaction against it, which failed—in the sense that romanticism has not endured or been replaced by any other expression of the religious view—the scientific view appears to be the dominating and overpowering intellectual force of the present day.

We must now try to show in some detail what role philosophy has played in this conflict. My contention will be that, if we ignore the technicalities of the philosophers of the modern period, if we cut through all that and get to their centers, we shall find that most of them can be classified under one of two heads. Either their philosophies, stripped of unessentials, express a vision of the world which is the scientific picture, or they express the religious picture. They may be unconscious of their central impelling visions, or they may be conscious of them. Both are dominated by science, the first because they are expressing the scientific view of the world, the second because their motive is a reaction against it. Both therefore illustrate the domination of the modern mind by science, the one by supporting, the other by opposing, the view of the world which has been derived from it. The major philosophers may accordingly be classified as shown in the following table.

Philosophies which express the scientific view of the world	*Philosophies of reaction and protest in favor of the religious view of the world*
Descartes	Descartes
Hobbes	Berkeley
Hume	Kant
Comte	Hegel and the post-Kantian idealists
Vaihinger	Romanticism
The logical positivists (e.g., Schlick, Ayer, Carnap)	The British and American absolute idealists (e.g., Bradley, Bosanquet, Royce)

There are several general remarks to be made about this broad scheme before it is explained in detail.

The left-hand column gives the dominant trend of the modern world. For a brief period in the nineteenth century the tendencies represented by the philosophers of the right-hand column regained a temporary ascendancy in Hegel, the post-Kantian idealists, romanticism, and the British and American absolute idealists. This ascendancy was lost again at the beginning of the present century.

We note that Descartes appears in both columns. His correct position is doubtful, and there might be justification for placing him only in the left-hand column. But some elements of both points of view are mixed in his philosophy. His ambiguous position is due to the fact that he lived at the very beginning of the modern period (1596-1650). In his time the lines of demarcation between the two views of the world had not been clearly drawn. The dominant tendencies of the modern mind had not been clearly formulated. The opposition of the two views had not crystallized. The battle lines were still confused. Hence it is not surprising that Descartes should appear sometimes to be in the one camp, sometimes in the other.

In a classification such as ours we must not expect great exactitude. It is not meant to be a rigid scheme with watertight compartments into which every philosopher will neatly fit. History is fluid and overflows boundaries. We must not try to force it onto any Procrustean bed. We are only dealing with general drifts and tendencies, and must expect to find exceptions and cases which are difficult to classify. For instance, Kant is difficult to classify because of the all-embracing character of his thought in which every side of modern culture is synthesized. He was not a one-sided, but a many-sided thinker. A case could be made out for putting him, like Descartes—although for quite different reasons —in both columns. For he tried to express in his philosophy both the naturalistic and the religious standpoints, and to reconcile them. But because he saw clearly—indeed was the first to see clearly—that the naturalistic view was undermining religion and morality, and was disturbed by this, and because one of the main motives of his philosophy was to find a place in a naturalistic world-view for "God, freedom, and immortality" without destroying or whittling down the claims of the scientific view of the world, it seems better to place him on the side of the protests and reactions. He did not protest against the naturalistic view as such. On the contrary, he supported it to the limit. But he sought, in spite of this, to find a theory of the world in which there should still be room for religion and morality.

Another difficult case is John Locke, whom I have omitted altogether. His philosophy is a direct product of the new science, yet it does not show the characteristic marks of the scientific view of the world as listed in the right-hand column on page 143. But neither does it show any strong religious bent, although—following the fashion of the time—he produces a "proof" of the existence of God, and subscribes to conventional theological doctrines. He does not perceive the essential antagonism of the two world-views, perhaps because he lived, like Descartes, too early.

Neither Spinoza nor Leibniz fits easily into the classification. Spinoza was a naturalist and determinist, yet the spirit of his philosophy was deeply religious, even mystical. Leibniz also combines elements of the naturalistic and religious viewpoints.

Vaihinger appears on our list, but it might be objected that he is not, in any sense, one of the great philosophers of the modern period. He is a relatively minor figure. This is probably true, but it happens that he illustrates very well some of the major tendencies of early twentieth century thinking. For this reason he is included.

Pragmatism, which is thought by many to be the characteristic philosophy of twentieth century America, is left out. The trouble with it is that it can be quoted on either side of the great debate. Indeed it seems that it can be quoted on any side of any debate. For its major doctrine is that we ought to hold as true whatever beliefs on any subject are most advantageous to us in the long run; and everyone is, of course, inclined to maintain that his own opinions on any matter are the most advantageous. Temperament, according to William James, decides, and should decide, the question. Hence pragmatists may appear either on the side of religion or against it, according to the temperament of the particular pragmatist. Accordingly, James produced a religious version of pragmatism, while Dewey has produced a naturalistic version. It is really impossible to classify so protean a philosophy in any way.

Thus we see that our classification pretends to be neither exhaustive nor exact. The battle between the religious and the scientific viewpoints is not unfairly represented by Matthew Arnold's lines:

And we are here as on a darkling plain
Swept by confused alarms of struggle and flight,
Where ignorant armies clash by night.

It is impossible to draw sharp lines. Yet if the reader should at this stage be inclined to conclude that our classification can have no value, I hope to show by the further elaboration of detail that this is incorrect, and that there is important significance in the picture of the general trends of modern thinking given in the scheme which I have proposed. To see this we must turn to the details.

8

NATURALISM

DESCARTES STILL RETAINS IN HIS PHILOSOPHY SOME MEDIEVAL modes of thought. Yet he represents on the whole a complete break with medievalism, and was the first great philosopher of modern times to do so. For this reason he is sometimes called the father of modern philosophy. He was himself a distinguished mathematician and scientist. He enthusiastically supported the new scientific spirit of inquiry, especially the mechanical interpretation of nature and the exclusion of teleological explanations from science. Like the actual founders of the scientific movement he did not disbelieve that natural phenomena are ultimately controlled by divine purposes. The view of the founding fathers, which Descartes shared, was that God's purposes are inscrutable, and that in any case a knowledge of them would be useless for the special purposes of science. What are its special purposes? It is often said that the function of science is to predict phenomena and so enable us, so far as possible, to control the future to our advantage. If you could know that an earthquake will occur at a certain place, you could not perhaps stop it, but you could at any rate take precautions against its effects. You could, for example, go to some other place. The science of meteorology aims at enabling you to know when to carry a raincoat. Physics can predict that if you do certain things with uranium you can achieve the obviously desirable result of killing a few millions of your fellow creatures.

This account of the function of science as being concerned only with prediction and control of events is probably an over-simplification. Why assume that science has only one function? But it is at any rate true that prediction is one of its most important aims. And knowledge of the purposes of events is no help in predicting them. Perhaps if one were omniscient and knew the entire world-plan as it exists in the mind of God, one might be able to predict what God will do next. But no one can attain this degree of knowledge. And it is useless to know merely that the sun exists to give men light by day, the moon by night. This will not enable one to foresee an eclipse. Nor will the knowledge that the purpose of rainbows is to remind us of God's promise not again to destroy us by floods be of any use in enabling us to know when and where it will please God to put a rainbow in the sky.

To predict phenomena what you have to know is, not their purposes, but their *causes* and the physical laws which govern them. If you know the causes of eclipses, and the laws of motion and gravitation, then and then only can you predict them. And it is the same with all other phenomena. The general causes of rainbows are now known. And the only reason why we cannot predict the exact moment and place at which a rainbow will appear is that the meteorological conditions which control them are, in particular cases, so complicated that it is impracticable to calculate them.

For these reasons the new science concentrated on causes and mechanical explanations, and excluded teleology. This, of course, did not prove, nor did the founders of science suppose that it proved, that there is no purpose in nature. How the mechanistic procedures of science gave rise to the conception of a purposeless world has already been explained. But Descartes, in supporting the mechanical interpretation of nature, gave a powerful impulse to the train of thought which led to that conception, and showed himself to that extent on the side of the scientific view of the world.

Nor was it only that he gave that view his general support. He injected mechanism and naturalism into the details of his philosophy in peculiarly emphatic ways. That he wished to push mechanism, and even materialism, to the limit, appears in his curious theory of animals. Animals, he maintains, are only automata. They act as if they are conscious, but in fact they are not conscious. They are nothing but physical machines. Man alone has a mind. The lamb may appear to be running away from the wolf because it feels fear. But in fact it feels nothing. It is a stimulus-response mechanism. Descartes did not, of course, use that language. His physiology was, from a modern point of view, crude. But his theory was, in spirit, identical with those modern views which would explain the behavior of animals without introducing the conception of an inner "consciousness" at all. Descartes did not include man in this theory. Men have minds. He believed this because he knew that he himself was conscious, had sensations and thoughts, felt pleasures and pains; and he supposed that other men must be like him in this respect. He would have thought it absurd to deny the existence of consciousness in men, and he therefore left that last extreme of absurdity to the more truly "scientific" thinkers of our own day.

Another motive which doubtless impelled Descartes to make an exception of man was that men are believed to have immortal souls, whereas animals do not have them. If this is so, the soul of a man must be non-material, since otherwise it could not survive the body.

In the end, of course, Descartes' philosophy is dualistic. The world is made of two radically different kinds of things, matter and mind—or three, if we add God. But he carries materialism and mechanism to the furthest possible limit, stopping short only where they would become, in his view, plainly absurd and untenable. This is the naturalistic side of Descartes.

We turn now to the religious elements in his system. One of them is his belief in an inner non-physical mind in human beings. It is true that a dualistic theory of human personality can be held without any religious implications. Consciousness might be entirely non-material, and yet it might not survive the body. The two might be interdependent and come to an end at the same time. But historically belief in a non-physical conscious mind has been loaded with religious implications connected with the idea of the immortality of the soul—which is one main reason why the modern mind, as exemplified by the scientific psychologists of our time, almost universally rejects it. Anything which in any way smells of religion is suspect and cannot possibly be "scientific." Belief in a non-physical mind does not necessitate belief in survival after death. It does, however, leave open the possibility of survival, whereas the denial of it renders survival impossible, or at least extremely unlikely. This is the logical connection between religion and a dualistic view of human personality, and justifies us in classifying Descartes' view as among the religious elements in his philosophy.

The position of God in his system is, however, its really important religious element. It is true that Hobbes who, on our view, is an entirely non-religious philosopher, also "believed in God." But there is a great difference between the two thinkers in this respect. Not that Descartes, any more than Hobbes, shows in his writings any religious feeling. His writing is coldly logical throughout, as well in its references to God as to anything else. God seems to be for him, as for Hobbes, a mere intellectual abstraction. But in Descartes' system the concept of God is necessary and central. The system would collapse without it; while in the philosophy of Hobbes God is an accidental appendage and, in fact, something of a nuisance. Hobbes believed that religion is "a pill which it is better to swallow without chewing." Professor Castell's remark that he "pays lip service to natural theology" hits off the position well. It is not meant that he was only pretending to believe in God. He was probably sincere. He believes that God has to be introduced as the first cause of the world-machine, but having said this he hurries on to what is obviously the only thing which genuinely interests him, the working of the machine itself. God might just as well be left out of his view of the world.

But with Descartes the position is quite different. He tries to construct a philosophy on the model of geometry. A system of geometry begins with a set of axioms which are its logical foundations. In Descartes' time the axioms were supposed to be "self-evident truths"—a position now abandoned by mathematicians. The geometrical system proceeds to deduce from the axioms a set of theorems by rigorous logical steps. Descartes thought the same thing could be done in philosophy. His system consists of three main steps. The first is the axiom, "I think, therefore I exist." The second is the theorem, "God exists," which he thinks he deduces by rigorous logic from the axiom. The third is the theorem, "matter exists" which is supposed to follow, again by rigorous logical steps, from "God exists." The details of the supposed logical steps from the axiom to the first theorem, and from the first theorem to the second, do not concern us here. But there are two points about the scheme which we should note.

The first is that the general result of the argument is to show that the universe consists essentially of three kinds of existences. The first is God. The second is mind—this is evident from the axiom, "I think, therefore I exist," since "I" am a mind. The third is matter.

The second point to note is the reason why the concept of God is essential to the philosophy of Descartes, and not merely accidental as with Hobbes. The proof that matter exists depends on the concept of God. One might ask how this can be the case when the existence of matter is proved by our senses. We see and touch stones and trees, which are material objects. But Descartes believed that these objects which we think we see and touch might not "really" exist. They might be no more than apparitions in a lifelong dream. Do we not seem to see and touch material objects in our dreams, while yet these objects do not really exist at all? He thought that the only way of proving that matter "really" exists is first to prove the existence of God. From this it would follow that matter really exists, and is not a dream; since if it were, we should have to accuse God of having given us instruments of knowledge—our senses—which systematically deceive us. This would make God a liar, which is inconsistent with the attributes of goodness and truthfulness which Descartes supposed his arguments proved God to possess.

Whatever we may think of this curious intellectual scheme, we see at least that the existence of God is logically necessary to it, and that without it the whole argument and the conclusion to which it leads—that the world is composed of the three things, God, mind, and matter—would fall to the ground, just as a system of geometry would fall to the ground if one of the steps of the chain of reasoning of which it consists were false.

We come now to Hobbes (1588-1679) who, according to our classification, is the first pure representative of the naturalistic or scientific view of the world. So much has already been said of him that we need do little more than summarize our previous comments and add a few points. His conventional references to God may be discounted. His general position in the history of thought is that he is the earliest translator of the new science into philosophy. He simply generalizes from the work of Galileo, Harvey, and other scientific discoverers. His first conclusion is materialism. What Galileo said about physical objects—that they are made of atoms in motion—Hobbes now says about the whole universe. Everything in the universe is made of atoms, and is therefore material. Minds, he holds, as against Descartes, are not non-physical.

Since all changes in the world, that is to say, all events, consist in nothing but changes in the motions of material particles, and since these motions are entirely explained by the laws of motion, Hobbes is necessarily a determinist. "Whatever effect is produced at any time, the same is produced by a necessary cause . . . so that all the effects which have been or shall be produced have their necessity in things antecedent."[1] Accordingly it is often said that Hobbes denied the existence of free will. This is a somewhat doubtful interpretation. But it is certain that he affirmed the rigid determinism which historically produced the denial of free will.

[1] Hobbes, *Selections,* Charles Scribner's Sons (The Modern Student's Library); pp. 95, 96 (no date given).

He held to a mechanical view of the world, including a mechanical view of human nature, the human body, and human society. The body is a machine. Human desires, including presumably man's loftiest aspirations, are nothing but motions of particles.

As already emphasized, Hobbes was one of the earliest philosophers to introduce the theory of the subjectivity of moral values. This implies that the world is not a moral order, although Hobbes did not express himself in those terms. He also draws from subjectivism the modern conclusion which affirms that morals are relative. Thus the whole paraphernalia of the scientific view of the world, as opposed to the religious view, are pre-eminently clear in Hobbes. And he drew these conclusions directly from the new science, which is one proof that that is their historical derivation.

Hobbes being one of the earliest exponents of the scientific view of the world is also one of the crudest. He does not see even the most obvious difficulties which beset his version of it. As time went on, these began to appear, so that later representatives of the dominant modern mentality, in trying to meet them, become increasingly more refined in their theories. But their theories are not in essence different. They are only more sophisticated.

David Hume (1711-1776) was in one respect the opposite of Hobbes. While Hobbes was the crudest of naturalistic thinkers, Hume was perhaps the most subtle and acute, and probably the greatest. He was the master builder of the naturalistic view of the world—so far as its expression in the abstract form of philosophy is concerned. He is the father of all positivists down to the present day. One and all of them are in reality no more than dancing to his tune. His thought is the very quintescence of the dominant philosophical trends of the modern world. So that if we once understand it, we shall have in our hands the key to the understanding of the main positions of the later naturalistic thinkers.

I shall concentrate on only one of Hume's contributions to

philosophy, which is, however, the most famous and character-istic—his theory of cause and effect. What, he asked, is meant when we say that one thing, C, is the cause of another thing, E? We say that a certain degree of cold causes water to turn to ice, and that a certain degree of heat causes it to turn to steam. We say that lightning causes thunder, or that bacteria cause diseases. Among all sorts of different kinds of phenomena there may exist this one kind of linkage or relation, which we call causation. What sort of a relation is it?

According to the traditional analysis of philosophers prior to Hume, to say that C is the cause of E means, or implies, two distinct things. First, it implies that *whenever C happens E happens,* or that any case of C is *always* followed by a case of E. Thus we believe not merely that today, at this particular place and time, a temperature of 212 degrees Fahrenheit will be followed by the boiling of this particular pot of water. We believe that whenever, other conditions being the same, water is raised to that temperature, it will boil. This is sometimes expressed by saying that the same causes always produce the same effects. This is a very rough statement. Someone might object that although striking a bell usually causes sound, it does not do so if the bell is in a vacuum, and that therefore the proposition that the same cause always produces the same effect is not true. What this means, however, is not that the proposition is false, but that it is very carelessly and imprecisely stated. It can be made accurate by inserting the necessary qualifications. The most important of these is that, if the proposition is to be true, all the necessary conditions of the effect E must be included in the cause. Thus the cause of the sound is not only the vibration of the bell. The presence of air is also part of the cause, and when this is realized, the absence of sound in a vacuum ceases to be an exception to our rule that the same cause always produces the same effect. Even so the rule is extremely difficult to state with a precision which will make it quite watertight. To do this is a technical problem which we must leave on one side here. The general idea which the rule expresses is a familiar one, and is certainly implied by a belief in causation. It may be called *regularity of succession*. Hume's own phrase was "the constant conjunction" of cause and effect.

The second thing supposed, according to the analysis traditional before Hume, to be implied by saying that C is the cause of E is what Hume called a "necessary connection" between C and E. It is not merely that whenever C occurs, then, as a matter of fact, E happens to follow, as if the connection between them were merely a coincidence. There must be some necessary connection between C and E, because if their conjunction were a mere coincidence, surely C might sometimes be followed by E and sometimes not. We must suppose therefore that there is something in C which *makes* E happen. We do not merely suppose that heat is followed by the melting of wax. We suppsose that this *must* happen, and that this *necessity* is why it always happens. The cause is not only followed by the effect; it *produces* the effect. One thing exerts *power* over another, the sun, for example over the wax. The flame has a *power* to boil the water. "Influence" is another word we use to express the same thing. One thing influences another. Another word which we use in certain cases is "force." Thus if a moving billiard ball collides with another ball which is at rest, and the second ball begins thereupon to move, we do not say merely that when one ball hits the other at a certain angle and velocity, the second will always, as a matter of fact, move off at a certain angle and velocity (regular succession), but we say also that the first ball exerts a force upon the second. Thus what Hume means by belief in necessary connection is the belief that C is necessarily followed by E, and that the connection is not mere chance. Such words as "necessity," "power," "producing," "making," "influencing," "compelling," "force," such phrases as that the effect not only does, but must follow the cause, all carry essentially the same meaning.

The traditional theory of causation was that it meant both of these two things, regular succession and necessary connection. Hume's new analysis was intended to show, however, that although regular succession is a fact, necessary connection is a fiction. There is no such thing in the world. More strictly put,

Hume's conclusion is that, as applied to nature, none of these words—"necessity," "power," "making," "producing," etc.—convey any idea to the mind; that they are all strictly speaking *meaningless*. The conception that many words and phrases used in language have no meaning, so characteristic of positivistic philosophies, makes with Hume its first appearance in philosophy. That various statements which men make are false had, of course, been often asserted. That they are often meaningless was a new idea, destined to play a great part in the subsequent history of thought.

The argument by means of which Hume sought to establish his conclusion about causation is based upon the theory of the origin of our ideas and knowledge which has come to be known as empiricism. John Locke had anticipated Hume in the statement of this theory, but Hume was the first to apply it with rigor. The theory is that all ideas which can exist in a mind have been proceeded by, and are derived from, "impressions." An impression is the direct presentation of something to the mind, as for instance when we see a color. There are, according to Hume, two kinds of impressions, those of sensation—such as seeing colors, smelling smells, etc.—and those of what he called *reflection,* by which he meant what we should now call introspection—perceiving one's own feelings, thoughts, or other operations of the mind. All our ideas about the physical world are derived from impressions of sensation, while ideas about psychological facts are derived from impressions of reflection. It is only the impressions of sensation which are important to us in considering Hume's argument about causation.

Since every idea which has reference to the physical world must have had its origin in impressions of sensation—or, more briefly, in sensations—you cannot have an idea unless you have previously had the sensations on which it is based. For instance, men born blind cannot have any idea of color. The idea of sound is for the same reason absent from the minds of those who have been born stone-deaf. Again, although bees perceive ultra-violet color, this color, which may be entirely different from any color which we can see, is to us wholly unimaginable because we have never had any sensation of it. In Hume's language, we cannot "frame the idea" of it.

It is true that we may have ideas of things which we have never seen or perceived with any of our senses, such as sea serpents, winged horses, or golden mountains. But it will be found that all such ideas are compounded out of ideas of sensations which we have had. We have seen wings and horses, so that we can combine them to form the idea of the winged horse. In this way even ideas of imaginary objects are derived from sensations, because they are built up out of materials which have been derived from sensations.

So far what has been stated is mere psychology—a generalization about the source of our ideas. But Hume proceeds to use it as a criterion for distinguishing meaningless words and phrases from those which have meaning. If we use a word to which there corresponds no idea in our minds, then this is the same as saying that the word has for us no meaning. For instance, color words can have no meaning for men born blind, though they will of course have meaning for those who can see. And if there are any words which are such that nobody has ever had any sensations from which the ideas for which they are supposed to stand have been derived, then there cannot in reality be any such ideas. In other words, these words must be entirely meaningless. There are, according to Hume, many such words and phrases. Necessary connection is one of them.

If it is suspected that a word is without meaning, the test to apply is: point out, or indicate in some way, the sensation or sensations from which the alleged meaning of the word has been derived. If you can do this, as the seeing man could if asked the meaning of the word "red"—he could point to red things—then your word will be admitted to have meaning. It has passed the test. But if you can in no way, either directly or indirectly, indicate the sensations from which the idea supposed to be conveyed by your word has been derived, then it will follow that you have in reality no idea in your mind at all, or in other words that your word is meaningless.

It is true that this raises a psychological problem which may seem to present difficulties to the theory of empiricism. How can a man use language and believe that this language stands for ideas, at least to himself, when he has in fact no ideas in his mind at all? We must be content to remark that, somehow or other, it certainly is the case that there is such a thing as "meaningless verbiage," as anyone who has made a study of political speeches, not to mention philosophical treatises, must know.

Hume applies his empiricist theory of ideas to causation in the following way. Causation was supposed to imply two things: regular succession and necessary connection. Regular succession can be observed, which is another way of saying that the idea of it is derived from sensations. You see C, and then you see that it is followed by E. You see the flame under the kettle, and then you see the water boil. This gives you the idea of succession. You can also observe that this happens regularly, that whenever C happens it is followed by E. This gives you the idea of regular succession. Since you have pointed out the sensations from which this idea is derived, it has passed the empirical test, and may be admitted to be meaningful.

But now try the test on the other supposed component of causation, necessary connection. Is it not obvious, not only that no one ever has had a sensation of it, but that no one ever could have such a sensation? For all that can ever be observed is a succession or flow of events, one thing following another. Watch what happens when you put the kettle on the fire. You see the flame and the water. First you see the water still, and then you see it bubbling. You see the cause, the fire; and then you see the effect, the boiling. You may, of course, see intermediate stages, such as the "simmering" of the water. But this makes no difference to the fact that all it would ever be possible to observe would be one thing following after another, that is to say, sequence, or succession. And as one event follows another, you could never

observe the supposed necessary connection between them. You
see the flame and then the boiling. But did you, or could you
ever, observe the flame *making* the water boil? Did you, or could
you ever, observe the "power" in the flame, or the "influence"
which it is supposed to exert? You may think that your inability
to have any sensation of necessary connection is due to the crudeness of your senses, and that science, with its sensitive instruments, will help you. But if you were to use an ordinary microscope, or even an electron microscope, or even if you could see
the individual electrons, it is obvious that all you could ever
observe would be a succession of movements, events, or things.
You could not observe any necessary connection between them.

Put the same thing in another way. You say not merely that
the water does boil, but that it *must* boil when a flame is put under
it. You say not only that, owing to gravitation, water does run
always downhill, but that it *must* do so. But have you ever observed this "mustness," this necessity? All you can observe, or
have a sensation of, is that water *does* boil, or *does* run downhill.
In short, all you can observe is facts, not the necessity of the facts.
This is the same as saying that it is impossible to indicate the
sensations from which the supposed idea of necessary connection
has been derived. The conclusion follows at once. *There is no
such idea.* The phrase "necessary connection" is entirely meaningless. Therefore when we say that C causes E, all that can possibly be meant is that there is a regular succession of C being
followed by E.

Hume's theory of causation has been the subject of furious
controversy. It is not necessary for us to go into this because,
for our present purposes, it does not matter to us whether Hume's
theory is true or not. What we have to note is that it has passed,
though not undisputed, into modern thought, and that it has been,
and still is, tremendously influential. It has become, on the whole,
the dominant view of causation as expressed in science. For instance, the practical disappearance of the concept of force from
recent physics, if not directly due to the actual writings of Hume
—most physicists have probably never read them—is at any rate

due to the empiricist spirit of modern thought which found its philosophical expression in Hume. Physicists may of course still use the word "force," as we continue to use the expression "the rising of the sun"—for convenience. But it is thought to be no more than a useful fiction. Newton's theory of gravitation uses the concept of gravitational force. But Einstein's theory dispenses with it altogether.

What, it will be asked, has Hume's theory of causation to do with the main themes of this book, or with what I have called the scientific view of the world? How does it in any way conflict with the religious view? There is in it no mention of God, purpose, freedom, or morals. But this first appearance is superficial and deceptive. We have to look below the surface. What kind of a universe, we must ask, is implied by Hume's analysis of the conception of cause and effect?

It follows from the denial of necessary connection that, although in our past experience one thing C has invariably been followed by this other thing E, and although, therefore, when we observe C again, we naturally expect E to follow, there is in fact absolutely no reason why it must follow or why we should expect it. When the kettle is put on the fire it always boils. At least this has always happened in the past. But how do I know that the water will boil the next time I put the kettle on the fire? According to Hume's own explicit and repeated statements there are no rational grounds whatever for my expectation. The expectations are founded, according to Hume, on nothing but habit or the association of ideas. It is a psychological fact that if two things have been constantly associated in my experience, then they become linked together in my mind in such a manner that the appearance of one always causes me to expect the appearance of the other. Since I have always in the past observed kettle-on-fire to be followed by boiling-of-water, the ideas of these two things have become so firmly associated that when I observe a new instance of the first I cannot help confidently expecting that it will be followed by an instance of the second. But the passage of my mind from C to E is a psychological, not a logical, transition. Hence there is no *logical reason* why I should expect C to be followed by E. For since there is no necessary connection between heat and boiling there is no reason why the sequence should be repeated. If there were something in the heat which *makes* the water boil, then I could know that the water will necessarily boil. But there is no such necessity. It is therefore merely luck, chance, or good fortune that the world so far has not disappointed our expectations, and that things have always happened in a regular and orderly fashion. For what is true of the fire and the boiling is of course equally true of every other causal connection of events. We have no more reason to believe that water will always freeze in the cold than that it will always boil under the influence of heat. We have no good logical reason to expect any orderly sequences in nature at all. The orderly universe might tomorrow become a chaos.

This is the source of the philosophical problem which I mentioned earlier: how do we know that the sun will rise tomorrow? We believe it because we assume that the causes which have so far operated to bring about the daily rising of the sun will continue to bring about the same effect in the future. We assume, in other words, that what we call the laws of nature, which means the regular sequences of causes and effects, will operate in the future as they have in the past. This assumption, we hope, will turn out to be true. But, if Hume is right, there is no rational ground for it. Therefore it cannot be "proved" that the sun will rise tomorrow. Nor can any other prediction about the future be proved. When the kettle was placed on the fire yesterday, it boiled. But for all I know, when I put it on the fire this afternoon, it may freeze, or fly away to the North Pole, or turn into a watermelon.

These implications of Hume's philosophy, which he himself clearly perceived and insisted upon, amount to saying—though he does not himself put it in this way—that there is no reason why anything happens as it does and that the universe is totally irrational and senseless in its proceedings. We can ask *what* happens, but to ask for a reason *why* it happens is to ask a meaningless question. Heat does as a matter of fact boil water, but there is no reason why it should, for it might just as well freeze it. To ask for a reason why will always involve somewhere the idea of a necessary connection between events. And there is no such thing in the universe. Hence there being no reason for anything; all we can say is that what happens happens. It just is so, and that is the end of the matter. Everything is just a brute fact. We live in a brute fact universe.

This has given rise to what is called the *descriptive theory of science*. Science can never, on this view, do anything except describe what occurs. It can never explain anything in the sense of giving a reason why it occurs. It is true that we talk, and scientists themselves talk, of "scientific explanations." But these turn out to be only generalized descriptions. For instance, suppose a savage brought from tropical Africa to America, having never seen ice, is astonished to see a pond freeze in the winter. He asks why the water turned solid. It is explained to him that this is an example of the "law" that water at sea level freezes at 32 degrees Fahrenheit. The law is the explanation. But all it tells anyone is that whenever the temperature falls to 32 degrees, water turns solid. This, however, is only to state *what always happens,* not to give any reason why it happens. But this, it may be said, is very crude science. For science does not stop at that elementary level. It goes on to explain why water always freezes at 32 degrees. The explanation will be in terms of molecules, atoms, or perhaps, if it is carried far enough, electrons and protons. The molecules, in the cold, move more slowly, perhaps. But this still only states what always happens without giving any reasons. It tells us that when it gets cold, the molecules always move more slowly. It is obvious that, however far science proceeds, its explanations can never consist in anything but descriptions of what happens, and can never tell us why. It cannot give "reasons" because—on the Humian view—there are none, and the very demand for them is without any meaning.

This then, the vision of a world without purpose, sense, or

reason, is the inner substance of Hume's philosophy. That philosophy plainly expresses, in its own fashion, the scientific view of the world, the modern *Weltanschauung* derived from science.

The train of thought just described is not, as a matter of fact, strictly logical. For there is an ambiguity in the word "reason." Sometimes it means purpose, sometimes it means cause. Thus we say that the reason why we caught a cold was that we were exposed to a draught. The draught was, in fact, the cause of the cold, and it is plain, therefore, that if we give it as the reason why we caught a cold, we are using the word "reason" as equivalent to the word "cause." But we might inquire why, or for what reason, a man sat in a draught. In that case we are probably asking what his purpose was, and if so we should think he had answered our question if he said: "I sat in the draught in order to get cool." Here plainly the word "reason" has been used as equivalent to the word "purpose."

If now we say that, according to Hume's philosophy the world is senseless and meaningless because there is, according to that philosophy, no reason why water should freeze when it does, rather than boil, we are probably using the word "reason" as equivalent to "purpose." By an irrational, senseless, and meaningless world, we probably mean a purposeless world. But that the world is purposeless does not strictly speaking follow from Hume's philosophy. What he shows is that there is no necessary connection between events. But necessary connection is not the same as purpose. Suppose we believe that all events are guided by God's purposes. This is not refuted by anything which Hume says. For he does not show that there is no such thing as purpose in events, but only that there is no such thing as necessary connection.

But this is simply an example of what has been so often illustrated in this book—that it is not logical, but psychological transitions, which govern men's minds. A brute fact world, a world in which anything might happen, in which water might tomorrow begin to run uphill, in which all the laws of nature might be turned upside down, is not necessarily irrational in the sense of being without purpose. For perhaps it is owing to the purposes of God that the world as a matter of fact does not become chaotic but follows regular laws. But the fact remains that Hume's world, in which any chaotic absurdity could happen at any time, *seems* to men to be a senseless and irrational world, and that they naturally identify the idea of such a world with the idea of a world which is senseless and meaningless in the sense of having no purpose. There cannot be any doubt that in this way Hume's world-picture is, or suggests, the typical world-picture of the modern mind.

Consider the impact of these thoughts on an age-old question —the famous "problem of evil." We ask why there is evil in the world. Why do the wicked prosper while the good are oppressed? Why are men born with hideous deformities which they have done nothing to deserve? Why are innocent children cut off, subjected perhaps to the miseries of cancer or inherited syphilis and then to early death? How do we explain these injustices? Why are they permitted?

But what does the word "why" mean here? What is it that we want to know about evil when we ask the "why" of it? Let us take what is no doubt a trivial example. A man has a toothache which, we will suppose, is entirely undeserved. Evil is sometimes classified as either moral or physical. Pain is a physical evil. And in view of the dreadful agonies which men suffer in the world this toothache is of course nothing. But this trivial example illustrates the principles of the problem of evil just as well as would all the miseries caused by a world war. The amount of the evil has nothing to do with the problem why there should be any evil at all. Why then is there this toothache?

But we put the same question again: what does this "why" mean? What is it that we want to know about the toothache when we ask why? Do we want to know the *cause* of the toothache? The dentist, no doubt, can explain that quite well. It is caused by an abscess, which was caused by bacteria, and so on back into the past. Is this what we wanted to know? We can apply the same thought to the human agonies suffered in a war. The causes of a war are much more difficult to discover than the causes of the toothache. But still there must be causes, and they must be theoretically discoverable. Suppose that we did discover all of them. Suppose we discovered all the causes of all the evil, physical and moral, which has ever existed in the world. Should we then feel that the problem of evil had been solved?

No. Because when we ask the "why" of evil we are not asking for its causes. What then are we asking for? Plainly what troubles us is the apparent injustice of most of the world's pain and evil. Admitting for the sake of argument that some men may sometimes deserve what they get, it still remains a fact that a vast amount of the sufferings of men, not to mention those of animals, are quite undeserved. What we want to know is how this injustice is to be explained. But this question assumes that somehow, in spite of all appearances to the contrary, the world-process must in the end work justice. Thus the problem of evil is based upon the assumption that the world is a moral order. But this is just what the modern world-view, which is embodied in the philosophy of Hume, denies. Hence the problem of evil, in the setting of the modern *Weltanschauung,* has no meaning at all. It is, as a philosophical problem, simply out of date. Such a question as why there is evil in the world can only be asked by a medieval mind. There is, in reality, no such question for the modern naturalistically-minded man. And it is accordingly treated as a pseudo-problem by the positivists who are the modern followers of Hume.

Another way of putting the same thing is to say that the problem of evil assumes the existence of a world-purpose. What, we are really asking, is the purpose of suffering? It seems purposeless. Our question of the why of evil assumes the view that the world has a purpose, and what we want to know is how suffering fits into and advances this purpose. The modern view is that suffering has no purpose because nothing that happens has any purpose. The world is run by causes, not by purposes.

The other philosophers on our list, Comte, Vaihinger, and the logical positivists may be dealt with in a short space because they are all spiritual descendants of Hume, and however their technical doctrines may differ among themselves, or from Hume, they are all at bottom expressing the same vision of the world as Hume expressed.

According to Auguste Comte (1798-1857) human knowledge necessarily passes through three stages, which he calls the theological, the metaphysical, and the positive. In the theological stage men explain events by gods or spirits. In the metaphysical stage they explain them by "abstract forces, personified abstractions." The essence of a metaphysical idea, in Comte's opinion, is that it is the idea of something *which cannot be observed*. For instance, if we say that two bodies "attract" one another—as Newton did—one can observe their motion towards one another, but one cannot observe the supposed attractive force. Comte agrees with Hume that a cause, in the sense of a force or necessary connection, is in principle unobservable. He calls it therefore a "metaphysical notion." Regularity of succession is the "positive" notion because it can be observed.

In the third or positive stage of knowledge all explanation is given in terms of what can be observed, and what is in principle unobservable is dismissed as metaphysical. The positive stage is the stage of science which, when fully attained, abolishes both metaphysics and theology. In the golden age of the future which the triumph of science is to usher in, nothing will be considered knowledge unless it is science. All education is to be scientific. And what science means is nothing except the establishment of natural laws, that is to say, regular sequences of events. If we know that whenever C happens, E happens, we know everything that there is to know. Everything else is either metaphysics or superstition. No science, and therefore no knowledge, can tell us *why* anything happens (in any other sense than giving its cause), because there is no why.

All this, plainly enough, carries the same world-picture as did the philosophy of Hume, from whom in fact it is obviously derived.

When Comte, or the present-day positivists, condemn as metaphysical the idea of anything which is not observable, they are merely repeating in other language Hume's empiricist doctrine that all ideas are derived from impressions and that there can be no idea without its antecedent impression. For to observe something is exactly what Hume meant by "having an impression" of it. The idea of red, according to Hume, is derived from the prior sense-impression of red, i.e., from having observed something red. Hence the sentence, "There is no idea of that of which we have had no impression," means the same as the sentence, "There is no idea of that which is unobservable, and any such alleged idea is metaphysical and meaningless." This makes clear the relation of Hume to positivism, whether that of Comte or that of the logical positivists of the present day.

Vaihinger is a transitional and no doubt not very important figure in the history of philosophy. But he illustrates the tendencies of the modern age. His contribution to philosophy consisted in his theory of fictions which he embodied in a book called *The Philosophy of As If,* published in 1911. Its essential doctrine is that only what is observed is real and that everything else, which we may conceive or imagine, is merely a fiction. Fictions may be either useful or useless. The man in the moon is a useless fiction. But "energy" is a useful fiction because it helps us to tie together our observations in an orderly system so that the mind can predict and control its experiences and so guide the organism through life successfully. Fictions are useful if the world behaves *as if* they were true, useless if this is not the case. For instance, neither the moon nor anything else in the world behaves as if there were a man in the moon. Hence the idea of such a man does not help us to predict phenomena, and is useless. But it is otherwise with the idea of the ether of space (which was still a part of physics in Vaihinger's time). The ether does not exist, for it cannot be observed. But light and heat, travelling from the sun to the earth, behave *as if* they were waves of such an ether. The ether is therefore a useful fiction, since it enables us to foresee the phenomena of light and heat.

Both our common-sense knowledge and our science are shot through and through with fictions. The sequence, visible lightning —audible thunder, is a fact. But the electricity which is said to explain it is a fiction. For the electricity, *apart from* its sensible manifestations in sounds, lights, etc.—which are commonly called its "effects"—could never conceivably be observed. God is a fiction which may be useful to some people if it enables them to fight the battle of life more courageously. Free will and moral responsibility are fictions, but they are useful, and even necessary, because without them society would be impossible. We must punish criminals, and in general hold people responsible for their actions, although these are, in fact, completely determined beforehand by their causes. For this reason we invent the fiction of free will. Atoms are fictions because they cannot be seen. But they are useful because in terms of them we can state chemical laws which make it possible to predict the future behavior of bodies. Even mathematics is full of useful fictions. Points which have no magnitude, lines which have no breadth, are obvious fictions. And geometers treat circles as if they were regular polygons with an infinite number of straight sides. This is plainly not true, but it enables the geometer to solve problems about circles.

Vaihinger calls himself a "critical positivist." He writes:

> From the standpoint of critical positivism, then, there is no Absolute, no thing-in-itself, no subject, no object. All that remains is sensations, which exist, and are given, and out of which the whole subjective world is constructed with its division into physical and psychical complexes. Critical positivism asserts that any other, any further claim is fictional, subjective, and unsubstantiated. For it only the observed sequence and co-existence of phenomena exist, and upon these alone it takes its stand. Any explanation going beyond this can only do so . . . through fictions.[2]

It is plain that Vaihinger's philosophy is derived from the great Humian doctrine that we can have no ideas except those which are based on impressions, and that it embodies in its nakedest

[2] *The Philosophy of 'As If,'* trans. C. K. Ogden (London: Kegan, Paul, Trench, Trubner & Co., 1924), Part I, chapter 18.

form the scientific view of the world as opposed to the religious view. For what is his world but a senseless drift of sensations which follow each other with endless and meaningless iteration? The "real" world is no more than what one may suppose some low-grade organism, a crocodile perhaps, to perceive; merely sensations of hot, cold, color, light, sound, hard, soft, pleasant or unpleasant smells and tastes, succeeding one another forever. In these sensations there are no doubt "regular sequences," that is, repetitions of the same following the same, which we dignify by the name "laws of nature." But how does that make the sensations any more sensible? Any suggestion that there is in all this any plan or purpose, or that the world so conceived is a moral order, must plainly be, on Vaihinger's principles, no more than a fiction.

The most popular school of philosophy in our own day is that of the logical positivists. In many technical problems of philosophy they have done original and useful work. In its mode of statement, and in the arguments which they use to support it, their version of positivism is quite different from that of Comte. They would certainly wish their philosophy to be distinguished from his, and they cannot be represented as merely his disciples. Nevertheless the spirit of the two philosophies is the same; and they both imply the same *Weltanschauung*.

Their original slogan was "the meaning of a statement is identical with its method of verification." This has been modified by a number of technical qualifications, but the principle remains the same in substance. It implies that a statement for which there is no possible method of verification is meaningless. And verification means either direct observation by the senses or indirect inferences from such observations. Thus the surface of the moon which is turned towards the earth can be directly observed, and many statements made about it can be verified by naked sight or by telescopes. But if an astronomer makes a statement about the other side of the moon, which no eye has ever seen, this cannot of course be directly verified, but it may be possible validly to infer it from facts which can be observed. Hence "There are mountains on the back of the moon," whether true or false, is not meaningless, since its truth or falsity might follow from observations which can be made. But if we say, "Energy is something which could never possibly be perceived, but which manifests itself in heat, light, electrical phenomena, motion, etc.," this will be meaningless if it is supposed to refer to some mysterious entity which has an existence of its own distinct from the heat, light, or other observable phenomena in which it manifests itself. For nothing but the heat, light, etc., could ever be observed, nor—for technical reasons of logic—is it possible validly to infer its existence from them. The energy just *is* its manifestations. And all that a statement made by a scientist about an energy which underlies heat and motion can mean is that there is a certain mathematically calculable equivalence between, say, the motion of a body and the heat which replaces it when the body is brought to a stop by friction. The scientist may quite legitimately use the word "energy," but this is all that his statements about it can mean. All that science can do, or aims to do, is to note the regular sequences of observed phenomena, including the equivalences referred to. Likewise the scientist may use such an expression as "attractive force" in gravitation, but this is only a handy way of talking about the observed tendencies of bodies to move towards one another according to certain mathematical formulas. For only the motion can be observed, not the force.

It must not be supposed that this view of scientific conceptions is necessarily unacceptable to the scientists. On the contrary, many scientists are themselves positivists, and not only accept it, but assert it with vigor. But it is not really a scientific question at all. It is a philosophical question. So long as the scientist can pursue his studies of atoms and electrons in his own way, and can by means of them state laws which will enable him to predict the future, it is of no importance to him whether they are fictions or solid realities.

One of the great ideas of the logical positivists—in which they agree with Comte—is that all metaphysical statements are meaningless. Their philosophical opponents are fond of saying that positivism itself implies, or rests upon, an unconscious meta-physics. Whether this is true or not depends upon what meaning one gives to the word "metaphysics." If a metaphysical idea is defined as one which refers to some hidden, forever unobservable "ultimate" reality, then it is probably true that positivism neither has nor implies any metaphysics. But if the term means only a general view of the nature of the world, a *Weltanschauung,* then positivism does imply a metaphysics, whether positivists are aware of the fact or not, whether they deny it or not. They must have a metaphysics in this sense because every thinking human being has one. And the nature of their view of the world is not hard to discern. It is the same as Hume's and Vaihinger's. The world is nothing but a stream of events. It is nonsense to talk of any purpose, order, or meaning in it. It is the function of science and mathematics, which alone are knowledge, to predict from one set of senseless events what the succeeding set of senseless events will be.

That the view of the world which is the inner meaning of current positivism is simply the modern *Weltanschauung* is made abundantly clear by the views of positivists on ethics and the theory of value. Consider the ethical statement, "Murder is wrong." How, asks the positivist, can you verify this by any conceivable observation? If a murder has been committed, there will have been a lot of facts about it which could have been observed if anyone were present. He might have seen the murderer raise the gun, point it, pull the trigger. He might have heard the explosion. He might have seen the victim fall to the ground and the blood ooze from his chest. But he could not have observed the *wrongness* of the action. Do you see, hear, or smell, wrongness? It is plainly unobservable. It cannot be verified either directly or indirectly. Therefore the sentence, "Murder is wrong," is meaningless.

Why then do people say such things? Because although they are meaningless in the sense that they do not state facts and cannot therefore be either true or false, yet they do express the *feelings* of those who utter them. To quote a prominent British positivist, Professor A. J. Ayer: "If I say to someone 'You acted wrongly in stealing that money,' I am not stating anything more than if I had simply said 'You stole that money.' In adding that this action is wrong I am not making any further statement about it. I am simply evincing my moral disapproval of it. It is as if I had said 'You stole that money' in a peculiar tone of horror, or written it with the addition of some special exclamation marks. The tone, or the exclamation marks, adds nothing to the literal meaning of the sentence. It merely serves to show that the expression of it is attended by certain feelings in the speaker."[3]

The point is that the moral utterance expresses an emotion, but does not state or deny any fact. Emotions simply exist. They are not true or false, nor can any words by which they are expressed be true or false. Factual statements, however, are always either true or false. An assertion of wrongness is therefore like saying "Ah!" This ejaculation may express my feeling of surprise, but to say "Ah!" is not to say anything which is either true or false. It does not state any fact. In the peculiar jargon of the positivists a sentence is said to have meaning only if it can be true or false. It is in this sense that, according to them, both "Ah!" and "Murder is wrong" are meaningless locutions. They do not intend to deny that they express feelings or attitudes or emotions which are really present in the speaker. Hence the statement that "murder is wrong" is meaningless, sounds more cynical and immoral than it actually is. For it uses the word "meaningless" in a technical sense. There is no reason to suppose that positivists approve of murder or are trying to condone it. There is no reason to doubt that they themselves approve and disapprove of most of the same things as other people, that they are themselves capable of high moral indignation and of high moral ideals.

This is not the point. The point is that this theory of morals is a subjectivistic one. And subjectivism implies, as we have seen, that the world is not a moral order. Professor Ayer has his own

3 From *Language, Truth and Logic* (2nd ed.: London: Victor Gollancz, 1948; New York, Dover Publications), chapter VI, by Ayer, reprinted by permission of Dover Publications, Inc.

definition of subjectivism, which differs from mine. According to his definition his view is not subjectivistic. That, however, is merely a matter of words. The positivistic view holds that moral utterances do not state facts, but merely express emotions, feelings, or attitudes. Morals therefore are dependent on human feelings, emotions or other psychological states, and this makes the theory subjectivistic in terms of the definition adopted in this book. Whatever word we use, the theory plainly implies that, since morals are only the expression of human feelings, they have no basis in the world outside the human mind. And that the world is not a moral order is one of the fixed points of the peculiar modern world-picture.

Positivists have made important contributions in the technical fields of logic, logical analysis, and semantics. It is these technical contributions which they themselves emphasize and care about. It is doubtful whether they would admit that these technical theories imply, or rest upon, the general view of the world which I have ascribed to them, or any general view of it. In such matters they are as a rule wholly uninterested. They talk about anything rather than the nature of the world. They talk about verbal analysis, logical rules, the nature of mathematics, the different uses of symbols, the meanings of the word "meaning." They discuss how we know that $2 + 2 = 4$, or that all crows are black. They dislike all world-views as savoring of metaphysics, to abjure which is a part of their creed. They may well be unconscious that their philosophy expresses any world-view. But the *Weltanschauung* of an age grips the men of the age and pulls the strings from behind the scenes. The little philosophers dance to its tune whether they know it or not.

The philosophers of the modern period seem all to be very different from one another. Philosophy is indeed often reproached for being nothing but a bedlam of conflicting opinions in which no order or pattern can be found. Descartes advocated dualism, the view that matter and mind are two wholly different kinds of thing. Hobbes taught materialism. Hume gave us an analysis of causation, Comte a historical theory of the different stages of culture, Vaihinger a theory of fictions, the logical positivists a theory of the meanings of sentences. Yet there is a pattern and an order to be found in all this if we look below the surface technicalities. There is this single world-view expressed by them all, each in his own way, the naturalistic or scientific world-view.

But the picture of modern philosophy which has been drawn in this chapter is one-sided. We have traced, from Descartes to the present day, only the dominant tendencies of the modern mind as they express themselves in philosophy. But the dominant trend has not been the only trend. There have been powerful forces working against it, and these forces too were certain to express themselves in philosophy, as also in art and literature. That there is no purpose in anything, that human life like everything else is futile and meaningless, that the world and all that is in it including human beings are governed by blind material forces, that there is no goodness, no beauty, nor any other kind of value in the universe save that only which men themselves have invented, that we are all carried along helplessly on pre-determined paths, that we have no choice and no control of our own destinies —this is a dismal set of doctrines. Protests and reactions against it were bound to make their appearance—among philosophers as well as among poets, artists, musicians, and scientists. The human spirit rebels against such conclusions. Rebellion will take the form of a return to a more religious view of the world. It cannot be indeed merely a revival of the medieval world-picture. That can never return. The religious spirit will express itself in forms suitable to the age in which it appears.

Religious men will be apt to say that revolts in favor of the religious view of the world are due to the fact that religion, in some form or other, is a divine truth which cannot therefore be suppressed by science or by anything else. They will ascribe to this divine truth an inherent power to triumph over all enemies. Skeptics, on the other hand, are likely to ascribe the protests and reactions against the scientific view of the world to wishful thinking. Men refuse to accept a truth which they do not like. They prefer to believe in comforting dreams and illusions. We have not yet reached a stage at which we can consider which of these two views is true. We are concerned at present only to record what has happened, and how the tensions of the modern mind have been produced. And we shall continue this story in the next chapter, giving there the missing half of the picture.

❊ 9 ❊

PROTESTS AND REACTIONS

ACCORDING TO THE RELIGIOUS VIEW OF THE WORLD THERE IS A purpose in the scheme of things, into which human life must presumably in some way fit, so that human life is itself meaningful as being a part of the cosmic plan. The world is governed "in the end" (whatever that phrase may mean) not by blind physical forces, but by spiritual forces which, in most actual religions, are conceived under the name, God. Moreover, the world is a moral order in which, in spite of all appearances to the contrary, goodness must prevail and justice be done. These are the three essentials of the religious view of the world as stated on page 143. Just as we find the opposite view, the view which contradicts all this, molding the dominant tendencies of the art, literature, and philosophy of the modern period, so we shall find the religious view embodying itself in a series of philosophies, art forms, and literary expressions. In this chapter I shall confine myself to its philosophical embodiments, except that I shall briefly mention its expression in the form of romantic poetry.

For easy reference I reproduce here the right-hand column of the list of modern philosophies given on page 147:

> *Philosophies of reaction and protest in favor*
> *of the religious view of the world*
> Descartes
> Berkeley

179

Kant
Hegel and the post-Kantian idealists
Romanticism
The British and American absolute idealists
(e.g., Bradley, Bosanquet, Royce)

The religious elements in the philosophy of Descartes have already been discussed, and I pass therefore to Berkeley who lived in the eighteenth century (1685-1753) and whose philosophy is the first definite protest against the prevailing naturalism of the modern world.

Since Berkeley lived before Hume, the form of naturalism which he opposed was the materialism of Hobbes. The motive of his writings, which he states plainly enough, is to counter the current "scepticism, atheism, and irreligion." Since Hobbes had advocated materialism, Berkeley preaches "immaterialism" or, as it is now more commonly called, "idealism." This latter label is not very fortunate because it would ordinarily be taken to mean an advocacy of high moral ideals. But this is not what the word means in the jargon of philosophers. It refers to a theory about the nature of the universe which has, as such, no reference to morals at all, although it does in the end usually imply some such view as that the world is a moral order. If materialism means the view that everything in the world is material, or a product of matter, idealism is the view that everything in the world is a product of mind. According to materialism matter produces mind; according to idealism mind produces matter. Berkeley's philosophy is only one version of idealism. There have been other versions which differ from his in important ways. What is common to them all is that mind or spirit is, in some sense or other, the ultimate source and controller of things.

If we want Berkeley's view of the nature of the universe put in a single sentence, it would be this: *The universe consists of minds and their ideas, and of nothing else.* What then, we ask, becomes of matter? What are the things which we call material objects?

A careful analysis will show, says Berkeley, that a material object is nothing but an idea in some mind. It should be carefully noted that he does not commit the absurdity, sometimes attributed to him, of denying the existence of material objects. He insists that on his theory the sun and the moon, the stars, the trees and the rivers, which we all perceive, are just as real as they are on any other theory. He insists that, on his theory, nothing in which common sense believes is in any way changed. Nature, and the laws of nature, remain what everyone has always supposed them to be. What he undertakes to prove is that this whole vast scheme of things which we call the material world, and which we undoubtedly perceive with our senses, is an "idea" which, as such, can only exist "in a mind." Ultimately, the mind in which all things exist as ideas is the mind of God. A tree or a mountain is an idea in that mind. But God can impress his ideas on minds other than his own, on human and animal minds. When he does so, then we perceive these ideas. We perceive, for instance, a mountain or a tree.

This theory, at first sight, is apt to appear fantastic and absurd. It seems to revolt common sense. But we should remember Whitehead's dictum that every great and new idea is apt to wear, on its first appearance, a certain air of foolishness. When we say that a conception is odd, queer, or even fantastic, this may only mean that it deviates widely from commonly accepted ideas. And commonly accepted ideas are often false. The Copernican hypothesis seemed ridiculous to men whose minds had been molded in the medieval pattern of thought. Common-sense opinions may very well be nothing but very deeply rooted prejudices. Recent physics seems to impress the same lesson. And, as Russell has said, the truth about the universe, whatever it is, *must* be queer. Thus the mere fact that Berkeley's opinion seems to conflict with what we naturally believe ought not to decide us against it. We ought to examine and weigh the reasons and arguments which he gives for it. University students, when they first encounter Berkeley's philosophy, usually tend to reject it out of hand as absurd. But they soon come, when they examine his reasons, to respect it. They may never come to accept it as true. But they learn that Berkeley was no crackpot, that he was possessed of an exceedingly acute mind, that he gives arguments for his opinion which are subtle and difficult to refute. At the present day there are perhaps no convinced Berkeleians among philosophers. But competent philosophers recognize Berkeley as a great thinker.

Berkeley does not rest his philosophy on any religious assumptions. He does not, for example, begin by "assuming" the existence of God. Had he done anything of that sort, his argument would have been circular. He would have begun by assuming that religious view of the world which it was the object of his philosophy to prove. He assumes at the start nothing except such plain facts as that men perceive mountains and trees and other material objects. He thinks that he can prove his case by a careful analysis of our ordinary acts of sense-perception. He uses a large number of arguments which it is impossible to reproduce here. But what is perhaps his main argument may be put in the following form:

A material object is nothing but the sum of its qualities.

Its qualities are all sensations (or "ideas").

Therefore a material object is nothing but a collection of sensations (or ideas).

Sensations and ideas can only exist in conscious minds.

Therefore material objects can only exist as collections of sensations or ideas in conscious minds.

Berkeley does not himself express his argument in this skeleton form. He elaborates each point at length. I have reduced it to its barest outline in order that we may have before us a series of logical steps which we can the more easily examine. It will be noted that, when it is put in this form, its premises do not include anything about God or religion. It rests, not on any religious assumption, but upon statements about such things as qualities and sensations.

The first proposition states that a material thing is nothing but a complex of qualities. This may seem at first sight a rather strange statement. The piece of sugar, you will say, is composed of atoms, not of qualities. But whether you take a whole lump of sugar or merely an atom of it, you have in either case, if Berkeley is right, a piece of matter which is nothing but a bundle of qualities which seem always to stick together and form one thing. The sugar is cubical, white, hard, cool, sweet. These are its obvious qualities as known to common sense. The chemist, no doubt, can tell us much more about it. But whatever he says will consist only in telling us other qualities or properties which we did not know about before. Whatever can be known about it must be something which could be observed by one or other of the senses aided, if necessary, by a microscope or other instrument. If it is observed by the eye, it must be a color or a shape; if by touch, it must be hardness, softness, hotness, coldness, roughness, smoothness, etc.; if by the ear, it must be sound; if by the nose, it must be a smell; if by the tongue, it must be a taste. And all these things—and nothing else but what has been or could be perceived by the senses can even be imagined—are qualities. Therefore the object just is this complex of qualities. If you say there must be something else which is not a quality, try to imagine what it could be. You will find that whatever you say of it will consist in imagining it with some new quality.

If this first proposition is clear, we can go on to the second. The qualities, Berkeley says, are all sensations. What is taste but a sensation in the tongue? What is smell but a sensation felt by the nose? What are hardness and softness but sensations which we have in our fingers, or in some other part of the body, when we press the object? Color is a visual sensation, sound an auditory sensation. There are some qualities which we perceive with more than one of our senses. Shape, for example, is perceived by both sight and touch. But this will make no difference to the argument. All it shows is that shape is both a visual and a tactual sensation.

If this is admitted, then the third proposition in the argument follows at once. A piece of matter is a complex of qualities. Qualities are sensations. Therefore a piece of matter is a complex of sensations.

It must be noted that Berkeley uses the word "idea" as a

synonym for the word "sensation." He uses both words indifferently. Hence he says that a material object is a complex of ideas,
and that the whole world of matter consists of ideas. This usage
of the word "idea," which he got from John Locke, is now wholly
out of date and seems very strange to us. It is, however, only a
verbal peculiarity of Berkeley's, and makes no difference to his
argument. Some critics have maintained that the fallacy of his
whole argument for idealism lies in his use of the word "idea,"
which, they say, is question-begging. But this criticism is a mistake since his argument is unaffected if we leave out the word
"idea" altogether and use only the word "sensation." He often
uses the latter word himself. And it is obvious that if a material
object is a bundle of qualities, and all qualities are sensations,
then a material object is a bundle of sensations, and it makes no
difference whether we call a sensation an idea or not.

Nor, if we leave out the word "idea" from the rest of his argument, which we have still to consider, does it make any difference.
The rest of the argument is easy. How can a sensation exist except
in a consciousness which feels or is aware of it? There cannot be
a toothache which nobody is having or a pain which nobody is
suffering. If in the middle of having a toothache you for some
reason become unconscious, you no doubt suppose that the abscess which causes it continues to exist, but the pain itself ceases
to exist. This is true of all sensations. The existence of a sensation
consists in its being felt. Therefore if there is no feeling—and
there cannot be a feeling unless there is a consciousness to feel
it—there cannot be a sensation. It follows that if a piece of matter
consists of sensations it can only exist in a consciousness which
is aware of it. With this Berkeley's argument is at an end. He has
proved, in his own opinion, that matter consists of ideas in minds.

It is evident that the crucial point of the whole argument lies
in the identification of qualities with sensations. Is a color really
a sensation in the same sense as a toothache or a tickling is a
sensation? It is true that even psychologists speak of colors as
"visual sensations." But may there not be some semantic muddle
here? Many philosophers have thought that there is.

Berkeley, however, has other arguments, besides the mere use of the word "sensation," to back up his contention that a quality is a sensation. The most important argument, which is certainly not verbal, is drawn from the fact that the qualities which are perceived in an object are different for different persons or even for the same person at different times. For instance, the same object which appears red to a person of normal vision will appear green—or at any rate not red—to a color-blind person. But it cannot be both colors at the same time. And the natural conclusion is that the same object is causing different sensations in the two different observers. It is no answer to say that the color seen by the color-blind man is a sensation, but that the one seen by the man of normal vision is the real quality which is in the object. For what the argument really shows is that any color at all is as much dependent upon the structure of the sense organ as it is upon the object seen. And this applies as much to the man of normal vision as to the color-blind man. This is also the reason why scientists have usually believed that atoms have no color. Color is produced by the interaction of the object and the sense organ. Hence without a sense organ there would be no color. But if so, color is a sensation in us and not a characteristic of the object. The same will be true of sound. In the world outside us there are, according to physics, vibrations, but not sound. Sound is a sensation which can only exist if there is an ear.

It is true that there is an inconsistency between Berkeley's view and that commonly held by science. The scientist will say that although colors, sounds, smells, tastes, are sensations which could not exist without sense organs, yet there are outside us atoms which really have such qualities as shape, position, motion, etc. Berkeley, on the other hand, says that shape, position, and motion, are also sensations which can only exist in us. And the reason he gives is that these qualities vary for different observers just as much as colors and tastes do. For instance, a penny appears round from one point of view, elliptical from another. And if the variation of apparent colors proves that colors are sensations, the variation of apparent shapes must prove that they too are sensations. This leads to a vastly complicated set of arguments and counter-arguments which it is quite impossible to follow through here. All I can hope to do is to make Berkeley's argument clear, and this has now been done. Matter is a complex of qualities; qualities are all sensations; sensations can only exist in minds; therefore matter can only exist as sensations in minds, and cannot exist without a mind. It would follow from this that material objects would cease to exist when we cease to perceive them, unless we admit that there is some mind which is always perceiving them. We must therefore admit this. And the mind which keeps all things in continual existence can only be the mind of God.

Criticism of Berkeley's reasoning has filled volumes. Most philosophers think that there are fallacies in it, but it cannot be said that there is agreement as to what the fallacies are. All sorts of logical puzzles are involved. What is important for us to see is that Berkeley's whole philosophy is an expression of the religious view of the world which he consciously puts forward as a counterblast to the naturalistic view which was derived from the scientific revolution, and which had come to be prevalent in Berkeley's time. For if mind, not matter, is the basic reality of things, then it will be true that the world is in the end run by spiritual and not by blind physical forces, which is the first article of the religious view.

The second and third articles of that view, that the world has a purpose and is a moral order, though they cannot perhaps be said to be "proved" by Berkeley's arguments, will naturally follow. We are reminded of the remark attributed to Socrates: "If mind is the disposer, it will dispose all things for the best." Purpose is a characteristic of mind, not of dead matter. Therefore if the world is run by mind it will be run by purpose, whereas if it is run by matter or material forces alone, it will be purposeless. Logically speaking this does not prove that it might not be run by bad purposes. A mind is not necessarily a good mind. But if we have once embraced the view that the world is governed by the purposes of an overruling mind, we are not likely to think that the world-purpose is an evil one.

Berkeley's philosophy, whatever its intrinsic value may be, did not stem the tide of naturalism. It deviated too far from common beliefs and prejudices to be widely accepted. Hence new attempts were made by other philosophers by way of protest and reaction against the scientific view of things.

The next philosopher we have to consider is the great German, Immanuel Kant (1724-1804), who lived roughly half a century after Berkeley. Seventy years elapsed between Berkeley's *Principles of Human Knowledge* and Kant's epoch-making *Critique of Pure Reason*. In the interval Hume had written; and as Berkeley's book was aimed at Hobbes, Kant's book was aimed primarily at Hume, although Kant's philosophy was so vast and all-embracing in its scope, so complicated a texture of motifs and philosophical reflections, that one cannot treat it as merely a reaction against Hume.

Kant differs from Berkeley in regard to the influence which he exerted. Berkeley was a lone thinker. He founded no school. He had practically no influence outside the narrow circle of professional philosophers, and even among them he never had any convinced disciples even in his own time. He deflected the general thinking of the modern world by scarcely a hair's breadth. His system certainly made no appeal to the masses of men. But Kant caused an upheaval in the history of human thought. He shook the world. Not only were most of the professional philosophers of western Europe, England, and America for a hundred years after his death his intellectual descendants. His spirit dominated the whole culture of the western world for that period. His influence was in the end only thrown off by a sort of intellectual counter-revolution which is well within the memory of living men. Even the poets of the nineteenth century, such as Wordsworth, Coleridge, Shelley, Keats, Tennyson, Browning, were in a sense his creations. Himself the most unromantic of men, a little dried-up university professor, almost a pedant, a writer of books phrased in a dreadful jargon of technical terms, famous for their difficulty and near-unintelligibility even to scholars, he nevertheless loosed upon the world that flood of ideas, attitudes, and emotions which collectively is called "romanticism." Perhaps historians of ideas do not commonly account Kant the founder of romanticism. And perhaps no one man can be really so entitled. And had Kant lived into the middle of the nineteenth century, it is probable that he would himself have disclaimed most of his intellectual descendants. Indeed he repudiated immediately some of the constructions put upon his thought by his purely professional disciples. But I shall try to show, later in this chapter, that the description I have given of him as an initiator of the romantic spirit is correct.

Hume and Kant are perhaps the two great philosophers, the master minds, of the modern period; Hume because he achieved the perfect expression of naturalism and became the intellectual ancestor of all naturalists and positivists since his time; Kant because he was the leader of the one great general revolt against naturalism which has occurred during the modern period, and which for a long time seemed likely to succeed. Berkeley protested, but his protest was ineffectual. In his day the time was not ripe for a great revolt. The forces of naturalism had not yet clearly expressed themselves, had not become organized into a consistent world-view, had not reached their peak. They did so in the philosophy of Hume. And it was only after Hume that a really great counter-attack was possible.

But it is time to turn to the actual content of the philosophy of Kant, leaving its effects on the world to be considered later. It is unfortunately impossible to give here even the barest outline of his philosophy as a whole. It is too vast an intellectual construction, synthesizing many different lines of thought, and having many different facets and aspects. I shall have to pick out one single thread of his thought, that one which is most immediately relevant to the story which we are telling.

Kant was perhaps the first thinker to perceive the deeper

aspects of the antagonism between the naturalistic view of the world and the religious view, and how the former had its roots in science. Other thinkers, Berkeley for example, had seen more special or more superficial aspects of the struggle. Berkeley saw that the crude materialism of Hobbes was inimical to religion, however much Hobbes paid lip service to the conception of God. Every country clergyman must have known that the skepticism of the eighteenth century was anti-religious. But Kant was the first thinker to whom the deep underlying tensions of the modern mind became plain. He did not concern himself with the superficial symptoms of the modern disease, with what men think about miracles, about the age of the earth, about the verbal inspiration of the Bible. He went to the source of the disease itself. He saw that Newtonian science had produced a general view of the world in which neither religion nor, as he thought, morality were basically possible, though they might linger on as habits. He perceived that there is no room for a living God in a naturalistic world mechanically governed by gravitation and the laws of motion; no room for free will, and therefore none for morality, in a deterministic world in which every detailed occurrence is the result of inexorable laws. He was deeply disturbed by these thoughts.

His philosophy, or at least that aspect of it which I am selecting for discussion, may fairly be represented as an attempt to reconcile the religious view of the world with the scientific view. But there was one great characteristic of his thought which forever distinguishes him from any of the common apologists for religion. Commonly the apologists admit the scientific picture up to a point, but then plead that the human spirit is somehow an exception to natural laws, or that in some way religion must be justified by picking holes in science or by insisting that there are exceptions to the naturalistic scheme. Even Newton did this. Although the solar system is, in general, run by gravitation and the laws of motion, yet exception must be made in the case of those irregularities to which he drew attention. They were corrected by divine interventions in the natural order. More commonly, and down to our own day, free will has been defended by asserting that, although nature in general is deterministic, man is an exception to this rule. Every physical event is wholly determined by causes, but the internal world of man's thoughts and volitions is not. It is an exception to the reign of law which is the basic pre-supposition of science. Even now, after Darwin, it is presumably believed by many that the minds of all animals cease to exist when their bodies die, but that man, although he too is an animal, has an immortal soul.

Kant perceived the shallowness and futility of all such attempts. If science is accepted, it must be accepted one hundred per cent, and all its implications faithfully faced. He was as anxious to defend science against the attacks of religious men as he was to defend religion against the destructive ideas introduced into the world by scientific men. And the method of defending religion by trying to pick holes in science, or by pretending that there are exceptions to its laws, is as fatal to religion as it would be to science if it succeeded. For it represents religion as crouched in a corner where it is allowed to exist so long as science does not press its claims too far, does not make its decrees universal but allows exceptions. At any moment the scientific axe may fall. And history has shown that this method of defending religion is fatal to it. Every new advance of science narrows the wretched corner in which religion is allowed to survive with its back to the wall. One after another the bastions fall. Something like this has been the actual history of the relations between science and religion. This is the inevitable result of trying to uphold religion by denying the universal application to the whole universe, including man, of the reign of scientific law.

Kant's approach to the problem is wholly different. He will uphold the claims of science one hundred per cent. But he will also uphold the claims of religion one hundred per cent. The whole of science must be true, and the whole of religion must be true, *even if they contradict one another*. For instance, he accepted a complete determinism. The reign of natural law, the determination of all events by their causes, must apply not only to the physical world but to the internal world of thoughts and volitions as well. The actions of men are as much determined as are the motions of the planets. And yet—there must be free will. Determinism, in Kant's own view, *contradicts* free will. And yet there must be some way in which both can be true. The same situation holds not only in regard to the problem of free will— which strictly concerns ethics rather than religion proper—but in regard to the problem of the relation of the scientific view of the world in general to the religious view in general. Kant did not set out the essentials of the two views in the same terms as I have set them out in this book. I have brought them to a focus in my own way in the three pairs of antithetical propositions: the world is governed by spiritual forces; it is not governed by spiritual forces, but by the blind forces of nature—it is guided by purpose; there is no purpose in it—it is a moral order; it is not a moral order. This has the merit that it makes clear the flat contradiction of the two world-views. Kant did not express himself in these terms, but he was perfectly aware of the contradiction—and faced it. Yet somehow both pictures of the world must be true. This is the problem as Kant saw it. And this is one reason for saying that he was the first thinker in the modern world to see the fulness and depth of the problem created by the tensions of the modern mind.

Now there is, as a matter of logic, only one way in which a problem so set can be solved. Contradictory characters cannot apply at the same time to the same thing. But they can apply to two different things. For instance, you cannot have one thing which is both square and circular. But you can have one thing which is square, and another thing which is circular. And you could have one world in which science is true, and another world in which religion is true. This, extremely crudely put, is the principle of Kant's solution. There actually are two worlds. Kant is not referring to, nor serving up again in a new form, the ancient and commonplace pious antithesis of "this world" and "the other world." He is not serving up the same old cabbage with a new sauce. And the word "world," as it is here used in reference to his thought, is a metaphor, and is not meant to be taken literally.

Kant argued roughly as follows. If we consider human knowledge, or any act of perception or thought, we find that two terms are involved, the subject and the object. On the one side is the mind which perceives, knows, or thinks. This is the subject. On the other side is the thing perceived, known, or thought about. This is the object. The object may be a material thing such as a stone. Or it may be a mind, that of another person or one's own. If one is aware of, or thinks about, one's own mind, then in that case one's mind as knowing or thinking is the subject, and, as known or thought about, it is the object. This is no doubt a special case in which the subject and object are one and the same thing. But the point is that in *all* perceiving, knowing, and thinking—whether the thing perceived or thought about is physical or mental—there is always this antithesis of subject and object.

Suppose that the object is a lump of stone. It is perceived as in space and time. It must exist at some place and at some date. But we not only perceive the stone with our senses. We also think about it or know it. And we think about it always in terms of what are called "concepts." Concepts are simply *general* ideas as distinguished from ideas of particular things. For instance, "man" is a concept as distinguished from "Socrates" which stands for the thought of a particular man. Kant emphasized certain very general concepts which we apply to absolutely all things, and not merely to some things. For instance, we only apply the concept "man" to men, and not to horses. We only apply the concept "stone" to stones, and not to trees. But there are some concepts which we apply universally to everything which exists. These absolutely universal concepts are distinguished by Kant from all others and given a special name. He calls them "categories." There are, according to him, exactly twelve categories. Among the most important are the following: unity (being one), plurality (being many), totality (being a whole), causality (being a cause or effect), action and reaction (acting on, and being acted upon by, other things).

If we think of anything in the world, we shall find that all these categories, or universal concepts, apply to it. For instance, the stone is *one* thing, *one* stone (unity). It is also *many,* for it is composed of many parts (plurality). It is also a *whole* (totality). Whatever exists is a whole thing. The stone is also a *cause* of effects of some kind; for instance, it depresses the ground on which it rests; and it is the *effect* of causes of some kind. Everything which exists is both a cause and an effect. The stone also *acts* and *reacts* with other things in the world. For instance, it exerts gravitational attraction and is also itself gravitationally attracted. Everything in the universe, in one way or another—gravitation is only one example—acts and reacts with other things.

Not only do the categories—I have mentioned five out of Kant's twelve—apply to all material things. They also apply to all minds and mental things. Every mind is *one* mind and has *many* thoughts, ideas, perceptions, and so on. Every mind is a *whole*. Every mind is a *cause* and an *effect,* and every thought or volition in any mind is causally determined (note that this implies complete determinism). Minds *act* and *react* upon one another, and presumably upon things in the physical world too.

The world which we have been describing, the world of things which are in space and time, and to which the categories apply, is *one* of Kant's two worlds. It may be called the space-time world. It is the world to which science applies, and in which science is one hundred per cent true, without any exceptions whatever. The naturalistic or scientific world-picture is the only truth about it. For this reason God, freedom, and immortality cannot be found in it. God is not to be found, for instance, by going backwards in time to a first cause. The whole conception of God as a first cause is erroneous. Nor is God to be found anywhere in space. That is why, though we sweep the whole heavens with our telescopes, we find no trace of him. God is not in space or in time at all.

It is at this point that we come in sight of the central thought of Kant's system. The space-time world, to which science applies, is not "reality"; it is only "appearance." This conclusion is reached by a number of highly technical arguments which he thinks prove it. They cannot be reproduced in any detail here. One of them starts from the analysis of our arithmetical knowledge which I mentioned earlier—the discussion of how we know that 7 + 5 = 12. Another urges that the very thoughts of time and space involve contradictions. He seeks to show by sheer logic that space and time must be both finite and infinite at the same time. And just as round squares cannot be real, because the thought of them contradicts itself, so space and time cannot be real, because the thoughts of them are self-contradictory. Kant concludes that this whole world of space and time cannot be real, but is only appearance.

Kant's view is that space, time, and the categories, are not what he calls "things in themselves." They are not the real things which exist outside us and apart from our minds. What are they then? They are the "forms" in which we perceive and conceive things. There must be real things outside the mind—here Kant differs from Berkeley—but they are not as we perceive them. They are not in time and space, nor do the categories apply to them. In saying that time, space, and the categories are "forms," he means that they are the forms which we impose on things by virtue of the structure of our own minds. They are *our* ways of perceiving and thinking about things, which we cannot avoid because our minds are so made.

Kant's difficult thought may be very crudely illustrated by supposing a man born with some peculiarity of his eye-structure such that everything appears to him green, although in reality many of the things which he sees are white or red or yellow or some other color. Then we might say that the greenness of everything in his experience is an "appearance" due to the structure of his optical apparatus, and that the things themselves are "really" of other colors. According to Kant, the space, time, unity, plurality, causality, which we perceive in everything are like the greenness in our illustration. They are due to the structure, not indeed of the eye or of any physical organ, but of the mind itself. Space and time are necessary forms of our perceiving faculty, while the categories are necessary forms of our conceiving or thinking faculty. Our minds are simply made in such a way that everything which comes to us from the real world outside passes through these forms of our minds and suffer their distorting influence. Therefore, just as the greenness in the illustration is not the reality, but an appearance, so the space, time, unity, plurality, and causality which we apprehend in things is not in things in themselves, is not reality, but appearance.

This means that the whole space-time world is an appearance, not a reality. What then is reality like? What are things in themselves? This, according to Kant, we can never know. Reality is unknowable. The very nature of our minds cuts us off completely from any such knowledge, just as the nature of our imaginary man's eye would cut him off from any knowledge of the real colors of things. Our mental structure makes us apprehend things as spatial, temporal, and enmeshed in a network of causes and effects, actions and reactions. The real world cannot be anything like this, but about what it is we can have absolutely no knowledge at all. We can say that it is not in space and time, that things in themselves are not unities, pluralities, totalities, causes or effects. We can know what they are not, but we cannot know what they are.

It is now generally believed by most philosophers that most of the *arguments* by which Kant tries to *prove* these remarkable conclusions are mistaken. But it by no means follows that the conclusions themselves are false, since true beliefs are often supported by bad arguments. Indeed we may suspect that great philosophers are often men who have a flair for intuitively divining—guessing, if you prefer it—some aspect of the truth, and that they then, in their anxiety to give it a firmer foundation, think up arguments, very often bad ones, to support it. The function played by intuition, not only in philosophy but in science, is very real, if also very mysterious. It is the characteristic of genius.

But to return to Kant's theory. His "real" world of things in themselves, which is wholly hidden from us by the way our minds are made, is the other of the two worlds to which I referred. There is the space-time world, which is the world of appearance, and the world of things in themselves, which is the real world. We cannot know, or prove, anything about this latter, but we can "postulate" that it is the world to which our religious intuitions refer and in which they hold true. Of the space-time world of appearance the naturalistic or scientific way of thinking will be one hundred per cent true. Of the world of reality, which is outside space and time, the religious way of thinking will be one hundred per cent true. This can never be proved by reason, but neither can it be disproved. For reason is itself a part of our mental structure which leads us to appearance, not reality. Reason, whether by way of proof or disproof, simply has no application to the real world.

This then is the way in which Kant seeks to reconcile the naturalistic view of the world with the religious view. He saw that they contradict one another. Hence they cannot both be true of the same thing. But science is true of the world of appearance, religion of the world of reality. Neither can interfere with the other. No conceivable scientific discovery could ever clash with religion, because all scientific discoveries have reference only to appearance. For the same reason in reverse no religious truth could ever conflict with the dicta of science.

Kant's philosophy lands him, or rather the human mind, as he well knows, in insoluble difficulties. For example, consider what he says about the question of free will. The mind as we know it is a stream of thoughts, feelings, perceptions, volitions, etc., which succeed one another in time. We have one thought now, another a minute later. Thus the mind, as we apprehend it, *is in time*. It is also subject to causality. One thought causes another to arise; or a thought is caused by an outside object, as when a picture of a house I know causes me to think of the house itself. Thus the mind as we know it is just as deterministically controlled by causes as is the motion of a stone falling under gravity. But for these very reasons, the mind, *as we know it,* is only an appearance. For whatever is in space or time, and is subject to the categories, such as causality, is appearance. The real mind, just like the real stone, is in the unknowable world of things in themselves. The real mind is therefore free. For its determination by causes is only an appearance. Thus the mind is really free, but appears determined and unfree. This is the solution of the problem of free will.

But Kant admits that it is impossible to understand this. How can the real mind, outside space and time, freely produce actions in the space-time world of appearance without interfering with the strict determinism of that world? This is incomprehensible. Hence Kant says that freedom is an idea "the possibility of which no human intelligence will ever fathom, but the truth of which, on the other hand, no sophistry will ever wrest from the conviction even of the commonest man."[1] Thus Kant's solution ends, on his own showing, in mystery and contradiction. But it must be pointed out that this is not an inconsistency in his philosophy. On the contrary, it is exactly what, if his philosophy is true, we must expect. For it is of the essence of his thought to believe that the very structure of our minds prevents us from knowing reality, and that the attempt to know it and understand it necessarily lands us in mystery and contradiction.

What is true of the problem of free will is also true of the problem of the nature of God. God, as the ultimate reality, is not in the world of appearance, in the space-time world, but in the world of things in themselves. Hence any attempt to understand what God is necessarily results in contradictions, because the structure of our minds gives us access only to appearances.

Whatever the difficulties or even contradictions of Kant's thought, it did at any rate inaugurate an epoch. In the realm of professional philosophy it produced the great schools of post-Kantian idealism, and later the schools of British and American absolute idealism. These come next on our list of protests and

[1] *Critical Examination of Practical Reason*, book 11, chapter 11, section vi, in *Kant's Theory of Ethics* (London: Longmans, Green & Co., 1889), trans. T. K. Abbott.

reactions against the scientific view of the world. Unfortunately, owing to the very abstruse character of their thinking, we can only mention them in the briefest way.

The German idealists who immediately followed Kant were in one respect his disciples, but also differed from him in a very radical way. They took from him his central idea, that the space-time world is an appearance only. They rejected his conclusion that reality cannot be known. They believed that it is possible for human reason to penetrate through the screen of appearances to the reality behind them. This reality, under the name of the Absolute, was variously conceived by different thinkers of the school. For example, according to Hegel, who is perhaps the greatest of these philosophers, the Absolute is a sort of universal or cosmic reason or rationality. In every case it was conceived as in some way a spiritual, not a material, reality. Even Schopenhauer who, though he differs in important respects from the others, is in a sense a member of this school, supposed that it is a kind of "will." The Absolute became for these thinkers—though one can hardly say this of Schopenhauer—the philosophical rendering of the popular conception of God. Thus everything in the universe is the product of mind, or of some spiritual essence, not of an individual or human mind, but of an absolute or universal mind. Spiritual forces, then, not material forces, ultimately rule the world. And this, it will be remembered, is the prime tenet of the religious view of the world.

These philosophers are called idealists because, in their view, mind, not matter, is the ultimate reality. Their idealism is very different from that of Berkeley. But idealism in any form is practically always associated with, and is a supporter of, the religious view of the world. German idealism can admit, as Kant did, that the scientific view is the whole truth about the space-time world of appearance, but it believes in a more real world of spiritual being which is, as it were, "behind" the appearances. And this is the world of which religion, in one way or another—possibly through myths, images, and allegories—speaks to us. For example, the God of popular religion may be a myth. But it symbolizes the Absolute.

The absolute idealism of the Germans, after conquering Germany itself, spread over to England and then to America. It produced in England the philosophies of Bradley and Bosanquet, and in America the philosophy of Royce. And in both countries there were many minor figures. These thinkers were not slavish followers of Kant or Hegel. They produced original points of view. But their basic vision—a world of appearance which is the sphere of science, but which is only the manifestation of a more real spiritual world which is behind and beyond—is always the same. Absolute idealism was the ruling philosophy in England and America throughout the latter part of the nineteenth century, although its influence has now almost entirely passed away. This movement of thought, stemming from Kant, also influenced in England such non-professional, non-technical, thinkers as Carlyle; and in America Emerson and the transcendentalists. Emerson's "over-soul" is nothing but the Absolute of the philosophers, suitably rendered in literary form.

This brings us to romanticism. Romanticism is one of the vaguest words in the vocabulary of culture, being surpassed in vagueness only perhaps by the word "humanism." Various writers have put forward different views as to what the "essence" of romanticism is. Sometimes it is conceived as a mode of thought which plays up the importance of feeling, emotion, or the heart in human life, and plays down the part of reason and the head. In this sense Pascal's famous words "the heart hath its reasons which the reason knows not of," though written two centuries before the rise of the romantic movement proper, might nevertheless be taken as its slogan. If so, Rousseau is likely to be produced as its typical exponent or even its founder. This view is not wrong. It draws attention to a real aspect of romanticism. But without quarreling fruitlessly about what is supposed to be the "essence" of romanticism, we may remark that the preference of the heart to the head as a way of knowing reality tells us nothing at all about the romantic's view of what the nature of reality is. There are two questions which have to be distinguished. The first is: what is the romantic's view of the world? The second is: how does he, in his own opinion, come to know the truth of that view? The second question he may answer by saying "the heart, the feelings, the intuitions." But this does not provide any answer to the first question. The heart may be the organ by which he knows, but it is not what he knows.

The question which is important to us here is the first. We want to know, not how the romantic reaches his vision—through the heart or through the head—but what his vision is. Is there a romantic view of the world, and what is it? My suggestion is that, according to the romantic, the world which we apprehend with our senses and our reason (or head), the world of space and time, is only an appearance or manifestation of a deeper hidden spiritual quality which lies behind. This, I shall even risk saying, is the "essence" of the romantic world-view. And this is obviously derived from Kant with his two worlds, one appearance, the other reality. This is why I said that Kant is the real founder of romanticism.

This view can hardly be fully documented here. But we can do something to establish it by means of a few quotations from the English romantic poets. I shall stick to common, even hackneyed examples, because the very fact that they are hackneyed means that men have perceived that in them the romantic vision is best expressed.

We will begin with Wordsworth's lines in which he attributes to poor Peter Bell a lack of vision about deeper things:

> A primrose by the river's brim
> A yellow primrose was to him,
> And it was nothing more.

This is not very good poetry. Perhaps it is doggerel. But it is instructive. We may ask prosaically: what more, besides being a primrose, can a primrose possibly be? What is the "something more" which Wordsworth himself, the man of vision, professes to see in the primrose? Shall we ask the scientist what more there is in the flower besides the petals, the stalk, the leaves, which we and Peter can see? Certainly the botanist can tell us much more than we know. He knows about the smaller parts, their mechanisms, their functions, and the way they act. The physicist perhaps can tell us about the atoms of which the plant is composed and how they move. But still, to the botanist and the physicist it remains, after all, nothing but a primrose. Neither of them can tell us what is the something more which the poet perceives.

Perhaps what he perceives is just the beauty of the flower, which is something that the scientist, as a scientist, says nothing about, and which perhaps Peter too has failed to appreciate. This is true. But it does not carry us very far. What *is* the beauty of nature which Wordsworth and the romantic poets are always talking about? It is here, in the answer to this question, that we come upon the essence of romanticism. For to Wordsworth, and the romantics generally, beauty is the shining through the dull envelope of matter of a spiritual reality behind. It is this spiritual reality shining through the veils of matter which is the something more which Wordsworth perceives. He writes:

> I have felt
> A presence that disturbs me with the joy
> Of elevated thoughts, a sense sublime
> Of something far more deeply interfused,
> Whose dwelling is the light of setting suns,
> And the round ocean and the living air,
> And the blue sky and in the mind of man;
> A motion and a spirit that impels
> All thinking things, all objects of all thought,
> And rolls through all things.

We may ask about the sunset what we asked about the primrose. What is the sunset to the scientist? It is a swirl of atoms and an interplay of vibrations. Note that this is the *whole* of what the sunset is. Every detail of it, without remainder, can be explained in these terms. And, for the purely scientific eye, there is nothing else. But for Wordsworth it is the dwelling place of a spirit. It may exemplify the "laws of nature." But there shines through it the ineffable light of that great presence whose dazzling raiment it is. It is that which is the something more.

Wordsworth does not deny the scientific view that the sunset is the scene of a violent commotion of particles. He simply ignores it as irrelevant. This brings out the relation of romanticism to Kant. Wordsworth could have admitted Kant's view that science is the whole truth about the world of space and time, while religion is true of that other world of spirit which lies behind.

From Wordsworth we may turn to Shelley. He writes:

> The One remains, the many change and pass;
>   Heaven's light forever shines, Earth's shadows fly;
> Life, like a dome of many-coloured glass
>   Stains the white radiance of Eternity.

One could not have a plainer poetic rendering of the Kantian and absolute idealist two-world view. The "dome of many-coloured glass" is the space-time world of appearance. Behind it, and shining through it, is the reality, "the white radiance of Eternity." But one notices a difference from Kant. For him the world of reality is unknowable; it fails to "shine through" so as to be apprehensible to the human mind. For him the dome is not many-colored, but black, cutting off all vision of the sun. Shelley, as well as Wordsworth, corresponds rather to the philosophies of Hegel and the absolute idealists according to whom the Absolute Spirit can be known by the human mind. This knowing by the human mind is the "shining through." But it was Kant, as we have seen, who originated this whole two-world view. The poets express in imagery what the philosophers state in abstract logical propositions. I do not mean of course that the poets first apprehend the logical idea and then mechanically translate it into images. The poets might perfectly well be entirely ignorant of the work of the philosophers, though in some cases they were not. I mean that the *Weltanschauung* which dominates them both clothes itself in the form of abstract ideas in the one case and in the form of imagery and feeling in the other.

The romantic vision passed down through the poets of the nineteenth century. Tennyson's well-known lines illustrate it again:

> Flower in the crannied wall,
> I pluck you out of the crannies,
> I hold you here, root and all, in my hand,
> Little flower—but *if* I could understand
> What you are, root and all, and all in all,
> I should know what God and man is.

The something more which is in the flower is here plainly named by the name of God. And according to the poem, if I knew all about the flower, I should know God. Yet this is not to be found in any textbook of botany. No scientific knowledge of the flower, even if it amounted to scientific omniscience, could ever find God in it. It would find only pistils, stamens, sap, tubes, leaves and, on further analysis, the atoms and electrons which are its smallest components. Thus the world of science does not disclose God either in its smallest or in its greatest parts. But there is another world of thought or knowledge into which the intuition of the poet—and of all of us in so far as we are poets— penetrates. It is thus Kant's thought of the two worlds, in one of which science reigns while in the other it does not, which is the ultimate source and inspiration of Tennyson's poem.

There is a famous line of Wordsworth's in which he speaks of

> The light that never was on sea or land . . .

We do not usually analyze the meaning of such an expression in cold, logical terms. We simply apprehend it intuitively. And this alone is what we should do so far as we are concerned with the esthetic appreciation of it. Nevertheless logical analysis will reveal something which it is worth while for us to note. The light of which the poem speaks never was "on sea or land." Clearly this "sea or land" is a poetic rendering of what the philosopher calls the world of space and time, which is the world of which science tells us. The light does not exist there. Yet it is surely for Wordsworth a greater reality than anything in space or time. It is not in the world of appearances, but in the real world behind.

The relation between philosophical idealism, with its jargon of technical terms, and the romantic poetry of the nineteenth century, is perhaps the clearest and most convincing example of the general conception of the nature of philosophy which I outlined in Chapter 7. Philosophy is the expression in abstract intellectual terms of the same ideas which express themselves elsewhere—notably in art and poetry—in the form of concrete imagery and feeling. The mere chronology of nineteenth century philosophy and nineteenth century poetry illustrates this in a striking way. There are two streams which run parallel in time, the philosophic and the poetic, each teaching in its own way the same view of the world. The philosophic stream begins with Kant, late in the eighteenth century, passes through the German idealists into the absolute idealists of England and America, Bradley, Bosanquet, and Royce, all of whom flourished and wrote their chief works in the last decades of the nineteenth century. This philosophic stream dried up just about the turn of the twentieth century. There was then a general revolt against idealism and the whole movement of thought which had been initiated by Kant. It was replaced by other philosophies: realism, pragmatism, and positivism. It is now almost wholly dead, claiming only a few minor adherents among older men who were brought up in an earlier climate of opinion.

The parallel poetic stream begins with Wordsworth, also in the late eighteenth century. The romantic spirit can no doubt be found in earlier poets such as Collins, Gray, and Blake. But the great outburst of poetic romanticism comes with Wordsworth.

It produced Coleridge, Shelley, and Keats—the first of whom, Coleridge, was consciously influenced by German metaphysics. It passed down through the nineteenth century, with gradually diminishing force perhaps, through Tennyson, Browning, and even Swinburne, although the last of these poets was, so far as his self-conscious theories were concerned, anti-religious. When did it peter out? Somewhere around the first decade of the present century when a revolt against romanticism took place among the poets and artists. Since then the poets and artists, with a few exceptions, have been anti-romantics. Romanticism in poetry was thus born into the world at roughly the same time as philosophical idealism, runs parallel with it for a hundred years, then meets with a revolt which comes at the same time as the philosophic revolt, and finally dies at almost the same moment.

How are we to interpret these facts? In my view romanticism in art and idealism in philosophy were born of the same movement of the human spirit. Together they constituted an unsuccessful counter-attack against the scientific view of the world. This movement, initiated by Kant, was the one great rebellion of the modern world against that view. And if we ask what, in addition to its negation of the scientific view, its positive content was, the answer is that it was plainly a return to the religious view of the world, though not of course to the particular version of that view maintained in the middle ages. In saying that the great counter-attack was unsuccessful I am not making a value judgment. I am not condemning it as a false or unjustified movement. I am merely stating the historical fact that it did not succeed, that it has suffered defeat at the hands of its enemy, the scientific view of the world.

If we look at what has happened since the collapse of idealism and romanticism we shall see this. How shall we characterize the first half of the twentieth century? In my view it has witnessed a return to the scientific view of the world, which constitutes again our present prevailing *Weltanschauung*. This appears both in the philosophy and in the art of our age. In philosophy there have been three movements, or schools, since the turn of the century.

All agree in scouting old-fashioned idealism. The first of the three, realism, was essentially a negative philosophy. What it maintained was that the material world is *not* mental, is not the product of mind. Thus, although it was not consciously or intentionally anti-religious, it repudiated the first article of the religious view of the world as that had been interpreted by the idealistic philosophies. The second school to make its appearance was pragmatism. This philosophy, as I have remarked, can appear on any side of any fence. But though it began, in James, in a religious tone, it has ended, in Dewey, in a full-fledged naturalism. The third movement of thought, positivism, which is now the most popular among the younger philosophers, is a return to Hume, the great master of naturalism.

In art and literature, I believe, the same tendencies can be observed. What is that realism which became fashionable with Zola and his followers and is still alive? The novelist's function as conceived by the realists is simply to describe, exactly and in detail, *what happens* in human affairs. He must not take sides with his characters, with the good or the bad. He must not praise or condemn. He must not see in what happens any significance or meaning, certainly not the interpretation of human life as permeated by any world-purpose. Hence the world which he depicts is the brute fact world of Hume where everything which happens does so without any reason, futilely, senselessly. It is also the artistic counterpart of the "descriptive" theory of science.

In art criticism, and in philosophies of art, the romantic view that beauty is the shining of spirit through matter is anathema. All current theories of art are naturalistic.

Does not much modern painting tell the same story? That the world or anything in it is a jumble of parts which make no sense seems in many cases to be the inspiring idea. A human body, for instance, is depicted as a jumble of arms and legs and eyes and teeth combined in some chaotic pattern. Very likely such painting may have its technical merits, which ought to be much admired. But the world-view which it reflects seems to be that the universe is a senseless chaos.

Modern poetry, whatever else is true of it, has certainly been anti-romantic. It may be said that there are signs of a contrary spirit. T. S. Eliot's *Waste Land* gave unforgettable utterance to the modern sense of the futility of everything. But this futility is obviously, even in that poem, deplored by the poet. And Eliot's later poetry is, of course, frankly religious.

What of the future? No one can predict. For my part I see no sign of anything but a continuance of the reign of science and of the naturalistic view of the world. If we map the history of the last three and a half centuries on a large enough scale, we see that a pattern emerges. The seventeenth century gave birth to science. In the eighteenth century the resulting religious skepticism organized itself into a consistent naturalistic world-view which found its most perfect expression in the philosophy of Hume. At the end of that century came a violent reaction in favor of the religious view of the world which lasted roughly throughout the nineteenth century. The beginning of the twentieth century saw its defeat and a return to the dominance of the scientific world-view. This revival of naturalism has held its own for fifty years, and we are still in the midst of it. There is nothing on the horizon which portends a change. The philosophy of Whitehead, it is true, was another protest against the mechanism of science, and sought to reintroduce into philosophy the conception of a world governed by purpose. It may fairly be regarded as a reaction in favor of a more religious view of the world. But Whitehead has had up to date almost no influence on the thought of our time. He was, in this respect, like Berkeley, a lone thinker. Berkeley's protest was overwhelmed by the triumphant naturalism of the eighteenth century, and Whitehead's has so far been overwhelmed by the triumphant positivism of our own, although one cannot say that it may not exert influence in the future.

Nor can we look to the current Neo-Thomism to stem the naturalistic tide. It is certainly a reaction against naturalism, and has attained popularity in some quarters. It offers a positive religious philosophy. But it contains no new insight capable of launching a great spiritual revival comparable to romanticism. On the contrary it goes back to the middle ages for its inspiration. Nor does it even restate the "eternal verities" on which it professes to rely in forms capable of being assimilated by the modern mind. Even truths which are in their essence eternal have to be continually reformulated in new expressions for each new age. But Neo-Thomism seeks only to reinstate ancient and outworn formulations almost without alteration. It is likely to remain the more or less official philosophy of the Roman Catholic Church, extending itself only to a few scattered sympathizers outside that organization.

Are there any other signs of a change of heart? It is said that the churches, empty in the twenties and thirties, are a little fuller now. It is said that students are more religious. There may be some movements in poetry and art which seem to speak with the same voice. But we must be careful not to mistake ripples on the surface for a major movement of the waters of time. We have had two great wars, and this fact is sufficient to explain the probably only momentarily increased religiosity. Such a cause is merely negative. It produces a sense of emptiness, a dissatisfaction with the philosophy of the time. It cannot of itself produce a positive new movement. A great movement of the human spirit requires some great idea—such as that which originated in the philosophy of Kant—to inspire it. No signs of the emergence of any such idea are at present discernible.

There is no doubt that naturalism, with its corollary of the futility of human life, has brought despair into the world. It is the root-cause of the modern spiritual malaise. It is impossible to say to what extent modern perplexities and problems have material—in the main economic—causes, and to what extent their sources are spiritual and intellectual. But at least the spiritual darkness of the modern mind has its source in the scientific view of the world.

Part III

Present Problems

✻ 10 ✻

THE PROBLEM OF RELIGIOUS TRUTH

THE PROBLEMS WITH WHICH WE HAVE BEEN CONCERNED IN this book, up to the end of the last chapter, have been in their nature historical. We have tried to show how the ideas which form the substance of the modern mind originated and grew up. We have been careful to avoid any discussion of their truth, or to attempt any assessment of their value. This holds true even of the many passages in this book in which we have examined the logic of an argument, in which, for example, we have inquired whether one idea logically follows from another. We have been careful to point out, for instance, that a purely naturalistic and anti-religious view of the world does not logically follow from science. But from this nothing follows as to the truth or falsity of naturalism. For we have to remember the old principle that a true conclusion is often supported by illogical arguments. The naturalistic view of the world may be true although the modern mind has reached it by a series of thought transitions in which the logic has been faulty.

In the remaining chapters of this book I shall change altogether our mode of approach. I shall endeavor to present reasonable conclusions about the great problems which face us. I shall attempt to weigh the truth or falsity of our beliefs. We have now on our hands, as a result of the history of the last three hundred years, a number of major spiritual and intellectual problems. They are the problems which are the root causes of the bafflement and perplexity of the modern mind. Their full solution must no doubt be the work of the ages before us. An individual is hardly likely to solve them completely. But I propose to offer, in the rest of this book, what contributions I can towards their solution.

If our analysis has been correct, there are two central problems and a sub-problem. The first problem is whether we are to accept the scientific view of the world as true and as the sole truth; or whether the religious view is true or contains some truth which the scientific view leaves out; or whether the two can be in any way reconciled. This is certainly the most important problem. The second problem concerns the foundations of morality, whether they are secular or religious, and if secular whether we are committed to a relativistic view of morals. The sub-problem is: have we any free will, or are we mere cogs in a world machine, unable, even in the smallest matters of our conduct, to alter by a hair's breadth the inevitable course of the world? I call this a sub-problem because it is subordinate to the problem of morals and really a part of it. For if there is no free will, there cannot be any morality.

I shall devote the present chapter to the question of religion and the final chapter to the questions of free will and morality.

In the modern epoch the two world-pictures, that which I have called the naturalistic or scientific view of the world and that which I have called the religious view, face one another in unresolved contradiction. I have said that modern culture has for its essence the conflict between them. It is not to be solved by amiable "reconciliations" between bishops and scientists. The notion that it has been settled because ecclesiastics now agree that the question of the age of the earth, of whether the heliocentric or the geocentric astronomy is true, of whether man is a "special creation" or is descended from simian ancestors, belong to the province of science and not to that of religion, is a sheer delusion. For science, as we have tried to show, is irrelevant to the problem. The problem is handed over to the philosophers because it is a matter of general world-views, and not of the details of any science. Moreover, any mere compromise, by which one part of the territory of the world is given to science, the other part to religion, is worthless and shallow. This was the great insight of Kant and of the romantic movement of the nineteenth century—whatever may be thought of the particular solutions offered by Kant and the romantics. Thus the problem still stands before us, unsolved by any rapprochements which have occurred, or are likely to occur, between scientists and religious men.

The question may perhaps be put in the form: is religion, or is anything in any religion, true? For it can hardly be the case that the religious view of the world in general is true, but that all particular religions are wholly false. And if the question be put in this form—is any religion true?—I should myself, until recently, have replied with an unqualified no. Religion, I should have said, is nothing but a mass of false ideas and superstitions of which the ultimate source is wishful thinking. We have believed a view of the world which we want to believe, namely, that is ruled by a power which is friendly to us and to the values of beauty and goodness which we cherish. As a result of further study and reflection I have modified this opinion. To the question asked I now find the answer to be a qualified yes.

To explain this is the object of the present chapter. I fear that its contents must appear, in a peculiar sense, no more than the very personal opinions of a single man. I offer them for what they are worth.

It will be helpful to begin by regarding the religious view of the world, not as a set of intellectual propositions about the nature of the world, but as importing a way of life. Of course any religion is, or implies, some complex of propositions about the universe. But every religion offers a way of life. And I shall consider religion in this aspect first, leaving its intellectual side, as a set of beliefs about the world, for consideration later in this chapter.

I will quote three passages from T. S. Eliot's play *The Cocktail Party*. They come from different parts of the play, but it is noteworthy that they are all three put into the mouth of the same character, whose utterances, in some sense, carry the main message of the drama. Whatever else there is in the play, it certainly teaches that there are two possible ways of life between which we have to make a choice. Says the character Reilly concerning human life:

> The best of a bad job is all that any of us make of it—
> *Except, of course, the saints.*[1]

In a later context he says:

> There *is* another way, if you have the courage.
> The first I could describe in familiar terms
> Because you have seen it, as we all have seen it,
> Illustrated, more or less, in the lives of those about us.
> The second is *unknown,* and so requires faith—
> The kind of faith that issues from despair.
> *The destination cannot be described;*
> *You will know very little until you get there;*
> You will journey blind. But the way leads towards possession
> Of what you have sought for in the wrong place.[1]

In the third passage, quoted from a later page, Reilly says:

> But such *experience* can only be hinted at
> In *myths and images.* To speak about it
> We talk of darkness, labyrinths, Minotaur terrors.[1]

[1] T. S. Eliot, *The Cocktail Party.* Quoted by permission of the publishers, Harcourt, Brace and Company, Inc. The italics in these quotations are all mine except the word "is" in the first line of the second quotation which is **Mr.** Eliot's.

There is then a "way," and an "experience," and a "destination." It is the way of the "saints." Nevertheless it is "unknown." Also it is only for those who "have the courage." The destination "cannot be described." The experience likewise cannot be described, but is only "hinted at in myths and images." I shall suggest that these words, a "way" or path, followed by the "saints," which leads to an "experience" and a "destination" which "cannot be known" except through "myths and images," stand for the conceptions which are the essential truth of all religions.

In every religion there is a way or a path, and there is a destination or experience to which it leads. "I am the way, the truth and the life," says the Jesus of St. John's gospel. The Buddhist speaks of "the noble eightfold path." The destination, the experience—which is hidden—is variously described as "salvation," "heaven," "nirvana," "union with Brahman." The different religions seem to refer to different paths and different destinations. I shall maintain that always and everywhere, in all the great religions, there is in fact only one destination, one experience, even —with some qualification—one path, but that it is "hinted at" by means of different "myths and images" which constitute the differences between the religions.

Mr. Eliot gives to his own words, if I understand him, a specially Christian interpretation. Thus the end of the play seems to teach that the "way" necessarily, or at least usually, leads through martyrdom which, if taken in its literal sense of death for the faith, is a peculiarly Christian conception. (All religions, of course, involve martyrdom, if by that is meant only the destruction in us of the desires of the world.) I do not know whether in this I interpret Mr. Eliot rightly. But in any case I shall not follow him in any specifically Christian interpretation he may give to his own words. I have made it clear before that in my view religion and the religious view of the world are not the special property of Christian peoples, but belong to the universal heritage of mankind. It does not matter whether the meanings which I shall give to Mr. Eliot's words are his meanings or not. I shall use them to express my own meanings. I shall give them a more universal scope than he perhaps intends. What he says, apparently only of one religion, applies, I shall contend, to all the great religions.

The myths and images by means of which we hint at the experience and the destination are, in my view, though perhaps not in Mr. Eliot's, the creeds and dogmas of the different religions. These vary and contradict one another, and herein lie the differences between the religions. The unity between them lies, in the first instance, in the path and the destination, the way of life, which is the way of the saints. By the word "saint" perhaps Mr. Eliot means to refer only to the Christian saints. But I shall mean the saints of any religion. Whether this way implies any common view of the nature of the world is something which I shall discuss later in this chapter. Thus there are three questions which we have to discuss:

(1) The conception of religious dogmas and doctrines as myths and images.
(2) The way of life, the destination, the experience.
(3) Whether the experience implies any special view of the nature of the universe.

That all religious doctrines and dogmas are myths and images means that none of them is *literally* true. To have perceived this is the contribution made to thought by the skeptics and the atheists, in fact by the scientific view of the world. But they have missed something. They have simply said that the dogmas are not true. In this they were right. What they failed to see was that the dogmas are not merely falsehoods, but that they are myths, images, allegories which hint at a way of life, a destination, an experience, and possibly also—this is the question referred to in (3) above, which is left for later discussion—some deeper truth about the universe. What we have first to show is that the dogmas are, if understood literally, false. Hence the contentions of the next few pages, which will be designed to show this, will seem like pure atheism and skepticism. But they must be understood in the light of the later parts of this chapter.

Naturally I cannot take all the dogmas of all the great religions and show that, if taken literally, they are false. Such a task would be almost endless. Nor is it at all necessary. Practically all religious people hold that the doctrines which are special and peculiar to religions other than their own are false. The Christian does not accept the Hindu doctrine of reincarnation. The Buddhist does not accept the Christian doctrine of the Trinity. The procedure I shall adopt will be to take only one dogma, which is common to most religions, and which will be thought by most people to be *the* most fundamental doctrine of religion, and show that, if it is understood literally, there is no reason to believe that it is true, and every reason to suppose that it is false. This is the doctrine that there exists a being, known as God, who is a person, a mind, a consciousness, who formed a plan in his mind, and who, in accordance with his purpose, created a world. I do not think that this can be "proved" to be false. It is conceivable that there might be such a mind who made the world as a watchmaker makes a watch. But I think it can be shown that there is no reason at all to think that there is such a being, and that the conception of him in fact involves such difficulties that we are compelled to give it up. That the doctrine of God may have a symbolic meaning, which is true, is something the discussion of which is postponed to a later page. It is only the literal meaning of it with which we are now concerned.

The first thing to say is that science has absolutely nothing to do with the matter. This should be obvious from what has already been said in earlier chapters. It does not make any difference to the doctrine of the existence of God whether the sun goes round the earth or the earth round the sun, whether the planets move in circles or ellipses, whether the laws of motion are what Galileo and Newton thought or not. The transition from the teachings of early science to a diminishing belief in God was a psychological, not a logical transition. In other words, it was a mistake. It is true that the scientific belief that all events are wholly to be explained by natural causes, and that there are no supernatural interventions, does make real difficulties for the more primitive and naïve ideas of God's action in the world. But even this, as was shown on page 92, can be overcome by a little logical ingenuity. We have only to suppose that God's existence is necessary to the continued existence of the world, and that he acts in it, now as in the past, always through and by means of, the operation of natural laws. And if Newtonian science contained nothing inconsistent with belief in God, neither does the science of today. No science ever could.

The kind of thought which is really fatal to literal belief in religious dogmas has always come from philosophers, not from scientists. The popular belief to the contrary, which is a delusion, is partly due to the mistaken transitions of thought already referred to, and partly to the fact that science is in everybody's mouth (the modern idol), while philosophy is unknown except to a few people.

In Chapter 2 I tried to pin down carefully the traditional meaning of the word "God," and of the conception of his creation of the world. For that word is nowadays used in all sorts of nebulous ways. I know a man who professes to believe in God, but who, if pressed, says that what he means by God is the sumtotal of all the good tendencies of human beings. This, at any rate, is not what the ages have meant by God. The ages have meant a mind, a spirit, a soul, a consciousness, which made and rules over the world. The conception, as shown in Chapter 2, is necessarily anthropomorphic. It is necessary to insist on this in order to understand what follows.

What reason is there to believe in the existence of such a being? There are a number of well-known so-called "proofs of the existence of God." These have been put forward from time to time in the history of thought from Plato onwards, by philosophers and theologians. It is impossible that I should here examine them all. Most philosophers—except Roman Catholic philosophers—and most philosophically instructed religious men themselves, now regard them as fallacious and outmoded; and religious thinkers tend to rely, more and more, not on these external, logical arguments, but on the internal light of religious experience in men's souls—of which more later. I have already examined, in Chapter 5, one of the most famous of these arguments, the argument from design, and shown that it is fallacious. I cannot do more here than briefly discuss a few other lines of thought which have been believed in the past to prove the existence of a divine being.

One of the most common has been that the world must have a first cause, which must be God. But why should not the chains of causes and effects run back into an infinite past with no beginning? This may be difficult to conceive, and some philosophers have thought that the idea of infinite time involves contradictions. But the point to be made is that the idea of God as a first cause presents exactly the same difficulties and contradictions and offers no solution of them. For the existence of God, on the traditional view, runs back into an infinite past in exactly the same way as the suggested chain of causes. It is true that some theologians, seeing this, have said that God's eternity is not an infinite extension of time, and that God created time along with the temporal world. But this leads to contradiction. For if it is true, then time had a beginning, and before it began there was no time. But the conception of time beginning *at* a time, which was not itself *in* time, i.e., had no time before it, is self-contradictory.

The main point, however, is that there is no reason to suppose that there must have been a first cause, since the chain of causes might go infinitely backwards into infinite time; and that *if* there is a difficulty in conceiving an infinite backward time containing an infinite series of causes, there will be exactly the same difficulty in conceiving an infinite backward time containing only one infinitely prolonged cause, namely, God.

Suppose we admit, however, that there must have been a first cause. Why should this first cause have been a mind? The argument that the chain of causes cannot have an infinite backward extension, even if accepted, shows nothing as to the nature of the primal cause. Why must it be a mental, rather than a material, existence? The only answer which has ever been given to this question is that the hypothesis of a mind is the only one which will explain the evidence of purpose, the adaptation of means to ends, which we find in nature. In other words, the argument that there is a first cause, even if it is admitted, is compelled to supplement itself by appealing to the argument from design in order to show that the first cause must have been a mind rather than anything else. But we have already shown that the argument from design is worthless.

It is rather late in the day to discuss the argument that miracles prove the existence of God. Not many people believe that miracles occur. But a word may be said on this subject. Suppose that some very astonishing event occurs which we are utterly unable to explain. Water is turned into wine, or a stone into bread. We are inclined to believe that a miracle has occurred. Now either the extraordinary event is due to the operation of some natural law which is not at present known, or it is a breach of natural law only to be explained as an intervention of God. If a miracle is defined as an event which we cannot yet explain by natural laws, but which could be explained if we knew all the laws of nature, then a miracle, not being a divine intervention, affords no evidence of the existence of God. But if it is defined as an intervention by God in breach of natural law, then we cannot use an astonishing event as an argument for God unless we already know all the laws of nature and know that the astonishing event in question could not be explained by them—which is to say, never. It may be the case, for all I know, that paralytics are sometimes cured at Lourdes. If there is sufficient trustworthy evidence of this—I do not know whether there is or not—then it ought to be believed. But it proves nothing. For we do not know all the natural causes and laws which affect human bodies. We are coming to know a little more about the powerful effects of unusual psychological states on the physical organism. "Faith" may well be one of these powerfully working psychological states. We are still woefully ignorant of such matters. But there is absolutely no reason to suppose that these cures, if they occur, are not due to natural causes.

If we admit that all the arguments for the existence of God are invalid, this does not, of course, prove that God does not exist. The fact that there is no evidence of the existence of a mountain thirty thousand feet high on the back of the moon does not prove that one does not exist. There might be such a mountain. In the same way there might be such a being as God, even though there is no evidence of the fact available to us. It is impossible to prove the non-existence of God. You can only say that there is no evidence of his existence. Let us suppose, then, that there is such a being.

What, now, does traditional religion tell us about his nature? First, he is a mind, a consciousness. In the Christian tradition this mind is infinite, eternal, omnipotent, and perfectly good. Let us consider some of these attributes. The word "mind" has to be taken in its literal sense as having the same essential meaning as it has when it is applied to human beings. Of course, the conception of the mind of God may have some symbolic meaning; it may be a myth or image which stands for something else. But we are now considering religious doctrines as taken in their literal meaning. And understood in this way the mind of God must be something like a human mind, although it is no doubt much more powerful, wise, and good. But the word "mind," taken in this literal way, means a stream of psychological states, flowing, changing, succeeding one another in a time-series. Consciousness, in the literal meaning of the word, cannot exist in any other way. It is not possible to conceive an unchanging consciousness, because consciousness depends on contrast, which is possible only if one thought or perception follows another with which it is contrasted; so that a consciousness which ceases to change ceases to exist and passes into the darkness of unconsciousness. Hence if God has consciousness in the only sense in which the word has meaning for us, it must be a changing consciousness. But that God's consciousness flows and changes in time contradicts that unchangeableness and immutability which is also, in all religious thought, attributed to God. It at once puts God in time, and contradicts the theological conception that he is above time and created it. And it also contradicts the infinity of God's mind. The infinite cannot change. For that which changes lacks at one time some state which it has at another time; and that which lacks anything is not infinite.

In all theological thought God is supposed to be infinite. The finite mind of man is contrasted with the infinite mind of God. But the more we think of it the more we see that we can attach no meaning at all to this language. Since a mind is a flow of changing conscious states, and change implies finitude, an infinite mind is a contradiction in terms. We can understand what is meant by infinite time or infinite space. But what is meant by the term "infinity" as applied to a consciousness? Since no answer can be given to this question, some writers have suggested that when we apply the word "infinite" to God we are merely using an honorific term. When we speak of God as infinitely good, infinitely wise, and so on, all we can really mean is that he is *very* good, *very* wise, etc.—much better and wiser than we are. If so, the difference between us and God is merely one of degree. This is certainly bad theology, and the theologian will insist that God is truly infinite. But in that case no meaning can be given to his language. Either he has to give up his doctrine of the infinity of God, or he has to use language which has no meaning.

God's activity and creativity also contradict his infinity. For action and creation involve change which, as we have just seen, are consistent only with the finite. Theological thought has always recognized that passing away is an attribute of the finite, which is the reason why God is said to be immutable and unchanging. But if so, God's consciousness cannot have changed from a perception of the absence of the world before it was created to the perception of its presence after he had created it.

There are also difficulties connected with the attribute of being all-powerful which is applied to God. Does this mean that he could create a square circle? No doubt this is absurd. But if so, what this means is that the laws of logic are as binding on the mind of God as they are on the mind of man. There *are* things then which he cannot do.

The reader may perhaps consider this last consideration trivial. But he cannot think this about the difficulties which arise in connection with the idea of the infinite or perfect goodness of God. For this is notoriously irreconcilable with the existence of pain and evil in the world, and has led to one of the most famous of theological problems, the problem of evil. If God is the ultimate source of everything, then he is the ultimate source of evil; and how is this consistent with his perfect goodness? Hume wrote:

> Epicurus' old questions are still unanswered. Is Deity willing to prevent evil, but not able? Then he is impotent. Is he able but not willing? Then he is malevolent. Is he both able and willing? Whence then is evil?[2]

The point to notice is that the whole force of Hume's argument depends on taking all the terms used in it literally. It is necessary perhaps to remind the reader of the fact that what we are attempting to show is only that the doctrine of the existence of God, *if taken literally,* is a myth. Hume's argument has no force unless such words as "able" and "willing" are taken in their ordinary human senses as meaning the same things as would be meant if we were to speak of a human being as able or willing to do this or that. And it has no force if God is not thought of as a person or a mind in the same sense as human beings are persons and minds. But if the terms and ideas are taken in their literal meanings, then Hume's argument is entirely unanswerable. But it does not show that the doctrine of God's infinite goodness may not be symbolic of some deeper truth. But if so, then it is what we have called a myth.

All attempts to solve this problem on the level of literal interpretation are obvious absurdities. Some have said that evil is not a positive, but only a negative fact. It is only the absence of goodness. It is therefore nothing, and God cannot be held responsible for creating a nothingness. But this is to assert that pain and evil do not really exist at all, which is absurd.

Others have urged that we should perceive no evil in the world

---

[2] *Dialogues Concerning Natural Religion* (New York: Hafner Publishing Co., 1951), part X.

if we could perceive the world as a whole. The appearance of evil is due to our limited and partial vision. A discord in a musical composition might be unpleasant if sounded alone. But when we hear it as a part of the whole piece we see that it contributes to the beauty of the whole. In the same way evil would cease to appear as evil if we could view the universe in a single all-embracing vision. But this contention, like the last, really amounts to denying the existence of evil. It is only an appearance, not a reality. Furthermore, if the appearance is due to our limited and partial view, then it will have to be admitted that at least our limited and partial view is a real, and not merely an apparent, evil.

Others, seeing the utter hopelessness of such prevarications and evasions, take refuge in the concept of mystery. The ways of God are a mystery to the human mind, and we must accept evil as one of these mysteries. But this is both illogical and inconsistent. For the same people will insist that the good and beautiful things in the world are evidence of God's goodness. But if so, by exactly the same logic, the evil things must be admitted to be evidence of either his badness or his impotence. Those who urge the concept of mystery upon us are therefore accepting the evidence when it favors their case, but refusing to accept it when it goes against them.

In these pages I have selected, as samples, only a few of the skeptical arguments which can be used to destroy such a proposition as: "There exists an infinitely good and powerful mind which created the world and runs it." Some of them may be more convincing, some less. It will always be possible, of course, to pick holes, to argue and dispute. But the total force of skeptical considerations of this kind, whether I have stated them impeccably or not, must in the end, I believe, prove irresistible to a mind which is both quite honest and quite impartial. What is the conclusion to which they point? Not, in my opinion, that all religion is false. Not even that the proposition just quoted is wholly false; but that such beliefs are not *literally* true, that they are at best "myths and images" which perhaps "hint at" some deeper truth. "To speak about it/We talk of darkness, labyrinths,

Minotaur terrors," that is to say, we talk of all-powerful minds, gods, devils, and what not.

What then—to turn to our second problem—is the way of life, the destination, the experience, which these myths and images are meant to symbolize? What is the deeper truth to which they point?

There are two ways of life, that which most of us follow, and which consists in "making the best of a bad job," and the "way of the saints"—the saints of any religion. What is this second way, and what is its destination? Since the way and the destination are, in Eliot's words, "unknown," since the destination "cannot be described," the present writer, who follows the first way, cannot be expected to know or describe them. No one can describe them, not even those who follow the way and have reached the destination. But I think that nevertheless something can be said. There do exist records, written by those who have followed the second way, which can be quoted. They too will be found not to express the literal and naked truth, not to "describe" the truth, because that truth is "inexpressible" in language. This is the reason why men invent myths and images which merely "hint at" it. The "experience," which is also the "destination," is "ineffable," which is the same as saying that "it cannot be described." But these direct records of the personal experience of saints and mystics are at least in some way nearer to the naked truth than are the official dogmas of the various creeds which have been, for the most part, the work of theologians, not of saints—although, of course, the theologian and the saint may in rare cases be the same person.

Buddha said: "It remains a fact and the fixed and necessary constitution of being, that all its constituents are misery."[3] Also it is said in one of the Upanishads: "In the Infinite only is bliss. In the finite there is no bliss."[4]

If we think candidly about them, both these statements are

[3] *Anguttara-Nikaya,* quoted *Buddhism in Translations,* H. C. Warren (Cambridge: Harvard Univ. Press, 1896), p. xx.
[4] *Chandogya Upanishad,* 7.23, in *The Hindu Scriptures* (Everyman ed.).

likely to appear to us as gross exaggerations, especially the first. It may be the case, we shall perhaps piously admit, that the highest happiness is found only in God, the Infinite, but there is, after all, a great deal of genuine happiness to be found in daily life. Yet expressions which are parallel to the verse of the Upanishad can be found in the literature of all religions. There is no happiness at all, the saints keep telling us, except in God. Even in Eliot's language, all that any of us can do, except the saints, is to "make the best of a bad job." This at least says that the normal way of life cannot ever be anything except a *bad* job. It cannot be made a good job by any of the ordinary means, such as money and possessions, or even poetry, music, science, philosophy, art. All religious men really say the same thing, that life in the finite world is bad, and that "in the Infinite only is bliss." They say it in stronger or in weaker terms. Buddha's language is the strongest, Eliot's perhaps the weakest.

But impartially considered, do not all these religious statements seem false? There is a great deal of happiness to be found in finite things. There are many innocent pleasures. There are flowers, sunsets, poems, concerts, plays like Mr. Eliot's. What is wrong, for the matter of that, with baseball and football? There are also good things to eat and drink. To take pleasure in these things may not be especially noble. There are no doubt higher and lower pleasures. There are pain and suffering too. Some may think that the pains outweigh the pleasures, some the opposite. But is it not simply false to say that there is no happiness in life at all, still more that all the constituents of being are misery? And yet—that there is *no* happiness except in God, *no* bliss except in the Infinite, is the constant refrain of the saints. Are they talking nonsense, denying plain facts? Or do they mean something which we have failed to understand even when, like parrots, we mumble their words in the church, the synagogue, the mosque?

I believe that what the saints say is true—not merely that there is some truth in it, but that it is wholly true.

It is correct that, as viewed from a certain level, there are plenty of pleasures and enjoyments available in the common way of life, and that many of them are perfectly innocent. The saint is not denying this. He is not denying that you can have a good time, and that having a good time is very enjoyable. But the level at which these things are said is superficial. At a deeper level we find that all this is hollowness, vacancy, and futility. Underneath the glitter of the tinsel there is darkness. At the core there is misery. That is why we are continually absorbing ourselves in ephemeral pursuits. To be absorbed is to forget what we ourselves, in the depths, actually are. We want to forget it.

This is not true of the animals. There is something in man which is not in the animals. It is at this something which the myth of an immortal soul is hinting. What is it? The question cannot be answered, because the something "cannot be described"; it is inexpressible. If we say that it is a "hunger for the Infinite" we use the language of myth, and we also use language which is trite and hackneyed. If we say that man's true home is God, that he is estranged, and this estrangement, being his essential nature as a finite being, is the inner misery of which we speak, we are using again hackneyed language and the language of myth. But something like this is all that can be said.

It is true that men can so completely forget this inner darkness of the soul that they become unaware of it and do not know what is meant when it is spoken of. And then it may be asked: how can a man be unhappy and yet not know it? If one feels happy, then one is happy. But even at the superficial level of daily life this is not true. It is possible to believe during a period of time that one is happy and afterwards to realize that one was not. And again one may ask whether, if a man is unaware of the darkness within him and is happy on the superficial level, it would not be better for him to remain in that state and be content with it. This is the same as the old question whether it is not better to be a pig satisfied than a Socrates unsatisfied. To which the answer is: No, not unless you are a pig.

The essential truth of religion, of every religion, is that from this darkness of life *there is a way out*, a way into the light. The destination of your present way is futility. The destination of the other way is "bliss" or "blessedness." This is not merely a higher degree of what men call happiness. It is not merely an elevated "pleasure." Blessedness and happiness—at any rate as the latter word is commonly understood—do not belong in the same order of things at all. According to all religions the way out is very long and hard. But it is possible, *if you want it enough*. What is this way?

It is generally supposed that the way of the saints consists in living a good life, that is to say, in morality. Is not a saint just a very good man? To this view corresponds the suggestion that the essence of religion is ethics. It may then be said that the essence of Christianity is the Sermon on the Mount. When we discount the dogmas, we are left with the ethics, for there is nothing else in a religion besides its ethics and its dogmas. The view that religion is "morality tinged with emotion" also makes ethics the essence of religion.

This whole way of thinking is a fatal blunder. It is hardly too much to say that it can only be the result of a sort of religious blindness. For just as there are men who are so esthetically insensitive that they appear to others blind—those, for instance, who have no sense of music, to whom music is no more than a jumble of sounds—so it is in religion. Nor are such men found only among skeptics. They are common enough among the conventionally orthodox.

Religion is not simply ethics. Nor is it just a mixture of ethics and dogma, or of ethics and emotion. There is a third something, totally different from either, which is its essence. It is true that religion always insists on a moral life. It is true that saints are usually good men. And this is not a matter of chance. It is a necessity. For love and compassion flow necessarily out of the peculiar vision, the peculiar experience, of the mystic or saint, are indeed parts of it, so that he cannot help being also a moralist. But his morality is not his religion.

The moral way alone will never lead to bliss, to blessedness, to salvation, or whatever the destination of the path may be called.

It is possible that it may lead to "happiness." Plato and others
have tried to prove that the good man is necessarily a happy man.
We may hope that this is true. And yet there is a peculiar kind of
disappointment, or disillusionment, which attends the life which
is *only* moral. A man may do his duty, and yet remain unhappy,
or at least basically unsatisfied. It seems in the end to have profited
him nothing and to have been no more than a heavy burden which
he has borne. And in any case happiness, even if the moral life
does ensure it, is only a superficial phenomenon, like pleasure.
It is not that blessedness which religion seeks.

What then is the way, what the destination? Strictly speaking,
they "cannot be described." They are ineffable. And this word
"ineffable" must be understood in its strict sense as meaning that
which cannot be said, cannot be uttered at all in any conceivable
words, in any conceivable language, and never will be. But it is
here that the records left by the saints themselves can be of some
use. Not that even they can say that which cannot be said. But
they can "hint at it" more clearly than the common dogmas of
religion do. Of course the saints themselves believed in and repeated the dogmas, Christian saints Christian dogmas, Hindu
saints Hindu dogmas, Muslim saints Muslim dogmas. They were
after all human beings conditioned in their intellectual beliefs by
the different cultures in which they were brought up. And in so
far as they repeated the doctrines of the particular religions to
which they were attached, they contradicted one another. But
sometimes they transcended these different cultures, and sought
to utter the pure essence of religion itself, and when they did so
their utterances show a surprising measure of agreement.

The essence of religion is not morality but mysticism. And the
way of the saints is the way of mysticism. Accordingly, I use the
words "saint" and "mystic" interchangeably in this book. If this
does not wholly accord with dictionary definitions, I cannot help
it. My contention is that all religion is ultimately mystical, or
springs from the mystical side of human nature. All religious men
are therefore mystics in greater or less degree. There is no sharp

line between mystic and non-mystic. Those who are commonly recognized as mystics, and who so recognize themselves, are only those whose mysticism is explicitly realized in the full light of consciousness. In the ordinary religious man that mysticism is implicit, lies below the threshold of consciousness, only faintly stirring the surface waters of the mind and not recognized as what it is either by himself or others. The "saint" is the religious man *par excellence,* and the substance of his life is therefore mysticism whether he, or others who watch and describe him, know it or not.

I shall quote a few of the utterances of mystics taken designedly from a number of different cultures and religions. What is common to all of them is the assertion that there is a kind of experience, a way of experiencing the world, in which all distinctions between one thing and another, including the distinction between the subject and object, self and not-self, are abolished, overcome, transcended, so that all the *different* things in the world become *one,* become identical with one another. We must suppose that they are still, in a sense, different; and yet they are not different but identical. Philosophical readers will be reminded of Hegel's famous "identity in difference." But whereas Hegel only talked about this, as a theory, the saints experience it—which is quite another thing. The affirmation of the possibility, or rather the actuality, of such an experience, raises at once a host of questions. But let us, for the moment at any rate, proceed to the evidence, or rather to that minute fraction of it which space allows me to reproduce here. I merely take a few samples from a vast literature.

A notable witness is Meister Eckhart, the Catholic mystic of the thirteenth century. A few passages from his writings follow.

> There all is one, and one is all. There to her [the perceiving soul] all is one and one is all. Herein lies the soul's purity, that it is purified from a life that is divided and that it enters into a life that is unified. All that is divided in lower things will be unified so soon as the soul climbs into a life where there is no contrast. When the soul comes into a life of reasonableness [the true insight] it knows no contrasts. Say, Lord, when is a man in mere "understanding"? I say to you: "When a man sees one thing separated from another." And when is a man above mere

understanding? That I can tell you: "When he sees all in all, then a man stands beyond mere understanding."[5]

In this passage our ordinary mode of experiencing the world, in which one thing is distinguished from another, is called understanding. In the true vision, which transcends it, there are no contrasts or distinctions, but "all is one."

In another passage Eckhart says:

All that a man has here externally in multiplicity is intrinsically One. Here all blades of grass, wood, and stone, all things are one. This is the deepest depth.[6]

And again:

When the soul comes into the light of the supersensual it knows nothing of contrasts[7]

In such an experience the mind has necessarily passed beyond time and space. For time and space are the very conditions of division, separation, multiplicity, contrast. Space divides things here from things there; time divides things now from things then. Hence the unifying vision in which all is one is an experience of the eternal, for eternity is not an unending length of time, but is timelessness. For the same reason it is an experience of the Infinite. For where all is one, there is nothing outside that one, and therefore nothing to limit or bound it. The notion of boundary is the essence of the finite. Only that which is bounded is finite. But for a thing to be bounded means to be bounded by something else. And if there is only one, there is no something else to bound it, and therefore it is infinite. This is the true meaning of the term "infinite" as it is used in religious thinking. And this is the solution of the paradoxes we earlier discovered in the notion of God as an infinite mind. We could give no meaning to this phrase so long as we understood infinite to mean mere endlessness—as when we speak of infinite time or space. An infinite mind, we now see, is a mind for which "all is one." This also provides the

5 Quoted, Rudolph Otto, *Mysticism East and West* (New York: The Macmillan Co., 1932), p. 45.
6 *Ibid.*, p. 61.
7 *Ibid.*, p. 61.

key to the meaning of the verse of the Upanishad which we quoted: "In the Infinite only is bliss; there is no bliss in the finite." This means that in the ordinary way of life, which views all things by what Eckhart calls the understanding, there is no bliss—though there may be pleasure and even happiness. Only in the super-consciousness, which is the second way of life, the way of the saints, is there bliss.

Our second witness will be a pagan writer, Plotinus. He wrote of that vision which he had himself attained:

> Our self-seeing There is a communion with the self restored to its purity. No doubt we should not speak of seeing, but instead of seen and seer speak boldly of a *simple unity*. For in this seeing we neither see *nor distinguish nor are there two.* The man is changed, no longer himself nor self-belonging; he is merged with the Supreme, sunken into It, *one with It;* only in separation is there duality. This is why *the vision baffles telling;* for how could a man bring back tidings of the Supreme as detached when *he has seen it as one with himself? It is not to be told, not to be revealed to any* that has not himself had the happiness to see. . . . *Beholder was one with beheld . . . he is become the Unity, having no diversity either in relation to himself or anything else . . . reason is in abeyance and intellection* and even the very self, caught away, God-possessed, in perfect stillness, all the being *calmed.* . . .
>
> This is the life of gods and of god-like and *blessed* men— *liberation* from the alien that besets us here, a life taking no pleasure in the things of earth—a flight of the alone to the Alone.[8]

The italicized passages carry the essential points which are the same in all accounts whether they proceed from Christians, Muslims, pagans, Hindus, or Buddhists. These are, first, that in this experience "all is one," there is no distinction of the seer from the seen (the distinction of subject from object) nor any distinction of any one thing from any other, no division or separation or discrimination; second, that in consequence the vision transcends intellection (Eckhart's "understanding"); third, that

[8] *Ennead VI.IX.II* (eleven) in *Works* (New York: Medici Society) trans. Stephen Mackenna. Italics mine.

for this reason it is ineffable—no words can speak it because all words depend on distinctions of one thing from another, that is to say upon the intellect; and fourth, that this experience is liberation, blessedness, calm, peace.

The pagan, we see, agrees with the Christian. Let us turn now to a wholly different culture, that of India. There the chief religions have been Hinduism and Buddhism. Their dogmas and doctrines are, of course, wholly different from those either of Christianity or ancient pagan philosophy. Nor can they be suspected of being influenced by these. They were indigenous products of purely Indian experience.

In Buddhism the unifying vision, that super-consciousness which is above mere "understanding" is called Nirvana. It is also called "enlightenment." In northern Buddhism it is sometimes called "the Buddha-mind," or again "Mind-Essence." It is a complete mistake to suppose that Nirvana is a sort of place or condition which one reaches after death. It is a state of the soul which can be attained by men who are still in the body and walking about the earth. Buddha attained it early in life, and lived and worked in the light of it for half a century. Ashvaghosha, who composed a Buddhist manual called *The Awakening of Faith,* about the first century A.D., distinguishes between the "discriminating consciousness" (Eckhart's "understanding," which distinguishes or discriminates between different things, and the "intellection" of Plotinus) and the "intuitive consciousness" or Mind-Essence in the attainment of which lies enlightenment. He says:

> Mind-Essence does not belong to any individualized conception of phenomena or non-phenomena. . . . It has no particularizing consciousness, it does not belong to any kind of describable nature. Individuations and the consciousness of them come into being only as sentient beings cherish false imaginations of differences.[9]

[9] A translation of *The Awakening of Faith* will be found in *A Buddhist Bible,* edited by Dwight Goddard (2nd ed.; Thetford, Vt.: Dwight Goddard, 1938). This passage appears on page 364.

In another passage of the same author:

> In its aspect of Enlightenment, Mind-Essence is free from all
> manner of individuation and discriminative thinking.[10]

Again:

> If any sentient being is able to keep free from all discriminative
> thinking, he has attained to the wisdom of a Buddha.[11]

Emphasizing what we should call the relation of the moral life
to the transcendent vision, the fact that the vision is the source of
ethical life, he says:

> The fourth significance [of enlightenment] is an affirmation of
> compassionate helpfulness, for being free from all limitations
> of selfness, it draws all alike into its all-embracing purity and
> unity and peacefulness, illuminating their minds with equal
> brightness so that all sentient beings have an equal right to
> enlightenment.[12]

Why does the unifying vision lead to love and compassion, the
sources of the good life? Because in it all differences are abolished,
including the difference between "I" and "you" which is the
source of egoism and selfishness.

The reference in this passage to peacefulness is also important.
We remember the Christian phrase "the peace of God, *which
passeth all understanding.*" Why does it "pass all understanding"?
We mumble this phrase in church knowing nothing of its meaning, or supposing that it is a pious ejaculation, or a superlative
which has no precise significance. On the contrary, it means
exactly what it says. Refer to Eckhart's use of the word "understanding." The peace of God, which is the same as the blessedness
which is the destination of the saint's way, the same as the "bliss
unspeakable" of Nirvana, is literally unintelligible to the discur-
sive consciousness, the discriminating mind, the understanding.
It has nothing to do with peace as that word is understood in our
ordinary modes of living and thinking, any more than blessedness
has anything to do with what is ordinarily called happiness.

[10] *Ibid.,* p. 365.
[11] *Ibid.,* p. 366.
[12] *Ibid.,* p. 368.

Referring again to egoism Ashvaghosha says:

> As soon as the mind perceives differences, it awakens desire, grasping, and following suffering, and then the mind notes that some relate to himself and some to not-self. If the mind could remain undisturbed by differences and discriminations the conception of an ego-self (the root of moral evil) would die away.[13]

From another northern Buddhist text *The Surangama Sutra,* out of many similar pasages I quote only one. Buddha, speaking to Ananda, the beloved disciple, says:

> Ananda, if you are now desirous of more perfectly understanding Supreme Enlightenment . . . you must learn to answer questions with no recourse to discriminating thinking. For the Tathagatas (Buddhas) in the ten quarters of the universe have been delivered from the ever-returning cycle of deaths and rebirths by this same single way, namely by reliance upon their intuitive minds.[14]

"Discriminating mind" is the "understanding" of Eckhart, the "reason" or "intellection" of Plotinus. Intuitive mind is the non-discriminating, non-conceptual mind, the unifying vision in which all is one, the "insight" of Eckhart.

From Buddhism we turn to Hinduism. The *Upanishads,* the work of unknown forest saints, which date back two thousand five hundred to three thousand years, have been the chief source of the best Hindu thought from their own time till now. The great theme of the *Upanishads* is the discovery by their authors that *"atman," which means the individual soul or self of a man, is identical with Brahman, which is the name of the Universal Self, or God.* I *am* God; or, to use the language of the *Upanishads* themselves, "That art thou." The difference which we make between ourselves and Brahman is *maya,* illusion. To overcome this illusion is salvation, for in the overcoming of it the soul passes into and becomes one with God. But the overcoming of the illu-

13 *Ibid.,* p. 369.
14 *The Surangama Sutra* is also translated in Goddard's *Buddhist Bible.* This quotation is from page 112.

sion is not an intellectual understanding of it. One may know as a matter of abstract thought that one's self is identical with God. But this does not destroy the illusion of the difference, the separation, between God and the self. One may compare this situation to any common optical illusion such as seeing a mirage. You see a lake of water in the desert. You may possess the scientific knowledge that no water is there. But this does not get rid of the illusion. You still see the water there. In the same way the intellectual knowledge that one's self is identical with the divine self helps not a whit in getting rid of the illusion of difference. The identity of one's self and God has to be actually *experienced*. Then only, in that supreme mystical experience, is the veil of illusion rent, and the soul passes into an immediate, experienced union with Brahman. It is of this mystical experience that the *Upanishads* everywhere speak. And it requires no great degree of understanding to see that this experience is identical with the unifying vision of Eckhart, the ecstatic state of Plotinus, the intuitive or non-discriminating mind of Buddhism.

In the *Mandukya Upanishad* we are told that there are four possible states of mind. The first three are waking, dreaming, and dreamless sleep.

> The Fourth, say the wise, is not subjective experience, nor objective experience, nor experience intermediate between these two, nor is it a negative condition which is neither consciousness nor unconsciousness. It is not the knowledge of the senses, nor is it relative knowledge, nor yet inferential knowledge. Beyond the senses, beyond the understanding, beyond all expression, is the Fourth. It is the pure unitary consciousness, wherein awareness of the world and of multiplicity is completely obliterated. It is ineffable peace. It is the supreme good. It is One without a second. It is the Self.[15]

In this passage the "Self" means Brahman, the Universal Self. The "One without a second" is another expression constantly

[15] The quotations given from the *Upanishads* are from the translation of Swami Prabhavananda and Frederick Manchester (Boston: Beacon Press, 1948). The expression here translated "not subjective experience, nor objective experience" is rendered by another translator (R. E. Hume) "not inwardly cognitive, not outwardly cognitive."

used in the *Upanishads* for Brahman. "Without a second" means that Brahman has nothing outside it, by which it is bounded or limited. It is therefore the Infinite in that precise meaning of the religious Infinite which has already been explained.

The essential character of this supreme vision, it will be noted, is that in it all discrimination, difference, multiplicity, are transcended. As with Eckhart, it is beyond the understanding. As with all mystics, to whatever religion they belong, it is ineffable, impossible to express in language,—"cannot be described" and is "unknown" in Eliot's words. And it is peace, bliss, blessedness, the supreme good, salvation. It is the "destination" of the "way." It is that for which, in Christian thought, the myth of a heaven after death stands.

From the *Mundaka Upanishad* I quote the following:

> The subtle Self [Brahman] is realized in that pure consciousness *wherein there is no duality*. [Italics mine.]

One of the commonest methods by which the *Upanishads* draw attention to the absence of all discrimination or difference in the mystic's experience of the divine is by insisting on the *formlessness* of Brahman. (It makes no difference whether we say the formlessness of Brahman or the formlessness of the mystical experience; for the two are one.) Form means any kind of character which distinguishes one thing from another. Gold, for instance, is distinguished from lead by having different characters—for example by the difference of yellow from gray. Since having form, having characters, is what distinguishes one thing from another, form is therefore the principle of differentiation and multiplicity. That in which there is no differentiation or multiplicity, in which "all is one," will accordingly be formless, and without any characters or qualities.

Hence we read in the *Katha Upanishad:*

> Soundless, formless, intangible, undying, tasteless, odorless, eternal, immutable, beyond Nature, is the Self.

And in the *Brihadaranayka Upanishad:*

The Self is to be described as not *this,* not *that.* It is incomprehensible, for it cannot be comprehended.

It cannot be comprehended, that is, it cannot be understood by the conceptual intellect, i.e., by Eckhart's "understanding," which always proceeds by discriminating this from that. But it can be experienced in the divine vision. It *is* the experience of the saint.

We many now draw together the main points of what has been said about the way, the path, the experience, the destination, of the saints in all the higher religions. Its essence is the transcendence of all multiplicity in the unifying vision of the One. In this experience not only is the distinction between this and that, for instance, between the stone and the wood, done away with, but also the distinction between the subject and the object, the experiencer and the divine which he experiences. The experience is also felt directly as being bliss, peace, blessedness. This is the source of all myths about a paradise to come. The experience also has the character of *eternality.* For since space and time are principles of division, and the experience is divisionless unity, it is therefore "above time and space." Even if the ecstatic vision lasts only a moment, which can, if we look at it from the outside, be dated, yet that moment, as seen from within itself, is timeless and eternal. For this is the meaning of eternity. It does not mean unending time, but timelessness. This eternality of the saint's experience is the source of all myths about the immortality of the soul, reincarnation, etc., in which eternity is symbolized by the notion of endless time. The experience has, finally, the character of *infinity* in the sense that there is nothing outside it to bound it, for in the vision in which all is one there cannot be any other to form a boundary. This infinity of the vision is the source of all myths about the infinite wisdom, power, and knowledge of God. In these myths infinity, like eternity, is distorted to mean mere endlessness. When so distorted the idea of God as an infinite mind gives rise to the absurdities and difficulties which were noted on an earlier page.

Now all this may seem like a tissue of fantastic dreams. It is quite easy to pound it with the battering rams of logic. If we are so disposed, we shall say as follows: It is not necessary to suppose that the saints and mystics are consciously saying what is not true. But they must be in some way deluded. The experience of which they speak is *impossible,* because it is self-contradictory. For consciousness of any kind depends on contrast, discrimination, difference. If discrimination of differences disappears, consciousness disappears with it; we simply become unconscious. Being aware of differences is therefore part of the meaning of the word "consciousness," just as "having four corners" is part of the meaning of the word "square." There cannot be a consciousness without awareness of differences for the same reason as there cannot be a round square.

But it must be pointed out that, by exactly the same sort of logic, a man born blind, who is aware of the world only by touch —we may ignore smell, taste, and sound—could prove that there cannot be such a thing as sight. His argument will go as follows: Consciousness means the awareness of things by touch. Therefore part of the meaning of consciousness is contact between the body and the thing which is being experienced. But these people who talk about sight say that it is an awareness of things at a distance, or without contact of the body. But this is self-contradictory because being in contact with the object is part of the meaning of experiencing or perceiving it.

Both of these arguments—the one against the mystical experience and the other against sight—are *a priori,* that is to say, arguments based on pure logic and not on experience. And they are both refuted in the same way, by experience. There simply is such a thing as sight, although it may seem contradictory to the blind man. And there simply is such a thing as the mystic experience, although it may seem contradictory to those who have not attained it. Of course you can say that the saint or the mystic is telling lies, or is at least in some way fuddled and deluded, as the blind man could say the same things of the man who sees. But it seems to me that, in view of the constant reiteration of the same things by innumerable mystics in different ages and countries and cultures, which are in many cases independent of one another and uninfluenced by one another, in view of their agreement with one another about the essentials of their vision—a vast literature of evidence of which I have only been able to give a few samples here—this explanation is not reasonable. The reasonable explanation lies in believing what they say.

We come to the third of the questions which we raised at the beginning of this chapter: whether the saint's experience implies any special view of the nature of the universe. There seem to be two possible views which can be taken. It may be held that the mystic's experience is real in the sense that he does have the experience, and it has the peculiarities which he asserts of it. But it is only a subjective experience in his own mind, so that it implies nothing about the real nature of the world outside him. It is, in this way, like a dream. A dream is real in the sense that it exists as a subjective state in the dreamer's mind. But it does not exist in the outside world, and implies nothing at all about that world. This may be called the subjectivist view of mysticism.

The other possible view is that the mystical experience does imply something objective. It may be held to imply that there is an objectively real being, a mind, a person, God, who is the creator of the universe. This is the view taken by most religions, and by most of the mystics themselves. For instance, in Hinduism the unifying experience is believed to be identical with Brahman, and Brahman is God—although it ought to be added that Hindu thinkers often do not think of God as a personal being. This may be called the objectivist view. Thus the question which we have to ask is: does the mystic experience imply what is ordinarily called "the existence, or objectivity, of God"?

Not all religions have taken the objective view. It is unsafe to speak with great confidence about what Buddha and his earliest disciples believed. But the earliest Buddhist writings seem to show that, although he certainly had the mystic experience—perhaps more clearly that any other man who ever lived—he did not objectify it. Brought up as a Hindu, he apparently denied the reality of Brahman, the Hindu equivalent of God. What he stressed was the state of enlightenment of the saint, which is Nirvana. On the face of it this seems like a subjectivist interpretation. It has been followed by the southern schools of Buddhism, those of Siam, Burma, and Ceylon, though not by the northern schools. This is the reason why Buddhism is sometimes called atheistic. And Buddhism is not the only Indian creed which takes a subjectivistic view of the mystic experience. The Sankhya and Yoga systems do the same. From this it seems to follow that theism is not a necessary implication of the experience of the saint. But that it is certainly a natural implication, which the majority of religious minds tend to follow, is shown by the emphatic insistence upon it of all the other great religions, Christianity, Hinduism, Judaism, and Islam.

It may appear that either the objectivist or the subjectivist view must be true, and that we are compelled to choose between them. My suggestion is that this is not the case, and that in fact neither is the truth; or, if we prefer to put it in another way, both are true, each from a different point of view. I will begin by pointing out that either view, if taken as the sole truth, is objectionable.

The religious man's objection to the subjectivist view will be that it destroys the truth of religion. We have seen that theological doctrines cannot be literally true; they can only be symbolic. This is the same as saying that they are myths which hint at a deeper truth. But if so, there must *be* a deeper truth to be hinted at. Of course, it is possible to say that what they hint at is simply the subjective mystic experience itself.[16] But it is utterly unsatisfactory to the religious consciousness. It amounts to saying that the doctrine, "God exists," means only that a certain mystical state of mind sometimes exists in some people.

No doubt the religious man can admit that the popular conception of a God who is a mind in the sense of a stream of psychological states, such as emotions, volitions, thoughts, succeeding

---

[16] This is the view I took in a paper under the title "Naturalism and Religion." I have since abandoned it.

one another in time, cannot describe the real nature of God, but is only symbolic. But, if religion is to be in any sense true, there must, he will say, be some real being who is thus symbolized.

The objection to the objectivist view is not so obvious, but it is just as important. If we look at the mystic experience itself, and ask what it implies, what we find is that it declares itself as neither subjective nor objective. This is stated in so many words in the *Upanishad* quoted above. "The Fourth [the mystic state of mind] is neither subjective experience, nor objective experience." And if it is objected that this is a Hindu, and not a Christian, thought, we must demur. For it is only what is implied by the most basic fact about all mystic experience, in whatever religion it is found, namely that it transcends the distinction between subject and object. And if it be added that what the mystic experiences is God himself, it follows that God himself is neither subjective nor objective.

This implies that God is not an object, and that it cannot properly be said even that he "exists." For both these words, "objective" and "existent," mean that what exists, or is objective, is one thing alongside of other things and therefore finite. But God is infinite and not one among other things. This is why all proofs of his existence fail. To prove that something exists means to pass by inference from *one* thing to *another*. Thus the proofs assume that God is "another thing." For instance, if God is the first cause, then there are other things besides God, namely the effects of which he is the cause, from which we pass by inference to him. The sun and the moon exist and are objective, and this means that they are parts of the natural order, i.e., the space-time order. But God is not a part of that order, and therefore is not existent or objective.

But from the statement that God is not objective it does not follow that he is subjective, or merely an illusory thought, or idea, or psychological state, in somebody's mind. For what the mystic experience teaches is that he is *neither objective nor subjective*.

That God should be neither the one nor the other may seem incomprehensible, but this should not surprise us since the incomprehensibility of God is asserted, in one form or another, in all the great religions.

Nevertheless something can be done to help the mind in this dilemma. We have become accustomed in science to the conception of frames of reference. For instance, suppose that two events, X and Y, occur. According to the theory of relativity, from the point of view of one space-time frame of reference, X may have occurred before Y, but from the point of view of another, Y may have occurred before X. Thus X may be both before and after Y. Until recently this would have been thought to be a contradiction. We should have said that there can be only one time order, and that, if the two events were not simultaneous, then either X occurred before Y, or Y occurred before X.

It is dangerous to press scientific and physical analogies too far in the religious sphere. No scientific analogy can properly express religious truth. But with this warning, and remembering that it is no more than an imperfect analogy, we may say that the contradiction between the naturalistic or scientific view of the world and the religious view is due to the fact that two frames of reference are being used. We may speak of the natural or temporal order, and the eternal order, as being the two frames of reference. The eternal order is revealed in the mystic experience of the saint. The natural order is the space-time world which is revealed to the intellect and to science. If we use the natural order as our frame of reference, then from that point of view the natural order is the sole reality, the mystic experience is subjective, and God is an illusion. This is the truth presented by atheism, skepticism, and naturalism. But if we use the frame of reference of the eternal order, then from that point of view God and the eternal order is the sole reality, and the world and the natural order are illusion. Looked at from outside itself, the mystic moment is a moment in time. But looked at from within itself, it is the whole of eternity. That God is an illusion is the standpoint of naturalism. That the world is an illusion is the standpoint of the eternal. This latter view finds actual expression in the Hindu doctrine of *maya,* and, in a less fully developed form, in all those

philosophies, such as those of Plato, Spinoza, the German idealists, and Bradley, who hold that the space-time world is "appearance," or is not "the true reality," or is "half real," or has a low
"degree of reality."

It will be observed that this view conforms to the great insight
of Kant that the solution of the religious problem cannot be a
compromise, but that scientific naturalism must be one hundred
per cent true and religion one hundred per cent true. Naturalism
is the sole truth about the natural order, and religion is the sole
truth about the eternal order. Neither order interferes with the
other. But the two orders may be said to intersect in the mystic
experience which is both eternal—from its own standpoint—and
a moment in time—from the standpoint of time. Man, as Kant
said, is an inhabitant of both worlds (orders). Kant's only mistake was his failure to recognize that man can have direct experience of the eternal order in the mystical vision.

If the solution of the religious problem here suggested is
accepted, there are still a number of questions which press on us
ordinary men who are not among the company of the recognized
mystics. Where, it may be asked, does all this leave us? It would
seem that the true religious vision is only possible to a few
extraordinary men. For the great mystic is rarer even than the
great poet. What then can religion mean to us? Are we not, on
the account here given, wholly cut off from it? And even though
we may believe that it exists, will it not be for us only a traveller's
tale, something which we cannot ourselves experience or know?
If so, it can mean nothing to us in our practical lives and we
might as well decide to ignore it.

The answer is that it is a mistake to suppose that there is a
sharp line to be drawn between the mystic and the non-mystic.
We easily recognize that there is no sharp line between the poet
and the non-poet. We are all poets in greater degree or less. This
is proved by the fact that when the great poet speaks our spirits
echo to his utterance and his vision becomes ours. We have that
vision in ourselves, but he evokes it. If it were not so, if we were
not ourselves inarticulate poets, his words would be nonsense

syllables to us and we should listen uncomprehendingly to them.

Something of the same sort is true of mysticism. All men, or at least all sensitive men, are mystics in some degree. There is a mystical side of human nature just as there is a rational side. I do not mean merely that we are potential mystics in the sense that we theoretically could, by living a life which is a practical impossibility for most of us, achieve the mystic consciousness. That would indeed be next to useless. I mean that we have the mystic consciousness now, although in most of us it shines only dimly. This is proved by the fact that, as with poetry, the utterances of the saint or the mystic call up a response in us, however faint it may be. Something in us answers back to his words, as also something answers back to the words of the poet. Why has the phrase of Plotinus, "a flight of the alone to the Alone," become famous and echoed down the ages? Why has it fascinated generations of men? It is not mere nonsense to men who, though they do not claim ever to have had anything which they would call a recognizable "mystical experience," yet possess spiritually sensitive minds. It must be that it stirs in them some depth of the waters of the soul which is ordinarily hidden, and which, by these words, is, if but for an instant, drawn up to, or near, the surface. Deep down in us, far below the threshold of our ordinary consciousness, there lies that same intuitive non-discriminating mentality which in the great mystic has come to the surface of his mind and exists in the full light of conscious recognition.

And it is reasonable to hold that when ordinary men have what they call "religious feelings" or "religious experiences" of any kind, whether with the conscious thought of God in their minds or without it, whether in prayer, in church, or amid scenes of nature, the wonder, the awe, the sublimity of the mountains, the sunsets, or the seas, such religious feelings, vague, unformed, unclear, hardly expressible, dim, misty, inarticulate, are a stirring of the depths of the mystic vision which, if only we could drag it up into the clear light of our surface consciousness, would *be* the full-fledged ecstatic vision of the great mystic. It is an ancient insight that at least some "feelings" are unformed and inchoate cognitions. And this is the justification of the religious feelings of common men. They are not sentimental and subjective emotions. They are faint mystic experiences. They are a dim vision of the eternal, appearing in the guise of feelings, or even emotions, because they are dim and vague.

It is here that the myths of the different religions have their function and justification. No doubt, taken literally, they are false. But whether the worshipper takes them literally or recognizes them as the myths they are, they perform the function of evoking within him those religious feelings which are in fact a far-off view of the divine. A man may feel in his heart or say with his lips that God is a God of love, and may pray to that God. It does not matter whether he simple-mindedly supposes that there is, somewhere unseen all about him, listening to his words, a great benevolent ghost who regards him with the human emotion which is called love, or whether on the contrary he knows that his language and his thoughts are symbolic expressions not to be taken literally; the inward effect in him, the evocation of the eternal, may in either case be the same.

This is the justification of the myths and images, and therefore of the creeds and doctrines, of the great religions of the world. No doubt they tend to degenerate on the one side into superstitions, on the other into mere intellectual abstractions spiritually dead and powerless. No doubt they may in this way become fetters on men's minds and even sources of intellectual and spiritual disorders. They become even shams and hypocrisies. It is then that the skeptics turn on them and rend them, and in this way the skeptic too performs a function which has value in the spiritual life, a spiritual purging. But basically most men will always require myths and images to evoke in them the divine vision. And when one set of symbols has degenerated into mere abstractions or debasing superstitions, another set arises. Even the great mystics who, one might suppose, would have no need of any mere metaphorical representatives of the eternal, since they have the eternal itself, yet for the most part use the symbols of the religion in which they were born and so attach themselves to this religion or that. It is in this way that what one mystic says seems to contradict what another says. For they use different symbols for the same reality.

A man may attach himself to any church, or to none. He may be disgusted with the superstitions into which institutional religions degenerate, and with the shams and hypocrisies which they engender. Or he may have seen the literal falsity of their creeds, and because he has been taught to take them literally and thinks there is no other way, because he fails to see their symbolic truth and function, he rests in a mere negation. He may then call himself an agnostic or atheist. But it does not follow that he is irreligious, even though he may profess to be. His religion may subsist in the form of a sort of unclothed religious feeling, unclothed with any symbols at all, inarticulate, formless. Each man, in an institutional religion or out of it, must find his own way. And it is not justifiable for those who find it in one way to condemn those who find it in another.

And if the theory of religion which I have outlined is accepted, it should at least cause those of us who cannot find a place within any institutional religion to understand the religious side of human nature, both that of themselves and of others, and the function and justification of religious creeds for those who can still hold them, creeds to which simple-minded men have clung, and which they, the more sophisticated ones, have perhaps too hastily condemned.[17]

[17] The view of religion which is baldly sketched in this chapter is more fully worked out in the writer's book, *Time and Eternity*.

11

THE PROBLEM OF MORALS

THE SECOND GREAT PROBLEM WHICH THE RISE OF SCIENTIFIC naturalism has created for the modern mind concerns the foundations of morality. The old religious foundations have largely crumbled away, and it may well be thought that the edifice built upon them by generations of men is in danger of collapse. A total collapse of moral behavior is, as I pointed out before, very unlikely. For a society in which this occurred could not survive. Nevertheless the danger to moral standards inherent in the virtual disappearance of their old religious foundations is not illusory.

I shall first discuss the problem of free will, for it is certain that if there is no free will there can be no morality. Morality is concerned with what men ought and ought not to do. But if a man has no freedom to choose what he will do, if whatever he does is done under compulsion, then it does not make sense to tell him that he ought not to have done what he did and that he ought to do something different. All moral precepts would in such case be meaningless. Also if he acts always under compulsion, how can he be held morally responsible for his actions? How can he, for example, be punished for what he could not help doing?

It is to be observed that those learned professors of philosophy or psychology who deny the existence of free will do so only in

248

their professional moments and in their studies and lecture rooms. For when it comes to doing anything practical, even of the most trivial kind, they invariably behave as if they and others were free. They inquire from you at dinner whether you will choose this dish or that dish. They will ask a child why he told a lie, and will punish him for not having chosen the way of truthfulness. All of which is inconsistent with a disbelief in free will. This should cause us to suspect that the problem is not a real one; and this, I believe, is the case. The dispute is merely verbal, and is due to nothing but a confusion about the meanings of words. It is what is now fashionably called a semantic problem.

How does a verbal dispute arise? Let us consider a case which, although it is absurd in the sense that no one would ever make the mistake which is involved in it, yet illustrates the principle which we shall have to use in the solution of the problem. Suppose that someone believed that the word "man" means a certain sort of five-legged animal; in short that "five-legged animal" is the correct *definition* of man. He might then look around the world, and rightly observing that there are no five-legged animals in it, he might proceed to deny the existence of men. This preposterous conclusion would have been reached because he was using an incorrect definition of "man." All you would have to do to show him his mistake would be to give him the correct definition; or at least to show him that his definition was wrong. Both the problem and its solution would, of course, be entirely verbal. The problem of free will, and its solution, I shall maintain, is verbal in exactly the same way. The problem has been created by the fact that learned men, especially philosophers, have assumed an incorrect definition of free will, and then finding that there is nothing in the world which answers to their definition, have denied its existence. As far as logic is concerned, their conclusion is just as absurd as that of the man who denies the existence of men. The only difference is that the mistake in the latter case is obvious and crude, while the mistake which the deniers of free will have made is rather subtle and difficult to detect.

Throughout the modern period, until quite recently, it was

assumed, both by the philosophers who denied free will and by those who defended it, that *determinism is inconsistent with free will*. If a man's actions were wholly determined by chains of causes stretching back into the remote past, so that they could be predicted beforehand by a mind which knew all the causes, it was assumed that they could not in that case be free. This implies that a certain definition of actions done from free will was assumed, namely that they are actions *not* wholly determined by causes or predictable beforehand. Let us shorten this by saying that free will was defined as meaning indeterminism. This is the incorrect definition which has led to the denial of free will. As soon as we see what the true definition is we shall find that the question whether the world is deterministic, as Newtonian science implied, or in a measure indeterministic, as current physics teaches, is wholly irrelevant to the problem.

Of course there is a sense in which one can define a word arbitrarily in any way one pleases. But a definition may nevertheless be called correct or incorrect. It is correct if it accords with a *common usage* of the word defined. It is incorrect if it does not. And if you give an incorrect definition, absurd and untrue results are likely to follow. For instance, there is nothing to prevent you from arbitrarily defining a man as a five-legged animal, but this is incorrect in the sense that it does not accord with the ordinary meaning of the word. Also it has the absurd result of leading to a denial of the existence of men. This shows that *common usage is the criterion for deciding whether a definition is correct or not*. And this is the principle which I shall apply to free will. I shall show that indeterminism is not what is meant by the phrase "free will" *as it is commonly used*. And I shall attempt to discover the correct definition by inquiring how the phrase is used in ordinary conversation.

Here are a few samples of how the phrase might be used in ordinary conversation. It will be noticed that they include cases in which the question whether a man acted with free will is asked in order to determine whether he was morally and legally responsible for his acts.

Jones I once went without food for a week.
Smith Did you do that of your own free will?
Jones No. I did it because I was lost in a desert and could find no food.

But suppose that the man who had fasted was Mahatma Gandhi. The conversation might then have gone:

Gandhi I once fasted for a week.
Smith Did you do that of your own free will?
Gandhi Yes. I did it because I wanted to compel the British Government to give India its independence.

Take another case. Suppose that I had stolen some bread, but that I was as truthful as George Washington. Then, if I were charged with the crime in court, some exchange of the following sort might take place:

Judge Did you steal the bread of your own free will?
Stace Yes. I stole it because I was hungry.

Or in different circumstances the conversation might run:

Judge Did you steal of your own free will?
Stace No. I stole because my employer threatened to beat me if I did not.

At a recent murder trial in Trenton some of the accused had signed confessions, but afterwards asserted that they had done so under police duress. The following exchange might have occurred:

Judge Did you sign this confession of your own free will?
Prisoner No. I signed it because the police beat me up.

Now suppose that a philosopher had been a member of the jury. We could imagine this conversation taking place in the jury room.

Foreman of the Jury The prisoner says he signed the confession because he was beaten, and not of his own free will.

Philosopher   This is quite irrelevant to the case. There is no such thing as free will.

Foreman   Do you mean to say that it makes no difference whether he signed because his conscience made him want to tell the truth or because he was beaten?

Philosopher   None at all. Whether he was caused to sign by a beating or by some desire of his own—the desire to tell the truth, for example—in either case his signing was causally determined, and therefore in neither case did he act of his own free will. Since there is no such thing as free will, the question whether he signed of his own free will ought not to be discussed by us.

The foreman and the rest of the jury would rightly conclude that the philosopher must be making some mistake. What sort of a mistake could it be? There is only one possible answer. The philosopher must be using the phrase "free will" in some peculiar way of his own which is not the way in which men usually use it when they wish to determine a question of moral responsibility. That is, he must be using an incorrect definition of it as implying action not determined by causes.

Suppose a man left his office at noon, and were questioned about it. Then we might hear this:

Jones   Did you go out of your own free will?
Smith   Yes. I went out to get my lunch.

But we might hear:

Jones   Did you leave your office of your own free will?
Smith   No. I was forcibly removed by the police.

We have now collected a number of cases of actions which, in the ordinary usage of the English language, would be called cases in which people have acted of their own free will. We should also say in all these cases that they *chose* to act as they did. We should also say that they could have acted otherwise, if they had chosen. For instance, Mahatma Gandhi was not compelled to fast; he chose to do so. He could have eaten if he had wanted to.

When Smith went out to get his lunch, he chose to do so. He could have stayed and done some more work, if he had wanted to. We have also collected a number of cases of the opposite kind. They are cases in which men were not able to exercise their free will. They had no choice. They were compelled to do as they did. The man in the desert did not fast of his own free will. He had no choice in the matter. He was compelled to fast because there was nothing for him to eat. And so with the other cases. It ought to be quite easy, by an inspection of these cases, to tell what we ordinarily mean when we say that a man did or did not exercise free will. We ought therefore to be able to extract from them the proper definition of the term. Let us put the cases in a table:

Free Acts	*Unfree Acts*
Gandhi fasting because he wanted to free India.	The man fasting in the desert because there was no food.
Stealing bread because one is hungry.	Stealing because one's employer threatened to beat one.
Signing a confession because one wanted to tell the truth.	Signing because the police beat one.
Leaving the office because one wanted one's lunch.	Leaving because forcibly removed.

It is obvious that to find the correct definition of free acts we must discover what characteristic is common to all the acts in the left-hand column, and is, at the same time, absent from all the acts in the right-hand column. This characteristic which all free acts have, and which no unfree acts have, will be the defining characteristic of free will.

Is being uncaused, or not being determined by causes, the characteristic of which we are in search? It cannot be, because although it is true that all the acts in the right-hand column have causes, such as the beating by the police or the absence of food in the desert, so also do the acts in the left-hand column. Mr. Gandhi's fasting was caused by his desire to free India, the man leaving his office by his hunger, and so on. Moreover there is no reason to doubt that these causes of the free acts were in turn caused by prior conditions, and that these were again the results of causes, and so on back indefinitely into the past. Any physiologist can tell us the causes of hunger. What caused Mr. Gandhi's tremendously powerful desire to free India is no doubt more difficult to discover. But it must have had causes. Some of them may have lain in peculiarities of his glands or brain, others in his past experiences, others in his heredity, others in his education. Defenders of free will have usually tended to deny such facts. But to do so is plainly a case of special pleading, which is unsupported by any scrap of evidence. The only reasonable view is that all human actions, both those which are freely done and those which are not, are either wholly determined by causes, or at least as much determined as other events in nature. It may be true, as the physicists tell us, that nature is not as deterministic as was once thought. But whatever degree of determinism prevails in the world, human actions appear to be as much determined as anything else. And if this is so, it cannot be the case that what distinguishes actions freely chosen from those which are not free is that the latter are determined by causes while the former are not. Therefore, being uncaused or being undetermined by causes, must be an incorrect definition of free will.

What, then, is the difference between acts which are freely done and those which are not? What is the characteristic which is present to all the acts in the left-hand column and absent from all those in the right-hand column? Is it not obvious that, although both sets of actions have causes, the causes of those in the left-hand column are *of a different kind* from the causes of those in the right-hand column? The free acts are all caused by desires, or motives, or by some sort of internal psychological states of the agent's mind. The unfree acts, on the other hand, are all caused by physical forces or physical conditions, outside the agent. Police arrest means physical force exerted from the outside; the absence of food in the desert is a physical condition of the outside world. We may therefore frame the following rough definitions. *Acts*

freely done are those whose immediate causes are psychological
states in the agent. Acts not freely done are those whose immediate
causes are states of affairs external to the agent.

It is plain that if we define free will in this way, then free will
certainly exists, and the philosopher's denial of its existence is
seen to be what it is—nonsense. For it is obvious that all those
actions of men which we should ordinarily attribute to the exercise of their free will, or of which we should say that they freely
chose to do them, are in fact actions which have been caused by
their own desires, wishes, thoughts, emotions, impulses, or other
psychological states.

In applying our definition we shall find that it usually works
well, but that there are some puzzling cases which it does not
seem exactly to fit. These puzzles can always be solved by paying
careful attention to the ways in which words are used, and remembering that they are not always used consistently. I have
space for only one example. Suppose that a thug threatens to
shoot you unless you give him your wallet, and suppose that you
do so. Do you, in giving him your wallet, do so of your own free
will or not? If we apply our definition, we find that you acted
freely, since the immediate cause of the action was not an actual
outside force but the fear of death, which is a psychological cause.
Most people, however, would say that you did not act of your own
free will but under compulsion. Does this show that our definition is wrong? I do not think so. Aristotle, who gave a solution
of the problem of free will substantially the same as ours (though
he did not use the term "free will") admitted that there are what
he called "mixed" or borderline cases in which it is difficult to
know whether we ought to call the acts free or compelled. In the
case under discussion, though no actual force was used, the gun
at your forehead so nearly approximated to actual force that we
tend to say the case was one of compulsion. It is a borderline case.

Here is what may seem like another kind of puzzle. According
to our view an action may be free though it could have been
predicted beforehand with certainty. But suppose you told a lie,
and it was certain beforehand that you would tell it. How could

one then say, "You could have told the truth"? The answer is that
it is perfectly true that you could have told the truth *if* you had
wanted to. In fact you would have done so, for in that case the
causes producing your action, namely your desires, would have
been different, and would therefore have produced different
effects. It is a delusion that predictability and free will are incompatible. This agrees with common sense. For if, knowing your
character, I predict that you will act honorably, no one would say
when you do act honorably, that this shows you did not do so
of your own free will.

Since free will is a condition of moral responsibility, we must
be sure that our theory of free will gives a sufficient basis for it.
To be held morally responsible for one's actions means that one
may be justly punished or rewarded, blamed or praised, for them.
But it is not just to punish a man for what he cannot help doing.
How can it be just to punish him for an action which it was certain
beforehand that he would do? We have not attempted to decide
whether, as a matter of fact, all events, including human actions,
are completely determined. For that question is irrelevant to the
problem of free will. But if we assume for the purposes of argument that complete determinism is true, but that we are nevertheless free, it may then be asked whether such a deterministic free
will is compatible with moral responsibility. For it may seem
unjust to punish a man for an action which it could have been
predicted with certainty beforehand that he would do.

But that determinism is incompatible with moral responsibility
is as much a delusion as that it is incompatible with free will. You
do not excuse a man for doing a wrong act because, knowing his
character, you felt certain beforehand that he would do it. Nor do
you deprive a man of a reward or prize because, knowing his
goodness or his capabilities, you felt certain beforehand that he
would win it.

Volumes have been written on the justification of punishment.
But so far as it affects the question of free will, the essential principles involved are quite simple. The punishment of a man for
doing a wrong act is justified, either on the ground that it will

correct his own character, or that it will deter other people from doing similar acts. The instrument of punishment has been in the past, and no doubt still is, often unwisely used; so that it may often have done more harm than good. But that is not relevant to our present problem. Punishment, if and when it is justified, is justified only on one or both of the grounds just mentioned. The question then is how, if we assume determinism, punishment can correct character or deter people from evil actions.

Suppose that your child develops a habit of telling lies. You give him a mild beating. Why? Because you believe that his personality is such that the usual motives for telling the truth do not cause him to do so. You therefore supply the missing cause, or motive, in the shape of pain and the fear of future pain if he repeats his untruthful behavior. And you hope that a few treatments of this kind will condition him to the habit of truth-telling, so that he will come to tell the truth without the infliction of pain. You assume that his actions are determined by causes, but that the usual causes of truth-telling do not in him produce their usual effects. You therefore supply him with an artificially injected motive, pain and fear, which you think will in the future cause him to speak truthfully.

The principle is exactly the same where you hope, by punishing one man, to deter others from wrong actions. You believe that the fear of punishment will cause those who might otherwise do evil to do well.

We act on the same principle with non-human, and even with inanimate, things, if they do not behave in the way we think they ought to behave. The rose bushes in the garden produce only small and poor blooms, whereas we want large and rich ones. We supply a cause which will produce large blooms, namely fertilizer. Our automobile does not go properly. We supply a cause which will make it go better, namely oil in the works. The punishment for the man, the fertilizer for the plant, and the oil for the car, are all justified by the same principle and in the same way. The only difference is that different kinds of things require different kinds of causes to make them do what they should. Pain may be the appropriate remedy to apply, in certain cases, to human beings, and oil to the machine. It is, of course, of no use to inject motor oil into the boy or to beat the machine.

Thus we see that moral responsibility is not only consistent with determinism, but requires it. The assumption on which punishment is based is that human behavior is causally determined. If pain could not be a cause of truth-telling there would be no justification at all for punishing lies. If human actions and volitions were uncaused, it would be useless either to punish or reward, or indeed to do anything else to correct people's bad behavior. For nothing that you could do would in any way influence them. Thus moral responsibility would entirely disappear. If there were no determinism of human beings at all, their actions would be completely unpredictable and capricious, and therefore irresponsible. And this is in itself a strong argument against the common view of philosophers that free will means being undetermined by causes.

We may now turn to the central question of the foundations of morality. In earlier ages morality was seen as grounded in religion. This view appeared historically, of course, in a variety of different forms according to what men's religious beliefs were, and according to their comparative naïveté or sophistication. Its most naïve form is the belief that what is right or wrong is simply determined by the will of God, God being conceived anthropomorphically as a great mind or consciousness which created and governs the world. And perhaps its most sophisticated form is found in the more abstruse and recondite systems of absolute idealism. The popular concept of God is in them replaced by the metaphysical Absolute. But this Absolute is, like God, the source of moral and other values. The one thing common to all forms of a religious basis of morals is the belief that the distinction between moral good and evil is in some way rooted in the concept of the world as a moral order.

The great advantage of such a religious view is that morals are given a firm foundation in the unchanging nature of the world, and not a shaky foundation in the shifting quicksands of human nature. Moral values and laws are necessarily objective in the sense in which I have used that word in this book. A value, on our definition, is objective if it is independent of any human ideas, feelings, or opinions. The will of God is independent of any human psychology. So is the world-purpose, if we assume that such a purpose exists. So also is the philosopher's Absolute. And if moral values are founded in any of these, they are objective.

Nor will it, on any such view, make sense to talk of the relativity of morals. There will be one set of moral values and standards valid for all men, not varying from age to age or from culture to culture. For those values and standards proceed from one unchanging God, or from one constant world-purpose, or from one eternal Absolute. Different ages, different cultures, may indeed have different opinions about what things are good and bad, as they may have different opinions about anything else. There will in this sense be a relativity of morals. But variations of moral opinion will be explained by any religiously or metaphysically based ethical philosophy in the same way as variations of opinion on any other subject. There can be only one truth about what is good or evil, just as there can be only one truth about the shape of the earth at a particular time, though opinions can vary on both subjects.

We have seen how the old views changed under the impact of the ever-growing dominance of the scientific view of the world. Objectivism in morals has given way to subjectivism. The beliefs in God, or in a cosmic purpose, though they may linger on in the minds of the majority, or on their lips, as mental or verbal habits, have been drained of effective meaning. The metaphysical Absolute—that thin abstraction substituted for God by a few intellectuals—never had any hold on men's minds. Therefore it became no longer possible to define morality in terms of divine or cosmic purposes. But since it has to be defined in terms of some purpose, there remained no alternative but to believe that what is good is what serves human purposes, and that what is bad is what obstructs them, and that good and evil have no other nature or meaning. This is at once to jump from objectivism to subjectivism, from the belief that the world is a moral order to the belief that it is not. This was the step which the modern mind took.

But if morals are subjective, are they not then necessarily relative? The apparent necessity of the transition from subjectivism to relativism lies in the consideration that all human beings do not have the same purposes; that purposes differ from person to person, or from social group to social group. If we define good as that which pleases men, or serves their purposes, or as that to which they have some subjective attitude of liking or approval, it would seem to follow of necessity that the same thing or action may be good to one person and bad to another, according to their respective likings or attitudes. And this is to say, not merely that men's opinions about right and wrong will differ—which is true on any view—but that what is actually right for one person will be actually wrong for another, that slavery was right in the ancient world, because the ancients approved it, though it is doubtless wrong for us because we disapprove it.

The collapse of moral theory, though perhaps not of moral practice, seems to follow. Does it not follow that although men may *think* some things good and others bad, there is in fact no objective distinction between good and evil at all? Moreover there is no room left, on such a theory, for progress in moral ideals. It is commonly supposed that there can be, indeed that there has been, such progress. Surely we have progressed in our moral ideals somewhat since the age of the cave man? We think that Confucius had better and higher moral ideas than those of some uncivilized and savage tribe. Or we think that Jesus effected an improvement in moral ideals. There was a time when "an eye for an eye" was the standard. Jesus preached unlimited forgiveness and love of one's neighbor. Even those who reject all supernaturalist conceptions of Jesus admit that this was a great moral advance. But belief in ethical relativity makes nonsense of all this. We cannot on such a basis say that one set of moral ideas is better than another, but only that they are different. For in a society which approved of an eye for an eye that standard was not merely thought right, it was right. It was just as right, therefore, as the Christian standard is among Christian peoples. Therefore Jesus, if he supposed that he was introducing *better* moral ideas, was deluded. He was in fact wasting his time. For he was not changing a worse into a better. He was merely preaching a different moral code which was no improvement on the old one. He was merely substituting Tweedledum for Tweedledee. Also, if we should now come to approve of the international morals, or immorals, of Hitler, Mussolini, or Stalin, or to approve of the reintroduction of the law of the jungle into human affairs, this would not be a deterioration, for these things would then become right and good. A reversion to slavery, witch-burning, or human sacrifice, would become right and proper if only we should all come to approve of them again.

These are the consequences of giving up our belief in a religious foundation of morals. Has the modern mind made any mistake? Can we either revert to a religious foundation for our moral ideals or, in the alternative, discover a firm secular foundation which will not yield the disastrous results of our present subjectivism and relativism?

The view which I shall attempt to maintain is that morality has in fact a secular basis which can be made reasonably solid, and which does not result in a chaotic relativism, i.e., that an ethics which is universal for human kind can be reached within the framework of a purely naturalistic and non-religious philosophy; but that nevertheless moral aspirations and ideals have a deeper foundation in, and ultimately flow from, religion. We can assume that moral values are subjective and the world not a moral order and still accept a universally valid ethics. But actually moral values are objective and the world is a moral order, so that the older view of morality as based in religion gives a truer and profounder understanding both of morals and of the world than does the merely naturalistic view. I believe that Bergson was right in suggesting that morality has two sources. One of these is the social pressure of purely utilitarian considerations. This source is, of course, secular and naturalistic. The other source is in mysticism, which is, for us, identical with religion. The moral aims which flow from these two sources fit into one another, harmonize and fuse together in human society, so that in this fusion they become indistinguishable and appear as a single homogeneous set of ideal ends, a single morality.

I will begin with the secular source of morals. We may agree that it is utility or, in other words, human happiness. I shall assume, for the sake of argument, a wholly naturalistic view of the world, according to which morals are entirely dependent on human purposes and have no cosmic significance whatever. I shall attempt to show that even if we dismiss religion as nothing but a set of falsehoods without even any symbolic truth, yet, even so, *the modern mind has made a mistake in thinking that all morals must be relative.*

The thinking of the modern world may be represented as having taken three steps. First, it accepted the naturalistic view of the world. Second, it deduced subjectivism from naturalism. For it argued that moral values must serve some purpose, and if there is no divine or cosmic purpose, the only remaining alternative is that their function is to serve human purposes, which constitute therefore their only foundation. And this view is, by definition, subjectivism. It took the third step when it deduced relativism from subjectivism, saying that, if morals are dependent on human purposes, they will be different for different men or different groups of men, because human purposes differ from man to man or from group to group. I shall not challenge the first two steps of the argument, but I shall challenge the third. I shall assume that morals are subjective—which they must be if there is no religious or cosmic basis for them—and that the world is not a moral order. But I shall maintain that relativism does not follow from subjectivism, and that the modern mind has made a radical error in supposing that it does. I shall say that, even if we place morality on a purely secular basis, there is yet a morality which is true for all men and not merely binding on this or that social group. Moreover, this secular morality will include not only the lower ranges of morality, the minimum of moral behavior required for survival, but even that universal love and compassion which are also commanded by the religious vision. For the two sources of morality do not conflict. They dovetail together, and fuse into one.

The essential reason for the transition which the modern mind has made from subjectivism to relativism lies in the proposition that the purposes of men are all different from one another. For it follows from this that there can be no common human morality. In one form or another the basic argument for moral relativity always founds itself on this one alleged fact of human nature, the variety of human purposes, wishes, needs, appetites, and aversions.

Now it is obvious at a glance that any such proposition as "human beings have different purposes" is utterly vague. Does it mean that no two human beings ever lived who shared a single purpose in common? If so, it is plainly false. Two or more men may agree to rob a bank. It is clear that, although there are certainly differences of purpose among men, the extent of these differences ought to be investigated if we are to have anything like an accurate picture of the human situation. Certainly groups of men may share a common purpose. And can we deny, without any investigation at all, that there may be purposes which all men share and which are common to the human race? Apparently the group-relativists of our own day must at least suppose that there are purposes which are in some sense common to very large social groups, to nations, and perhaps to whole cultures and civilizations. For they tell us that there are moral rules which are binding within the social group. This can only be true if in some sense the social group is united in a common purpose—perhaps in the sense that a great majority of its members share the purpose, though there may be a few who do not. But if a whole culture may share some purposes, why is it impossible that the whole human race may share some purposes?

What is the importance of this question? It lies in the fact that any purpose which is common to a number of men, whether the number is small or large, will give rise to rules of conduct which all those men must obey if they are to achieve their purpose. For instance, if a band of men agree to rob a bank, this will impose on them all certain rules. For example, none of them must tell the police of their design. We should not call this a moral rule— though the robbers might—but it is a rule of conduct. And it is obligatory on all the members of the group if they are to succeed in their purpose. In the same way, if there are any purposes which are common to all humanity, this fact will give rise to rules of conduct—not necessarily moral rules—which all men ought to obey if they are to achieve those purposes. I believe that there are at least three such common human purposes which are the sources of universal rules of conduct. They are:

(1) *Self-preservation:* This is the source of a number of universal rules of conduct which may be called *rules of prudence or safety*.

(2) *Physical Health:* This common human purpose gives rise to a vast body of rules, which are the same for all men, under such heads as sanitation and diet, and which also includes the rules of medical science. These may be called *medical rules*.

(3) *Happiness:* This may also be called by such names as welfare, richness of living, self-realization, abundance of life, power, health of the soul, etc. The rules which are founded in it are called *moral rules*.

These three ends constitute a hierarchy in the sense that the second includes and advances beyond the first, while the third includes and goes beyond the second. The rules of conduct to which all of them give rise are universal and common to all men, and in no way relative to any age, culture, or civilization. The reason for this is the same in each of the three cases, namely, that they are common human ends which require common means, that is, common modes of conduct to achieve them.

To begin with self-preservation. All men desire their self-preservation in the sense that each desires at least his own. I am not committing the fallacy of supposing that all men desire self-preservation in the sense that each desires the preservation of the lives of all the others. As a matter of fact men do commonly desire the continued existence of at least some other persons, for instance, their children and other people in the society immediately surrounding them. But this is not necessary for my argument. The same remarks apply to the other two common ends.

Of course there are occasional cases of men who do not desire to preserve their own lives. Suicides are the obvious example. But it is true that all men want to preserve their own lives in the same rough or general sense in which it is true that all men have two legs, two eyes, etc. There may be men born without any legs. But all normal men have two legs. And all normal men normally, that is throughout most of their lives, wish to continue in existence.

This fact is the foundation of many rules of conduct. Here are a few:

Do not jump off the top of the Empire State Building.
Do not cross the street without looking.
Do not eat poison.

These are no doubt negative rules. Positive ones would be:

Eat enough food to keep you alive.
Keep on breathing.
Put out a fire which starts in your house.

All this seems very trivial. But the more obvious it is the better it supports my argument. There are two points to be made. First, it cannot be denied that these are genuine rules of conduct, of things which we ought and ought not to do. We should not call them moral rules. They are rules of prudence or safety. Secondly, they are universal in their scope. They apply to all men—except suicides. It would be absurd to say that they are relative to an age, a social group, or a culture. It would be absurd to say that, although it is bad for an American to jump off the Empire State Building, it is quite all right for a Frenchman to do so. It is conceivable—though not at all likely—that there might be a whole tribe or other social group which rejected one or other of them. They might have some different code of safety, and in that sense codes of safety might be called relative to different social groups. But if any man, or group of men, or even all men, should be mad enough to think they could safely jump off the Empire State Building, they would be mistaken. These rules are binding upon all normal men everywhere, and in all ages and societies, because they are necessarily corollaries of a common human purpose, self-preservation.

The next common human end is physical health. All normal men desire their own health—not necessarily that of other men. There may be men, for all I know, who want to have cancer. But they are very few. Notice that this end includes and transcends the end of self-preservation. He who wishes to keep in good health must at least first of all wish to retain bare existence. But he also wants something more. He wants not only bare existence, but a happy life so far as the mere physical condition of his body will ensure it. For this is the meaning of physical health. What is health, and what is disease? Health is that condition of the body which ensures continuance in existence as long as possible and ensures during such continuance a happy and pleasant life so far as that depends on nothing but the condition of the body. Disease is any condition of the body which leads to death or to pain, misery, discomfort, and so on. (This, of course, is not meant to include as disease a painful condition of the body which a surgeon may have to induce temporarily in order to achieve greater health in the end.)

If we admit that, in the sense explained, all men desire their own health—apart from abnormal cases—this, because it is a common human purpose, will give rise to many rules of conduct which will be applicable to human beings generally. Here are a few:

Do not overeat or overdrink.
Take a balanced diet.
Take enough exercise and fresh air.
Be clean.
Take proper sanitary measures for the disposal of sewage.

These are rules of conduct. We should not ordinarily call them moral rules—perhaps dietetic, sanitary, hygienic rules, and so on. We notice also that, except in regard to a point shortly to be mentioned, they are none of them relative. They are rules which all men, in any age or culture, ought to follow if they wish to be healthy. No one would say that overeating and overdrinking are bad for the health of Americans, but may be good for the health of Chinese. It may be the case, as with the rules of safety, that there may be disagreements about them in different cultures, and in that sense relativity. I believe that the ancient Egyptians thought that the urine of a cow applied to the eyes would cure blindness. They had a different medical rule from ours. But their rule was mistaken.

Yet we should notice that, in spite of these considerations, there is a slight element of genuine relativity about some of these rules. For they contain words like "enough" and "too much." Even "Be clean" must, I suppose, be interpreted to mean "Be clean enough." For no one would advise a man to spend ten hours a day brushing his teeth. And it is at this point that an element of relativity seems to enter the picture. For "enough" and "too much" are vague words. What is enough for one person may be too much for another. Some people, for maximum physical health, require more food, some less; some more exercise, some less; and so on. This means that such and such an amount of food may be "good" for me, but "bad" for you. This is a sort of relativity. The doctor will take account of individual differences of constitution. He may order more for one person, less for another. But the rule, "Don't overeat," will still be universal and and non-relative. The *general* rule is universal and non-relative, but because it is vague and imprecise, it has to be applied differently in different cases when it comes down to details. And this may be called relativity, not merely of opinion, but of the rule itself. This is very instructive because we shall find exactly the same situation, due to the same sort of causes, in the sphere of morality.

We should also notice that not only more or less common-sense rules of diet and sanitation flow from the common purpose of health, but the whole of the laws of medical science including those which are unknown to laymen; and that these medical rules are universal and non-relative for the same reason as the others. If you have cancer, tuberculosis, or Bright's disease, then you should take such and such treatments. These are rules of conduct. You may say that they are rules for the doctor to follow, not for you. But that is chiefly because you do not know the rules yourself and have to get the doctor to apply them to you. These rules are not relative to cultures. If the cure for appendicitis is to cut out the appendix, this will be just as true for a Hottentot as for an Englishman. Of course there will be different opinions in different ages and countries about the best cures. There may even be differences between doctors in the same country at the same time. This is like the differences of opinion about moral questions.

Moreover there is, in matters of detail, an area of relativity here. Some people may require more of a drug, some less. In particular cases a drug which generally does good may do harm. There are people who cannot take penicillin or quinine without unpleasant results. The doctor knows the general rules, but will apply them somewhat differently according to individual needs. Only the general rules are universal and non-relative.

We come finally to moral rules. These depend on the common end of happiness. This is at least common in the sense that each man desires his own happiness, whether he also desires that of other people or not. Philosophers have become very impatient with the word "happiness," because they say that no one knows what it means. This is true in one sense, false in another. There are two quite different levels of "knowing what a word means." One is to know the definition of it, and this may be called scientific or philosophical knowing. The other consists in being able to recognize the object or situation for which the word stands, so that you know when to apply it and when not to apply it, and do not make mistakes in this. This does not usually require any knowledge of definitions and may be called common-sense knowing. For instance, not being a biologist, I do not know the biological definition of a horse. In fact I do not know any definition, not even that which a farmer or owner of horses might give, if they could give any definition at all. In this sense it may be said that I do not know the meaning of the word "horse." But I know how to apply the word. I use it rightly. I apply it only to horses, never to elephants. In this common-sense way I know the meaning of the word.

Do we know the meaning of the word "happiness"? When the philosopher says that we do not, he means that no one has ever yet discovered exactly how to define it, though some philosophers have tried. In this he is probably right. But everyone who knows the English language has a common-sense knowledge of the meaning of the word. We can use it appropriately. We usually know when we are happy and when we are not. We know the difference between a happy marriage and an unhappy one. I therefore think that, in spite of the philosopher's objections, the word "happiness" is just as respectable as the word "horse." Hence I propose to continue using it. But if anyone prefers to speak of welfare, or the enrichment of life, he is welcome.

Every man—except perhaps a few abnormal individuals—desires at least his own happiness. It is therefore a common human end in our sense of the phrase, and must give rise to universal non-relative rules, though there may be different opinions about what these are. It may be objected that "happiness" is a blanket word which is applied to different things by different people. What makes one person happy makes another unhappy. And if so, the assertion that we all desire the *same* thing may seem to be false, or only true in a verbal sense. I will postpone this objection for later discussion.

Just as physical health includes and transcends bare self-preservation, so happiness includes and transcends physical health. It includes health, for although sick people may sometimes be happy, they would usually be happier if they were not sick. Physical health is in a general way a condition of happiness. But happiness transcends health because it involves something more. What more? Perhaps one may say that what it includes, over and above a happy condition of the body, is a happy condition of the personality, and I think that we shall have to include a man's personal relations here, for instance his relations with his wife and children and with other human beings with whom he comes in contact. Perhaps this is rather to extend the common meaning of the word "personality," but this does not seem to matter. A man's happiness at any rate will include not only bodily health, but health of personality as well as happy personal and social relations. It may also include ordinary amusements and pleasures, and the satisfactions to be derived from music, poetry, science, philosophy, if he happens to care for these things.

If happiness is allowed to be a common human end, shared by all normal men, to what rules of conduct, applicable to all normal men, will it give rise? I will mention a few:

Love your neighbor.
Get rid of hatred, malice, jealousy, envy, and so on.
Do not steal, lie, break faith, etc.

These are not rules of prudence or safety or diet. They are what are commonly called moral rules. It is much more difficult to show that all men should follow these rules if they wish to be happy than it is to show that they should follow rules of safety if they wish to preserve their lives, or medical rules if they wish to be healthy. But I believe that this is true. I believe that moral rules simply *are* rules of human happiness. And if so, they will be universal and not relative to any culture in exactly the same way, and for the same reason, as rules of safety and of health are so.

I think it is not possible to prove this—at any rate at present— in the sort of exact and rigorous way in which scientific truths are established, but that it is nevertheless supported by general human experience. And it would seem that the great moralists, such as Jesus, Buddha, and Socrates, have been the best interpreters of that experience. Perhaps more intuitively than by any conscious process of generalizing from experience they divined that obedience to such precepts is the best way of achieving happiness, best for society at large, and best for each individual.

The connection of some moral rules with happiness is more obvious than that of others. It is pretty clear that lying and stealing lead in general to unhappiness in a society, while their opposites tend to increase human welfare. It is perhaps less obvious that if you wish to be happy you should love everybody, though it seems fairly clear that a life based on malice and hatred produces misery not only in others but in the man who indulges in them.

We must not claim too much. It is possible that a dishonest man may be happy, and we have all known happy liars. Some people seem to get along pretty well even though they lead immoral lives. Perhaps what we may claim is something of this sort —that although a particular man may sometimes "get away with" a dishonest way of living, and perhaps not suffer at all, yet this is an utterly unsafe and unsound way of conducting one's life. It is certain that a general rule which prescribed all-round dishonesty and untruthfulness would be disastrous, and that a general rule which prescribes honesty and truthfulness will, if carried out, increase human happiness. After all, it is the same with rules of health, which we nevertheless recognize as universal and non-relative. You may possibly get away with bodily uncleanliness, and with unbrushed teeth, without suffering in your health. But to be cleanly is the only sound rule, and this is universally true for all men and in no way relative to any particular culture or age. Even the man who neglects it with impunity acts wrongly and ought to have obeyed it if he wished for health. And the same is true of the man who disobeys moral rules without suffering.

It was admitted that it is more difficult to show some moral rules to be rules of happiness than others. What about the rule of universal love? Is that universal and applicable to all men? It is non-relative because it is true of all men, regardless of race or period or culture, that if the rule of love were followed, if we got rid of all anger, hatred, and envy, all men would be the happier. To be for a moment Utopian, suppose that this rule were followed as between nations, that they got rid of all international grasping and selfishness, is it not obvious that this would be a far happier world? The command to love all men is held before us as a remote ideal, in the direction of which we can hope to move, although we shall never reach the end. Its non-relativity lies in the fact that it is an ideal equally for all men in the sense that the more they approximate to the moral ideal the nearer will they come to the common end of happiness which they all desire.

Let us put the matter in another way. Agricultural scientists discovered that certain kinds of chemicals increase the health and productivity of plants, while other substances destroy their health. This is not a relative truth. It is true in all ages and countries. The great moralists have made a similar discovery. It is that hatred increases human misery, and that love increases human happiness. Neither is this dependent on culture or color of skin. It is a general truth about human beings everywhere, just as the other is a general truth about plants everywhere. It is true that you can subject the proposition about fertilizers to laboratory tests in a way which can hardly be applied to the proposition about love. Yet the latter too is not without its evidence, which lies in the general experience of humanity. The world is the laboratory of the moralist.

And suppose that some social group should deny this moral truth. There may be some Melanesian tribe which believes that hatred is for them the best way to happiness. Does this prove relativity? Not at all. All it shows is that those people are making a disastrous mistake about *their own* happiness. It is true of them, as of us, that the rule of love, if followed, would lead them to a happier life. The rule of love is therefore one that they too ought to follow if they wish to achieve their own greatest happiness.

It is sometimes said that a man or group is the best, or even the only, judge of his or its own happiness. There is of course some truth in this. But it is more important to point out its element of falsehood. Men just as often make mistakes about what will lead to their own happiness as about what will conduce to their physical health. That is why we need moralists as well as doctors.

There is a point in our argument which needs clearing up. It was asserted that happiness is a common purpose shared by all normal men in the sense that each man desires his own happiness at least. But how can this give a reason for attending to the happiness of other people, and not only to his own? And this amounts to asking why he should love his neighbor. This is the crucial question for any naturalistic or secular ethics. For instance, J. S. Mill in his famous *Utilitarianism* told us that doing right consists in doing actions which produce the greatest amount of happiness. He adds: "The standard is not the agent's own happiness, but the greatest amount of happiness altogether. . . . The greatest happiness principle is the greatest happiness of mankind and of all sentient creatures." No doubt this is a perfectly correct *description* of the moral principle. To care for the happiness of others as well as my own is just what morality is. But Mill fails to give any foundation, either religious or secular, for this duty. Why a man should work for his own happiness is obvious. Selfishness is a sufficient answer. But why should he work for the happiness of others? Unless some reason can be given we have failed to discover the secular foundation of morals.

So far as I can see the only answer which the naturalist can give is that the great discovery of moral geniuses such as Christ and Buddha was precisely this: that the selfish life is not the happy life, and that the best road to one's own happiness is to forget one's happiness and work for that of others. Why this should be so it is perhaps impossible to say. It is just a fact about human nature. And probably the only reason which can be given for it is found in the famous words of John Donne: "No man is an Iland, intire of it selfe; every man is a peece of the Continent, a part of the maine; if a Clod bee washed away by the Sea, Europe is the lesse, as well as if a Promontorie were, as well as if a Mannor of thy friends or of thine owne were; any mans death diminishes me, because I am involved in Mankinde: And therefore never send to know for whom the bell tolls; It tolls for thee." It is impossible for a man to be happy while all around him are miserable, because he is "involved in mankind," and their happiness *is* his happiness. Therefore if he wishes to be happy himself, he must work for their happiness. The man who asks, "Why should I care for any happiness except my own?" wrongly supposes that he is a human atom independent of other human atoms; that he is an "island," and not part of the continent. He starts from an atomistic conception of human nature which is simply false.

It may be said that this gives the wrong reason for being good. It appeals to self-interest. I am to love others out of selfishness. And this is precisely what the good man does not do and must not do. To do this is simply to be selfish and *not* good. Thus this whole explanation of morality does violence to morality. It gives a non-moral reason for being moral.

This criticism is not wholly fair. We must distinguish between the *motive* for being good and the intellectual *reason* for being so. It is not suggested by the naturalist who gives the above account of the matter that the good man should be *motivated* by a desire for his own happiness. If he acts from that motive he will defeat himself. His motive should be pure self-disregarding love. It is of the essence of the good man's state of mind that he forgets his own happiness. But the question asked was not about motives, but about reasons. It is an intellectual question asked by the philosopher. The good man as such simply does not ask such a question at all. He does not have to be convinced by arguments, either by this or any other. And if the philosopher is also a good man, neither will he, in his capacity as a moral man, ask any such question. But although he does not, in acting, ask for a reason or argument to convince him, he may surely as a thinker be interested to discover whether any intellectually convincing argument *could* be given. And if a man does ask this legitimate question of theory, then the answer suggested by the passage from Donne is the only one that can be given on a secular or naturalistic basis.

In discussing rules of health we saw that although they are universal and non-relative, yet when we come down to their detailed application we run into an area of relativity. The physician can say, "Do not overeat." This is a universally valid rule for all men. But when we come to apply it we find that more food is necessary for the health of one man and less for that of another.

The same thing is true in moral matters. The moralist, who is the physician of the soul, can lay down general rules which are valid for all men, but their detailed application is relative to the different constitutions of different individuals. "Do unto others as you would that they should do unto you." This is universal. But its application is relative to the needs and natures of the "others." What is it that I should do to others? Not identically the same things to all, and not identically the same things as I should want done to me. I do not insist that because being a professor gives me the sort of life I want, everyone in the world should be a professor. I do not insist that because X likes chocolate I should force chocolate on Y who hates it. "Do unto others . . ." means that we should do to each according to his needs or desires. And the needs and desires of men differ.

This means that only very general, even vague, moral rules are non-relative. The Sermon on the Mount inculcates general moral attitudes, and gives specific illustrations of some of them. Detailed injunctions lie in an area of relativity. But the thoroughgoing ethical relativist makes the mistake of supposing that there are no universally valid moral rules at all.

This too is the answer to the criticism, mentioned earlier, that "happiness" is only a blanket word which covers a multitude of different things. It is true, the critic says, that all men desire happiness, but it is false that this gives a common end which all men share, and which will give rise to universally valid rules. For happiness lies in different things for different people, so that in fact they all desire different things, and there is no common end.

Up to a point this is true. Some men are happy as engineers, others as musicians. Some like dinner parties, others do not. But there are certain things which are universally conditions of the best happiness of all men. And it is regarding these that the great moral precepts hold. Being an engineer is not a condition of happiness for all men, though it may be for a few. But being justly treated is such a universal condition. Therefore being an engineer is not a part of morality, but being just is. Love, unselfishness, justice, honesty, the keeping of faith, are universally conditions which will increase human happiness. Hatred, selfishness, injustice, dishonesty, faithlessness, are universally conditions which increase human misery.

To say these things is not to suggest an "absolute" standard of morals. That "there are no absolutes nowadays" is one of those unintelligent parrot-cries which are commonly mistaken for thought. But we need not insist on this here, for we are not claiming that an absolute ethic can be founded on secular considerations. We may call the view here taken "non-relative." By an absolute moral standard I understand one which would be absolutely and eternally valid throughout the universe like the mathematical truth $2 + 2 = 4$. This would be true whatever human beings are like, or even if there were no human beings in existence. Fifty billion years ago two and two made four. They make four on the remotest nebula in space. But the moral law that one should love one's neighbor depends—on the naturalistic view which I am here explaining—on human nature. That love tends to increase happiness is just a fact about human nature which might not be true if human nature were wholly different. It might not be true of beings living on Mars; and it might not be true of our own descendants a million years hence if they have evolved into creatures quite different from ourselves. We may say if we like that the great universal moral laws are relative to human nature. But they are not relative to particular cultures or periods, which is what is usually meant by saying that morals are relative.

The view which I have suggested avoids the disastrous consequences of the common relativism. For instance, we saw that on the relativist view it is impossible to say that the moral standards of one culture are better or higher than those of another. We can only say that they are different. And from this it followed that there could be no progress in moral standards, and that "love your neighbor" cannot be considered an advance on "an eye for an eye." But on the view suggested here what is right does not depend on what individual men or social groups feel or think. It depends upon facts about human nature as such, not on regional idiosyncrasies. That love increases human happiness is a fact which is true for all men. Those therefore who preach hatred, or even an eye for an eye, are not merely taking a different view. They are mistaken. And those who discovered that love is the best source of happiness are taking a better and truer view, and are making an advance. Progress in moral ideals is therefore a reality.

Thus there is a possible secular basis for morals even if we accept subjectivism. The view that morality is founded in human happiness is subjectivistic in our sense because it makes morality depend upon human purposes, on human psychology, and not on the nature of the world outside man. Hence what has been shown is that relativism does not follow from subjectivism, and that the modern mind has made a mistake in thinking that it does. And it has been shown that morality can be given a secular basis which will save it from the collapse of moral theory implied by relativism.

We may turn finally to the religious foundation of morals. It is no longer possible to discover this by taking literally the creeds and dogmas of any particular religion. For these creeds are myths. We cannot found morals in a crude anthropomorphic conception of "the will of God," nor even in the idea of a world-purpose.

Since for us the essence of religion is found in the mystic experience of the saint, the only possible solution of our problem is that a basis for morals must lie in that experience. The moral urge must be seen as flowing out of that experience. And undoubtedly this is true. For the experience is, according to the account of all who have it, not merely cognitive or emotional, but above all a value-experience. It is blessedness, calm, peace. It is also, or contains as an integral part of itself, an infinite compassion and love for all men. And such compassion and love are the fountains of all higher morality.

But it is not enough to state the mere fact that love flows out of the mystic vision. For if no reason is given for this, it might in that case be a mere accident. The mystic vision is the unifying vision in which "all is one," in which all distinctions are transcended. What, it might be asked, has this peculiar state of mind, wholly unpractical and visionary, got to do with practical life? The love of man for man is after all a practical affair having to do with the daily routine of our lives. And if it is true that mystics do feel, as a result of their ecstasy, an increased love for their fellow beings, may not this be a mere superficial phenomenon? The mystic may have a sense of emotional uplift which will cause him, at least for the moment, to feel kindly to his fellows in much the same way as an intoxicant does? And can any such mere emotional afflatus be made the foundation of ethics?

But the connection between mysticism and love is not thus accidental and superficial. There is a necessary metaphysical relation between the two. The foundation of this relation lies in the fact that in the mystic vision all distinctions, and therefore the distinction between one man and another, are transcended. Selfhood, in the sense in which I am one self and you are another, is gone. But it is out of such selfhood that all moral evil, especially hatred and envy of others, arises. He who achieves the vision sees that his self is the self of all men, that he is in them and they in him. There is for him no such distinction between an "I" and a "you" as would cause him to seek something for the "I" and deny it to the "you," to hate another while loving himself, to cause pain to another while grasping at pleasure for himself. He lives in all men and all men live in him. His desire, his love, therefore, is not for himself but for all men. It is this which makes mysticism the source of the moral life and provides the religious foundation of ethics.

This is why, although the way of the saints is not simply the moral way—to say this is to leave out its specific religious essence —yet it always includes and results in a moral life. The saints are good men, although this is not the essence of sainthood. It is a fact that the divine vision normally transforms the lives of those who have it, making them centers from which radiate enhancements of moral aspiration and illumination among their fellow men.

But of what use, it will be asked, is this to the masses of men who have had, and can have, no glimpse of that unifying vision of the saints and mystics? *Their* morality cannot flow from an experience which they do not have. The saint may find a basis for morals in this experience, but how can we who lack it do so? And in particular how can this help in regard to the problem of relativity? How does it help to show that what is good is good for all men, and that what is evil is evil universally? The saint's vision is essentially private to himself. Hence what seems good to the saint will be good for the saint, but what reason is there to say that it will be good also for us? We could find a basis for a universally valid morality only in a universal value experience. And the saint's experience, so far from being universal, is perhaps the rarest of any experience known to man. Hence the solution proposed does not solve the problem of relativity. Nor does it give any foundation at all for morality, even a relative morality, for those who lack the mystic experience.

I have already given the answer to this sort of objection in the last chapter. The principle there stated in the context of religion has only to be applied in the context of morality. Not only is the saintly experience potentially in all men in the sense that all could have it in certain conditions—for instance, if they subjected themselves to some rigorous and long discipline. It is actually present in all men now, though in a low degree in most of us. What ordinary men call religious feeling is a dim "seeing through a glass darkly" of what the saint sees in brilliant illumination.

If this is so, moral aspiration will flow out of the religious experience common to all men in proportion as it is dim or bright. And since that experience is basically the same in all men—the differences being differences of degree—the morality which flows out of it will be the same everywhere, the same for all men, though some will apprehend it more clearly, others more obscurely. Perhaps something like this is the truth which lies at the bottom of the old myth of "conscience." It is a myth if it is taken literally as meaning a magical and infallible inner voice which tells a man on every occasion what he ought to do. But it is true if it is taken symbolically as standing for an inner light of the divine vision shining clearly only in the very few, more dimly in the rest of us.

And we may also think that what some philosophers have called moral "intuitions" are in reality an influx into our ordinary consciousness of elements from that radically different kind of mentality, intuitive and non-discriminating, of which mystics speak, which in most of us is sunk in the depths of the unconscious. This would explain the apparently mysterious character of such intuitions, and would also explain many of the paradoxes with which ethical philosophers have wrestled.

Does the view which has here been expressed justify the statement made earlier in this chapter that although, even if we take the naturalistic view that moral values are subjective and that the world is not a moral order, a sound basis for morality can be given, yet actually moral values are objective and the world is a moral order? Are we not compelled to think that even if ideal and moral aspirations flow out of the religious experience of the saints and, more dimly, out of that of common men, yet this experience being itself no more than a human thing, morals will still be subjective and the world not a moral order?

To answer this question we have to refer again to the conclusions reached in the last chapter. That the mystic vision is merely subjective is the sole truth if we take our stand within the order of time and make that our frame of reference. But there is another equally legitimate frame of reference. If we take our stand within the mystic moment itself, if we view it from within instead of from the outside, then it alone is the truth; and it is, rather, the time-order which is subjective illusion. The same will be true of the moral ideals, the value experiences, which are enclosed in the religious vision and which overflow from it into our daily lives in time. From a naturalistic standpoint they are merely subjective. But in that other frame of reference, which is the eternal order, they are eternal truths. Properly speaking we should say of them, as we did of God himself, that they are neither subjective nor objective. But we may also say of them that they are both subjective and objective since the universe contains both frames of reference. The error of the naturalist is to admit the reality only of the time-order. But the eternal order is as much a part of the universe, and therefore of reality, and therefore the moral values which belong to it are in the same sense real and objective. This means that from the standpoint of time the world is not a moral order, but that from the standpoint of the eternal it is a moral order. And both truths have an equal right to our acceptance because we live in both orders.

It is not true that moral ideals are merely human devices for achieving survival and increased pleasure or happiness. They do indeed serve these ends, and can be naturalistically justified thereby; but that is not all. A naturalistic ethics can at best only lamely explain why, if morality is nothing but this, men will face torture and death—which are surely not an increase of comfort or security—for the sake of ideals. In the long and tragic struggle of life on this planet from lower to higher forms; in the terrible sufferings of mankind reaching upward to grasp at nobler ways of living, constantly falling backward, yet as constantly striving higher; in the vague aspirations of men for immortality, for a more blessed mode of existence, for God, for a life which shall be not merely animal but also divine; in all this can be seen, not merely the futile, because ultimately purposeless, efforts for survival or pleasure by an animated piece of clay, but an influx into the darkness of such a life of a light which has its source in that which is eternal.

INDEX

283